AWS Development Essentials

Design and build flexible, highly scalable, and cost-effective applications using Amazon Web Services

Prabhakaran Kuppusamy

Uchit Vyas

[PACKT] enterprise
PUBLISHING
professional expertise distilled

BIRMINGHAM - MUMBAI

AWS Development Essentials

First published: November 2014

Production reference: 1191114

Published by Packt Publishing Ltd.
Livery Place
35 Livery Street
Birmingham B3 2PB, UK.

ISBN 978-1-78217-361-8

www.packtpub.com

Credits

Authors
Prabhakaran Kuppusamy
Uchit Vyas

Reviewers
Joe Johnston
Robert M. Marks
Somanath Nanda

Commissioning Editor
Kunal Parikh

Acquisition Editor
Larissa Pinto

Content Development Editor
Manasi Pandire

Technical Editors
Indrajit A. Das
Shashank Desai

Copy Editors
Sarang Chari
Dipti Kapadia

Project Coordinator
Suzanne Coutinho

Proofreaders
Simran Bhogal
Ameesha Green
Amy Johnson
Jonathan Todd

Indexers
Mariammal Chettiyar
Priya Sane

Graphics
Abhinash Sahu

Production Coordinator
Komal Ramchandani

Cover Work
Komal Ramchandani

About the Authors

Prabhakaran Kuppusamy is a Hadoop ecosystem specialist and cloud enthusiast who is currently working as a senior systems engineer and developer, Cloud and Infrastructure Services unit, at Infosys Limited. He is passionate about teaching and writing. He loves to play cricket during his leisure time. He joined Education & Research at Global Education Centre, Infosys, where he trained and evaluated thousands of freshmen in Java, Big Data, and cloud technologies. During his tenure in the Education & Research department, he provided training to students from Coventry University and to professionals from Costa Rica on Big Data and cloud technologies, such as Hadoop, MapReduce, Hive, Elastic MapReduce, Google App Engine, DynamoDB, and CloudStack.

Prabhakaran has a Bachelor of Engineering degree in Instrumentation and Control Engineering from Anna University. After completing his degree, he started providing workshops and training sessions on Big Data and cloud to several engineering colleges. He is an IBM Certified Cloud Computing Architect. He has more affinity towards private clouds and a greater working knowledge about them. Currently, he is working on MarkLogic, Storm, and XQuery. He keeps on trying new things, even if it burns his fingers. He loves to interact with students and teachers, and his Twitter handle is `@prabhakar28dec`.

Prabhakaran has also authored *DynamoDB Applied Design Patterns*, *Packt Publishing*.

I dedicate this book to my niece, Harrsatha Sri, and my sister, Kalaiselvi Sathishkumar. I would like to thank Sarika Ghawle, Abhishek Kumar Sharma, and Bhupendra Bajpayi for providing favorable conditions to write this book. Also, I would like to thank my GEC colleagues, Krishna Prasad, Uchit Vyas, Sureesh Joseph, and Ravindran Balachandran, for shepherding me technically and personally. Special thanks to Kshitiz Jain, my manager and friend, who has always been there to help me.

Uchit Vyas is an IT industry veteran, a cloud technologist at heart, and a hands-on Lead DevOps at Clogeny Technologies for cloud automation. He is responsible for the delivery of solutions and services as well as product development. He explores new open source technologies and the defining architecture, roadmaps, and best practices for enterprises. He has consulted and provided training on various open source technologies, including cloud computing (AWS Cloud, Rackspace, Azure, CloudStack, OpenStack, and Eucalyptus), Mule ESB, Chef, Puppet, Liferay Portal, Alfresco ECM, and JBoss to corporations around the world.

Uchit has done his engineering in Computer Science from Gujarat University. He was in the Education & Research Team as a senior associate at Infosys Limited; during this time, he has worked on private clouds, cloud security, and virtualization.

Uchit has also authored books on Mule ESB and AWS DynamoDB, and he continuously writes books on open source technologies such as Storm, Python, and so on.

He hosts a blog named Cloud Magic World (`http://cloudbyuchit.blogspot.com`), where he posts tips and phenomena on open source technologies mostly relating to cloud. His Twitter handle is `@uchit_vyas`.

I would like to thank my better half for helping me a lot in writing this book and providing me with continuous support throughout the period of writing this book. I would also like to thank my Infocian colleague, Prabhakaran Kuppusamy, for his help.

About the Reviewers

Joe Johnston is the co-author of *Programming Web Services with XML-RPC* and *Unix Power Tools, 3rd Edition*, both by O'Reilly Media. He builds cloud-hosted applications for the human resources market.

> I would like to thank my wife, Sally, and son, Angus,
> for their support.

Robert M. Marks is an experienced software developer and has spent over 12 years of his career working for a variety of software companies, ranging from large companies such as IBM to small start-ups. He is passionate about crafting well-tested software using best practices, such as TDD, layered design, dependency injection, and so on. He has contributed to various open source projects and is the creator of Java Online Gaming Real-time Engine (JOGRE).

Robert is currently the Head of Engineering at Adoreboard, a unique platform that measures how the world feels about your brand so that marketers can make better business decisions. In his work at Adoreboard, he is a key pioneer for the development of real-time scalable architectures using a combination of technologies, including Enterprise Java, Spring Framework, cloud computing, and NoSQL databases such as MongoDB, Elasticsearch, Solr, and Redis.

Somanath Nanda is a young and dynamic technical speaker, an experienced tech-savvy professional with more than 3 years of IT experience, who is interested in learning new, upcoming technologies and providing cutting-edge design solutions. He started his career as an embedded engineer, and at present, he is working at Cognizant Technology Solutions Pvt. Ltd. with the product development team as a core team member. He has completed his BTech in Electronics and Telecommunication Engineering from Biju Patnaik University of Technology.

He loves to read novels and watch documentaries related to God and science. He has an interest in Big Data technologies, including Apache Spark and Apache Hadoop. He has worked on various technologies, including Struts Framework, Spring Framework, iBatis, and Hibernate; databases such as Oracle and MySQL; NoSQL databases such as HBase; as well as analysis tools such as R and Microsoft Excel. He has a comprehensive knowledge of applied statistical methodologies, including regression analysis (univariate and multivariate linear regression, nonlinear regression, including logistic, Poisson, and negative binomial regressions), linear models (generalized linear model, hierarchical linear models, including mixed effect, random effect, and fixed-effect models), statistical data analysis, and statistical modeling.

I would like to thank my parents and my friends for their help in making this review successful.

www.PacktPub.com

Support files, eBooks, discount offers, and more

For support files and downloads related to your book, please visit www.PacktPub.com.

Did you know that Packt offers eBook versions of every book published, with PDF and ePub files available? You can upgrade to the eBook version at www.PacktPub.com and as a print book customer, you are entitled to a discount on the eBook copy. Get in touch with us at service@packtpub.com for more details.

At www.PacktPub.com, you can also read a collection of free technical articles, sign up for a range of free newsletters and receive exclusive discounts and offers on Packt books and eBooks.

https://www2.packtpub.com/books/subscription/packtlib

Do you need instant solutions to your IT questions? PacktLib is Packt's online digital book library. Here, you can search, access, and read Packt's entire library of books.

Why subscribe?

- Fully searchable across every book published by Packt
- Copy and paste, print, and bookmark content
- On demand and accessible via a web browser

Free access for Packt account holders

If you have an account with Packt at www.PacktPub.com, you can use this to access PacktLib today and view 9 entirely free books. Simply use your login credentials for immediate access.

Instant updates on new Packt books

Get notified! Find out when new books are published by following @PacktEnterprise on Twitter or the *Packt Enterprise* Facebook page.

Table of Contents

Preface

AWS Development Essentials is a single place where you can find solutions for all of your issues with Amazon Web Services. This book will explain how to begin and manage eight different services using the AWS SDKs and APIs as well as the AWS Management Console, a browser-based graphical user interface to interact with the services. It will include a significant number of examples that can be used by anyone, from a newbie to an expert. Using the examples of this book, users can perform advanced-level programming and gain the advantages of AWS SQL and NoSQL databases in their application at significantly lower costs. The final chapter of this book is purely dedicated to how you can create an application having EC2, VPC, RDS, SNS, and S3 services as the backbone of the application and how you can deploy and manage this application using Elastic Beanstalk.

What this book covers

Chapter 1, *An Introduction to Amazon Web Services*, helps you to start accessing AWS through the Management Console and shows the steps required to set up and configure the IDE and SDK tools.

Chapter 2, *Working with AWS Storage Services*, makes you aware of the different storage techniques available in AWS and how to access them through the IDE.

Chapter 3, *Computing and Networking Services*, teaches you about the creation and management of EC2 instances in different regions and VPCs.

Chapter 4, *Managed Services and the Databases*, makes you familiar with the Relational Database Service and DynamoDB, a NoSQL database service.

Chapter 5, *Deployment and Management*, teaches you how to use Amazon IAM for identity management and how to deploy an application using Elastic Beanstalk.

Chapter 6, Working with the AWS Simple Notification Service – SNS, helps you to dive deep into different notification and messaging options, explaining the challenges and troubleshooting in detail.

Chapter 7, Working with AWS SQS, helps you to explore different queuing options, explaining the challenges and troubleshooting in detail.

Chapter 8, Building an Application Using AWS, teaches you how to create, deploy, and manage an application that uses multiple AWS services.

What you need for this book

To start using this book, you need the following things:

* An AWS account
* Java 1.6 or higher
* Eclipse (Juno or Kepler)
* The AWS SDK
* AWS CLI tools
* MySQL Workbench

Who this book is for

This book is ideal for programmers who want to move their existing infrastructure to the AWS Cloud and start using AWS services in all the application tiers using services such as compute, file storage, database, queuing, messaging or mailing in an application, and finally, hosting this application in AWS too. Readers should have a basic knowledge and understanding of Java programs.

Conventions

In this book, you will find a number of styles of text that distinguish between different kinds of information. Here are some examples of these styles, and an explanation of their meaning.

Code words in text, database table names, folder names, filenames, file extensions, pathnames, dummy URLs, user input, and Twitter handles are shown as follows: "To use the low-level API, refer to the `AmazonGlacierClient` class, which provides each and every method that maps REST calls for Glacier."

A block of code is set as follows:

```
//s3_KEY is name of file we want to upload
PutObjectRequest request = new PutObjectRequest();
request.WithBucketName(BUCKET_NAME);
request.WithKey(s3_KEY);
request.WithFilePath(pathToFile)
client.PutObject(request);
```

Any command-line input or output is written as follows:

```
aws sns --topic-arn <topic-arn> --protocol <protocol-name> --
notification-endpoint <endpoint>
```

New terms and **important words** are shown in bold. Words that you see on the screen, in menus or dialog boxes for example, appear in the text like this: "Now, click on **Libraries** and add **External Jar**."

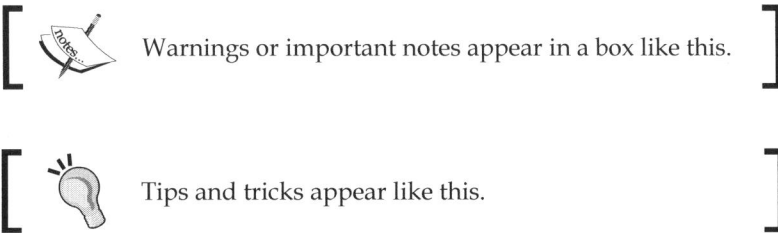

Warnings or important notes appear in a box like this.

Tips and tricks appear like this.

Reader feedback

Feedback from our readers is always welcome. Let us know what you think about this book—what you liked or may have disliked. Reader feedback is important for us to develop titles that you really get the most out of.

To send us general feedback, simply send an e-mail to feedback@packtpub.com, and mention the book title via the subject of your message.

If there is a topic that you have expertise in and you are interested in either writing or contributing to a book, see our author guide on www.packtpub.com/authors.

Customer support

Now that you are the proud owner of a Packt book, we have a number of things to help you to get the most from your purchase.

Downloading the example code

You can download the example code files for all Packt books you have purchased from your account at http://www.packtpub.com. If you purchased this book elsewhere, you can visit http://www.packtpub.com/support and register to have the files e-mailed directly to you.

Errata

Although we have taken every care to ensure the accuracy of our content, mistakes do happen. If you find a mistake in one of our books—maybe a mistake in the text or the code—we would be grateful if you would report this to us. By doing so, you can save other readers from frustration and help us improve subsequent versions of this book. If you find any errata, please report them by visiting http://www.packtpub.com/submit-errata, selecting your book, clicking on the **Errata Submission Form** link, and entering the details of your errata. Once your errata are verified, your submission will be accepted and the errata will be uploaded on our website, or added to any list of existing errata, under the Errata section of that title. Any existing errata can be viewed by selecting your title from http://www.packtpub.com/support.

To view the previously submitted errata, go to https://www.packtpub.com/books/content/support and enter the name of the book in the search field. The required information will appear under the **Errata** section.

Piracy

Piracy of copyright material on the Internet is an ongoing problem across all media. At Packt, we take the protection of our copyright and licenses very seriously. If you come across any illegal copies of our works, in any form, on the Internet, please provide us with the location address or website name immediately so that we can pursue a remedy.

Please contact us at copyright@packtpub.com with a link to the suspected pirated material.

We appreciate your help in protecting our authors, and our ability to bring you valuable content.

Questions

You can contact us at questions@packtpub.com if you are having a problem with any aspect of the book, and we will do our best to address it.

1
An Introduction to Amazon Web Services

Amazon Web Services (AWS) is a leading public cloud provider. One good thing with AWS is the abundant number of services and tools offered, which helps the programmer to use them in an easy and customized way. There are different tools and methods available to perform the same operation with different, varying complexities. Various options are available, depending on the user's level of experience. In this book, we will start with an overview of each service, learn about the various tools available for programmer interaction, and finally see the troubleshooting and best practices to be followed while using these services. In the final chapter, you will learn how to develop an application using AWS services. AWS provides a handful of services in every area. A separate book can be written for each service. For this reason, we will discuss one service in each section and learn how to use it.

In this chapter, we will cover the following topics:

- Navigate through the AWS Management Console
- Describe the security measures that AWS provides
- AWS interaction through the SDK and IDE tools

A background of AWS and its needs

AWS is based on an idea presented by Chris Pinkham and Benjamin Black with a vision toward Amazon's retail computing infrastructure. The first Amazon offering was SQS, in 2004. Officially, AWS was launched and made available online in 2006, and within a year, 200,000 developers had signed up for these services. Later, due to a natural disaster (June 29, 2012 storm in North Virginia, which brought down most of the servers residing at this location) and technical events, AWS faced a lot of challenges. A similar event happened in December 2012, after which AWS has been providing services as stated. AWS learned from these events and made sure that the same kind of outage wouldn't occur even if the same event occurred again. AWS is an idea born in a single room, but the idea is now made available and used by almost all the cloud developers and IT giants.

AWS is greatly loved by all kinds of technology admirers. Irrespective of the user's expertise, AWS has something for various types of users. For an expert programmer, AWS has SDKs for each service. Using these SDKs, the programmer can perform operations by entering commands in the command-line interface. However, an end user with limited knowledge of programming can still perform similar operations using the graphical user interface of the AWS Management Console, which is accessible through a web browser. If programmers need interactions between a low-level (SDK) and a high-level (Management Console), they can go for the **integrated development environment** (**IDE**) tools, for which AWS provides plugins and add-ons. One such commonly used IDE for which AWS has provided add-ons is the Eclipse IDE. You will learn about the AWS plugin for the Eclipse IDE in the last section of this chapter. As of now, we will start with the AWS Management Console.

The AWS Management Console

The most popular method of accessing AWS is via the Management Console because of its simplicity of usage and power. Another reason why the end user prefers the Management Console is that it doesn't require any software to start with; having an Internet connection and a browser is sufficient. As the name suggests, the Management Console is a place where administrative and advanced operations can be performed on your AWS account details or AWS services. The Management Console mainly focuses on the following features:

- One-click access to AWS services
- AWS account administration
- AWS management using handheld devices
- AWS infrastructure management across the globe

One-click access to the AWS services

To access the Management Console, all you need to do is first sign up with AWS. Once done, the Management Console will be available at `https://console.aws.amazon.com/`. Once you have signed up, you will be directed to the following page:

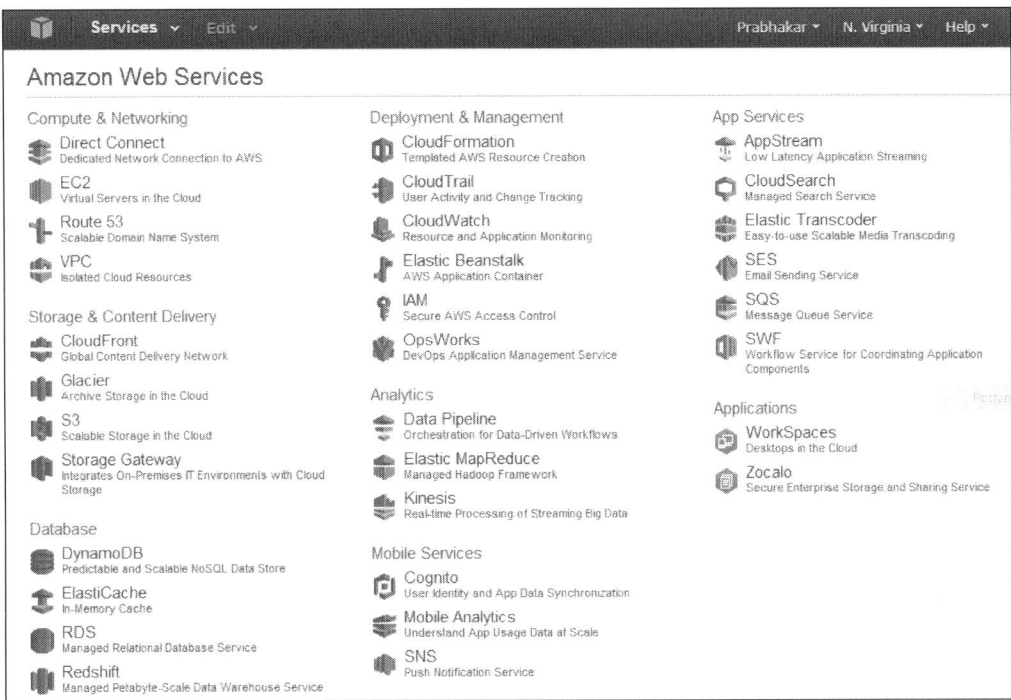

Each and every icon on this page is an Amazon web service. Two or more services will be grouped under a category. For example, in the **Analytics** category, you can see three services: **Data Pipeline**, **Elastic MapReduce**, and **Kinesis**. Starting with any of these services is very easy. Have a look at the description of the service at the bottom of the service icon. As soon as you click on the service icon, it will take you to the **Getting started** page of the corresponding service, where brief as well as detailed guidelines are available. To start with any of the services, only two things are required. The first one is an AWS account and the second one is the supported browser. The **Getting started** section usually will have a video, which explains the specialty and use cases of the service that you selected. Once you finish reading the **Getting started** section, optionally you can go through the DOC files specific to the service to know more about the syntaxes and usage of the service operations.

AWS account administration

The account administration is one of the most important things to make note of. To do this, click on your displayed name (in this case, **Prabhakar**) at the top of the page, and then click on the **My Account** option, as shown in the preceding screenshot. At the beginning of every month, you don't want AWS to deduct all of your salary by stating that you have used these many services costing this much money; hence, all this management information is available in the Management Console. Using the Management Console, you can infer the following information:

- The monthly billing in brief as well as the detailed manner (cost split-up of each service) along with a provision to view VAT and tax exemption
- Account details, such as the display name and contact information
- Provision to close the AWS account

All the preceding operations and much more are possible.

AWS management using handheld devices

Managing and accessing the AWS services is through (but not limited to) a PC. AWS provides a handful of applications for almost all or most of the mobile platforms, such as Android, iOS, and so on. Using these applications, you can perform all the AWS operations on the move. You won't believe that having a 7-inch Android tablet with the installed AWS Console application from Google Play will enable you to ask for any **Elastic Compute Cloud** (**EC2**) instance from Amazon and control it (start, stop, and terminate) very easily. You can install an SSH client in the tablet and connect to the Linux terminal. However, if you wish to make use of the Windows instance from EC2, you might use the **Graphics User Interface** (**GUI**) more frequently than a command line. A few more sophisticated software and hardware might be needed, for example, you should have a VNC viewer or remote desktop connection software to get the GUI of the EC2 instance borrowed. As you are making use of the GUI in addition to the keyboard, you will need a pointer device, such as a mouse. As a result, you will almost get addicted to the concept of cloud computing going mobile.

AWS infrastructure management across the globe

At this point, you might be aware that you can get all of these AWS services from servers residing at any of the following locations. To control these services used by you in different regions, you don't have to go anywhere else. You can control it right here in the same Management Console. Using the same Management Console, just by clicking on **N.Virginia** and choosing the location (at the top of the Management Console), you can make the service available in that region, as shown in the following screenshot:

You can choose the server location at which you want the service (data and machine) to be made available based on the following two factors:

- The first factor is the distance between the server's location and the client's location. For example, if you have deployed a web application for a client from North California at a Tokyo location, obviously the latency will be high while accessing the application. Therefore, choosing the optimum service location is the primary factor.

- The second factor is the charge for the service in a specific location. AWS charges more for certain crowded servers. Just for illustration, assume that the server for North California is used by many critical companies. So this might cost you twice if you create your servers at North California compared to the other locations. Hence, you should always consider the trade-off between the location and cost and then decide on the server location.

Whenever you click on any of the services, AWS will always select the location that costs you less money as the default.

AWS security measures

Whenever you think of moving your data center to a public cloud, the first question that should arise is about data security. In a public cloud, through virtualization technology, multiple users might be using the same hardware (server) in which your data is available. You will learn in detail about how AWS ensures data security.

Instance isolation

Before learning about instance isolation, you must know how AWS EC2 provisions the instances to the user. This service allows you to rent virtual machines (AWS calls it instances) with whatever configurations you ask. We will discuss EC2 in detail in *Chapter 3, Computing Services and Networking*.

Let's assume that you requested AWS to provision 2 GB RAM, a 100 GB HDD, and an Ubuntu instance. Within a minute, you will be given the instance's connection details (public DNS, private IP, and so on), and the instance starts running. Does this mean that AWS assembled 2*1 GB RAM and 100 GB HDD into a CPU cabinet and then installed Ubuntu OS in it and gave you the access? The answer is no. The provisioned instance is not a single PC (or bare metal) with an OS installed in it. The instance is the outcome of a virtual machine provisioned by Amazon's private cloud. The following diagram shows how a virtual machine can be provisioned by a private cloud:

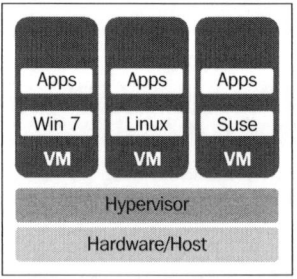

Let's examine the diagram from bottom to top. First, we will start with the underlying **Hardware/Host**. Hardware is the server, which usually has a very high specification. Here, assume that your hardware has the following configuration: 99 GB RAM, a 450 TB HDD, and a few other elements, such as NIC, which you need not consider now. The next component in your sights is the **Hypervisor**.

A hypervisor or **virtual machine monitor** (**VMM**) is used to create and run virtual machines on the hardware. In private cloud terms, whichever machine runs a hypervisor on it is called the host machine. Three users can request each of them need instances with 33 GB RAM and 150 TB HDD space. This request goes to the hypervisor and it then starts creating those VMs.

After creating the VMs, a notification about the connection parameters will be sent to each user. In the preceding diagram, you can see the three **virtual machines** (**VMs**) created by the hypervisor. All the three VMs are running on different operating systems. Even if all the three virtual machines are used by different users, each will feel that only he/she has access to the single piece of hardware, which is only used by them; user 1 might not know that the same hardware is also being used by user 2, and so on. The process of creating a virtual version of a machine or storage or network is called virtualization. The funny thing is that none of the virtual machines knows that it is being virtualized (that is, all the VMs are created on the same host). After getting this information about your instances, some users may feel deceived, and some will be even disappointed and say, *has your instance been created on a shared disk or resource?* Even though the disk (or hardware) is shared, one instance (or owner of the instance) is isolated from the other instances on the same disk through a firewall. This concept is termed as instance isolation. The following diagram demonstrates instance isolation in AWS:

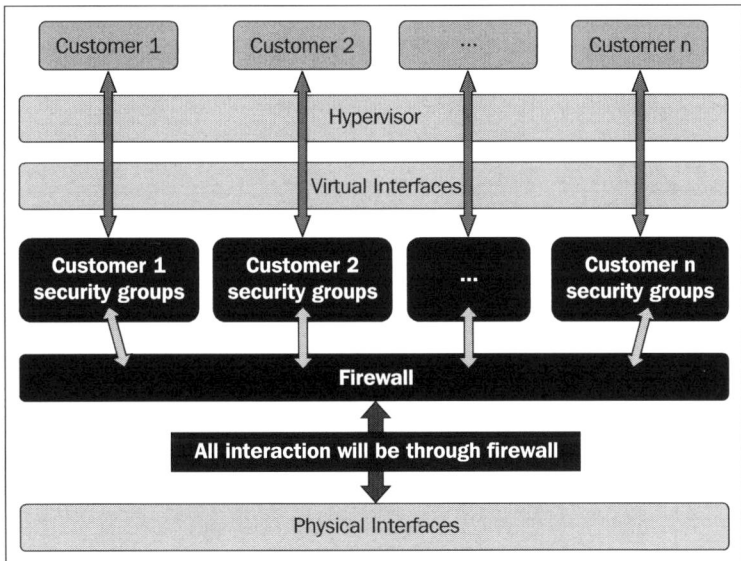

The preceding diagram clearly demonstrates how EC2 provides instances to every user. Even though all the instances are lying in the same disk, they are isolated by the hypervisor. The hypervisor has a firewall that does this isolation. So, the physical interface will not interact with the underlying hardware (machine or disk where instances are available) or virtual interface directly. All these interactions will be through the hypervisor's firewall. This way, AWS ensures that no user can directly access the disk, and no instance can directly interact with another instance even if both instances are running on the same hardware. In addition to the firewall, during the creation of the EC2 instance, the user can specify the permitted and denied security groups of the instance. These two ideologies provide instance isolation.

> In the preceding diagram, **Customer 1**, **Customer 2**, and so on are virtualized disks since the customer instances have no access to raw or actual disk devices. As an added security measure, the user can encrypt his/her disk so that other users cannot access the disk content (even if someone gets in contact with the disk).

Isolated GovCloud

Similar to North California or Asia Pacific, GovCloud is also a location where you can get your AWS services. This location is specifically designed only for government and agencies whose data is very confidential and valuable, and disclosing this data might result in disaster. By default, this location will not be available to the user. If you want access to this location, then you need to raise a compliance request at `http://aws.amazon.com/compliance/contact/` and submit the FedRAMP Package Request Form downloadable at `http://cloud.cio.gov/document/fedramp-package-request-form`. From these two URLs, you can understand how secure the cloud location really is.

CloudTrail

CloudTrail is an AWS service that performs user activity and changes tracking. Enabling CloudTrail will log all the API request information into your S3 bucket, which you have created solely for this purpose. CloudTrail also allows you to create an SNS topic as soon as a new logfile is created by CloudTrail. CloudTrail, in conjunction with SNS, provides real-time user activity as messages to the user.

 **Simple Storage Service (S3)** allows AWS users to store files. S3 will be discussed in *Chapter 2, Working with AWS Storage Services.* Similarly, **Simple Notification Service (SNS)** permits the AWS user to be notified (by an e-mail or SMS) when a condition occurs. You will learn more about SNS in *Chapter 6, Working with the AWS Notification Service – SNS.*

Password

This might sound funny. After looking at CloudTrail, if you feel that someone else is accessing your account, the best option is to change the password. Never let anyone look at your password, as this could easily compromise an entire account. Sharing the password is like leaving your treasury door open.

Multi-Factor Authentication

Until now, to access AWS through a browser, you had to log in at `http://aws.amazon.com` and enter your username and password. However, enabling **Multi-Factor Authentication (MFA)** will add another layer of security and ask you to provide an authentication code sent to the device configured with this account. In the security credential page at `https://console.aws.amazon.com/iam/home?#security_credential`, there is a provision to enable MFA. Clicking on **Enable** will display the following window:

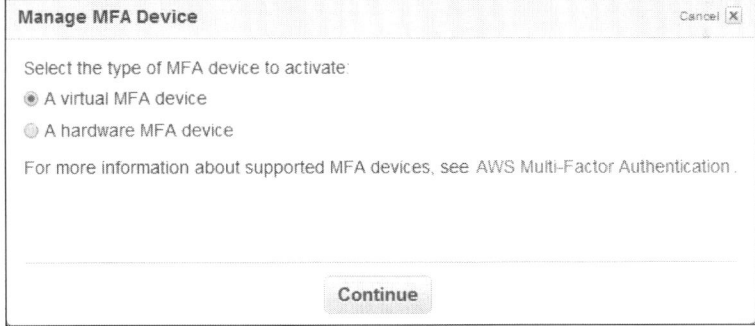

Selecting the first option **A virtual MFA device** will not cost you money, but this requires a smartphone (with an Android OS), and you need to download an app from the App Store. After this, during every login, you need to look at your smartphone and enter the authentication token. More information is available at `https://youtu.be/MWJtuthUs0w`.

Access Keys (Access Key ID and Secret Access Key)

In the same security credentials page, next to MFA, these access keys will be made available. AWS will not allow you to have more than two access keys. However, you can delete and create as many access keys as possible, as shown in the following screenshot:

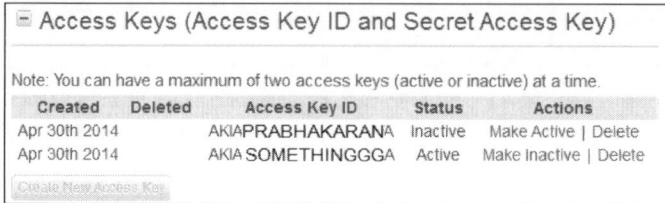

This access key ID is used while accessing the service via the API and SDK. During this time, you must provide this ID. Otherwise, you won't be able to perform any operation. In other words, if someone else gets or knows this ID, they could pretend to be you through the SDK and API. In the preceding screenshot, the first key is inactive and the second key is active. The **Create New Access Key** button is disabled because I already have a maximum number of allowed access keys. As an added measure, I forged my actual IDs.

It is a very good practice to delete a key and create a new key every month using the **Delete** command link and toggle the active keys every week (by making it active and inactive) by clicking on the **Make Active** or **Make Inactive** command links. Never let anyone see these IDs. If you are ever in doubt, delete the ID and create a new one.

Clicking on the **Create New Access Key** button (assuming that you have less than two IDs) will display the following window, asking you to download the new access key ID as a CSV file:

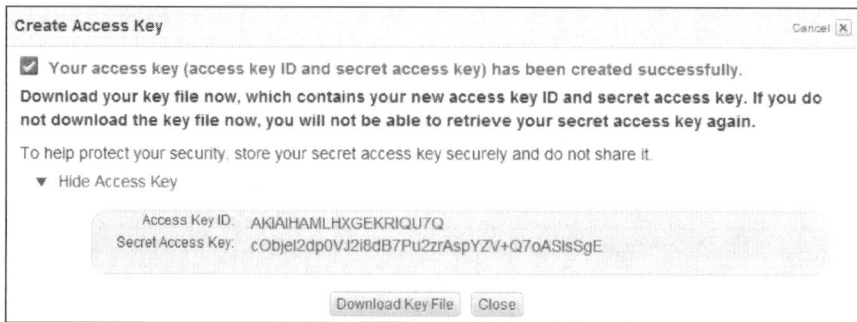

The CloudFront key pairs

The CloudFront key pairs are very similar to the access-key IDs. Without these keys, you will not be able to perform any operation on CloudFront. Unlike the access key ID (which has only an access key ID and a secret access key), here you will have a private key and a public key along with the access key ID, as shown in the following screenshot:

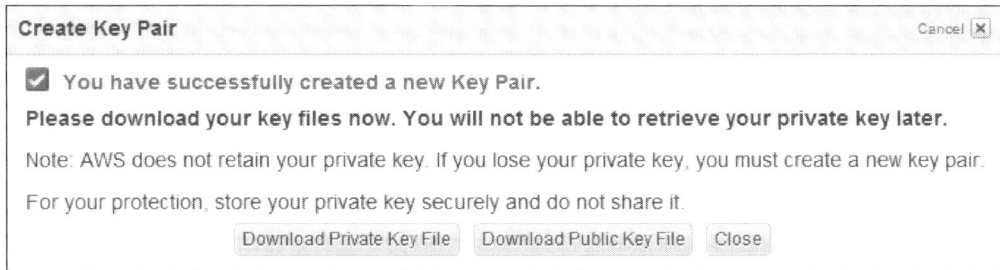

If you lose these keys once, then you need to delete the key pair and create a new key pair. This is also an added security measure.

X.509 certificates

X.509 certificates are mandatory if you wish to make any SOAP requests on any AWS service. Clicking on **Create new certificate** will display the following window, which performs exactly the same function as discussed in the previous section:

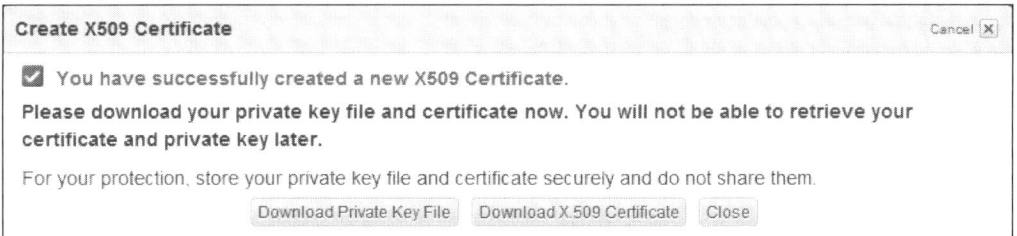

Account identifiers

There are two IDs that are used to identify ourselves when accessing the service via the API or SDK. These are the AWS account ID and the canonical user ID. These two IDs are unique. Just as with the preceding parameters, never share these IDs or let anyone see them. If someone has your access ID or key pair, the best option is to generate a new one. But it is not possible to generate a new account ID or canonical user ID.

AWS interaction through the SDK and IDE tools

As discussed, AWS has a bit for everyone with respect to the kind of knowledge or expertise that the user has. An end user might find the Management Console useful. From a programmer's point of view, the SDK will be helpful. AWS provides SDK for most of the commonly used languages, such as Java, Ruby, .NET, PHP, Node.js, and Python. More information about these tools is available at `http://aws.amazon.com/tools`. For an Eclipse IDE addict, IDE tools will be very supportive. Now that we have discussed enough about the Management Console, we can spend some time on the SDK and IDE tools.

The first IDE tool – the Eclipse plugin

Eclipse is one of the most commonly used open source IDEs, and it provides a plugin to work with AWS. Almost all the Java developers use Eclipse for application development. Eclipse can be downloaded from `www.eclipse.org/downloads`. Try to download the latest version. Throughout the book, you will see Eclipse Juno. To get started with Eclipse, visit `www.eclipse.org/users`. To configure the AWS plugin in the Eclipse IDE, follow these steps:

1. Open Eclipse and select **Install New Software** from the **Help** menu, as shown in the following screenshot:

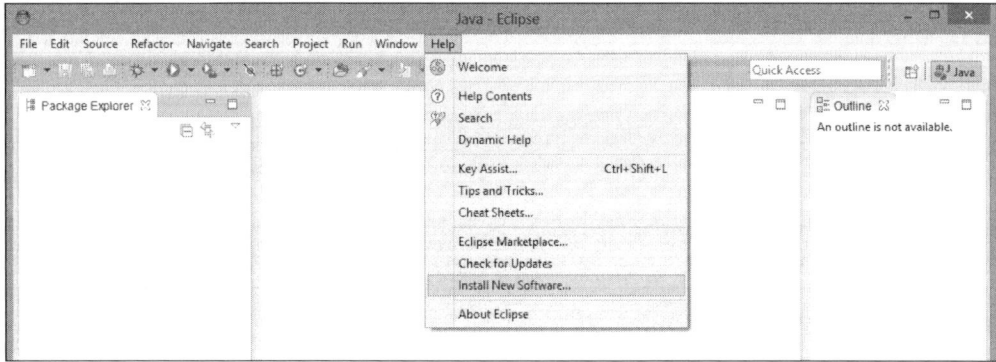

2. In the following screenshot, you need to enter `http://aws.amazon.com/eclipse/` and press the *Enter* key. It will display all the available plugins for AWS. You can either install everything or only the necessary components (it's better to install everything because there will be dependency between these plugins).

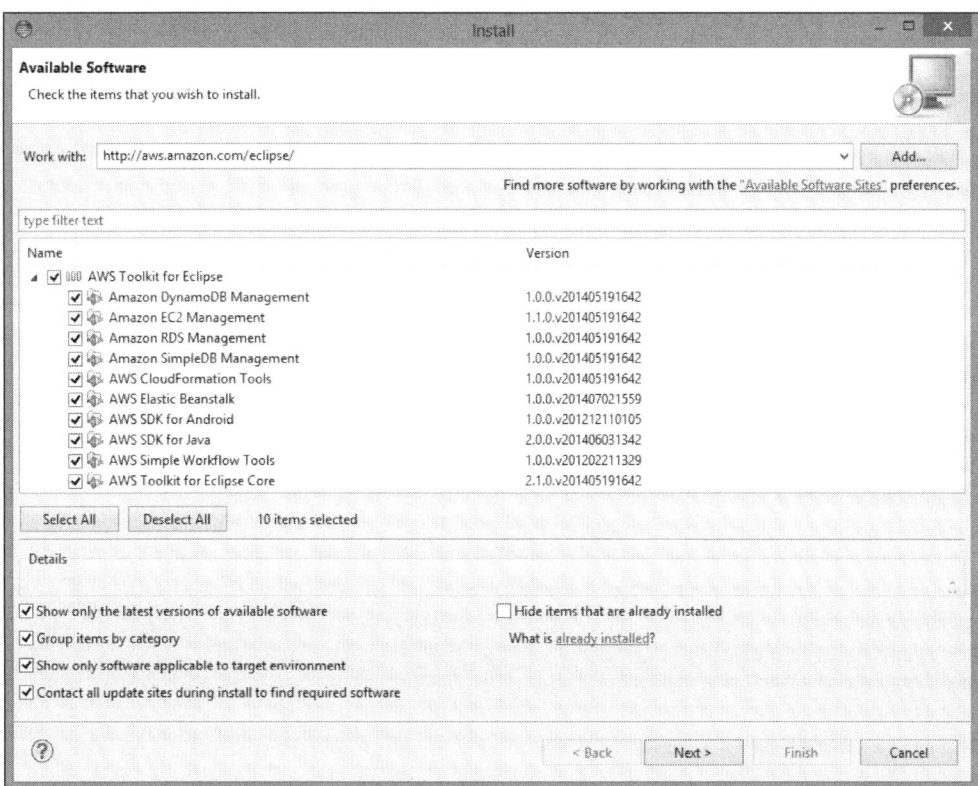

3. The following page will display the components that will be installed on Eclipse. Confirm it and then proceed.

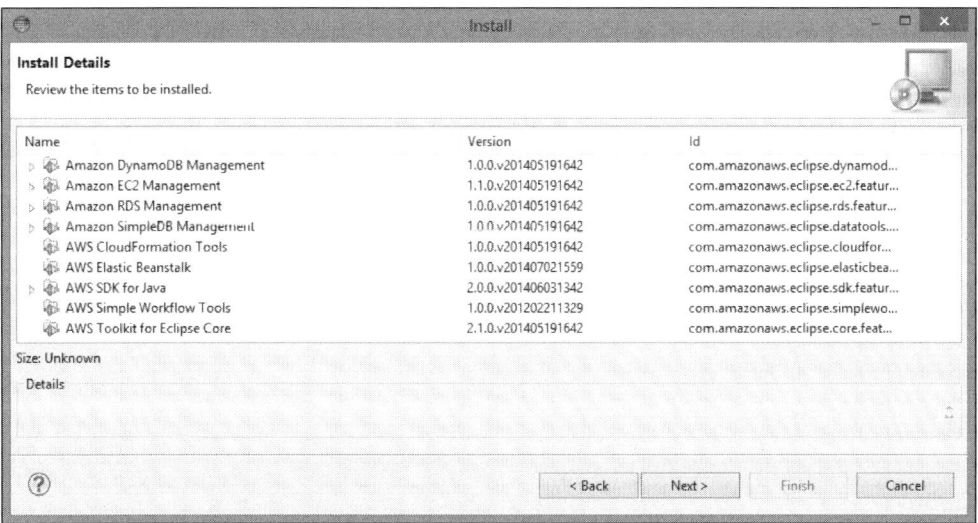

4. The following page will show the invalid components (in this case, **AWS SDK for Android**). If the component (not installed) does not cause any trouble, just proceed with the installation.

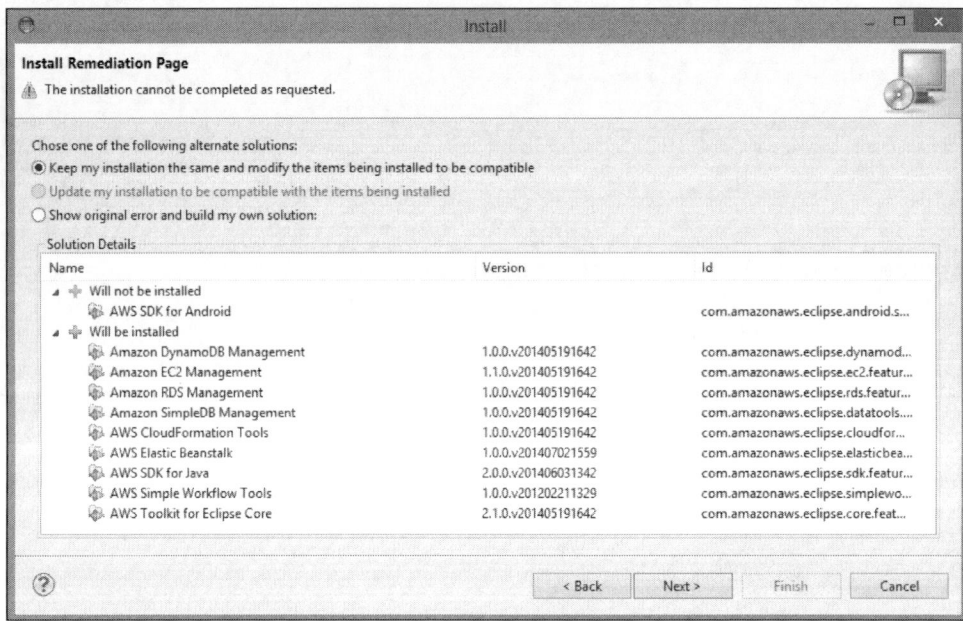

5. To proceed with the installation, you must accept the Apache license and the Eclipse foundation agreement. Check the **I accept the terms of the license agreements** condition, and click on the **Finish** button to complete the installation, as shown here:

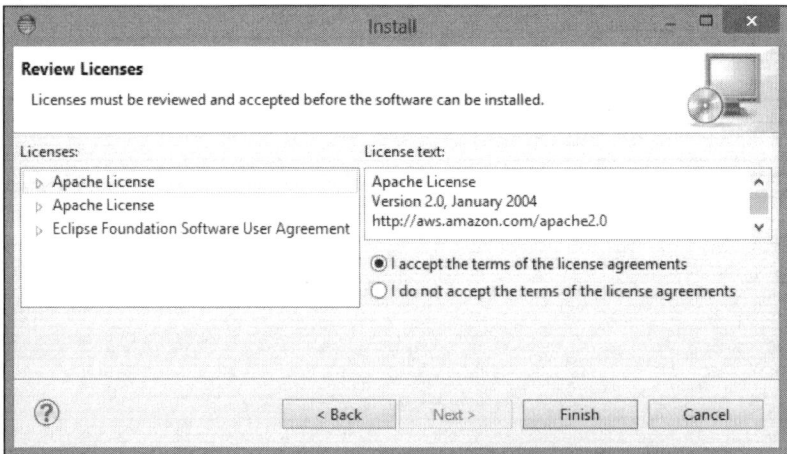

6. Due to the dependency among packages, there might be some dependency errors thrown while setting up the plugin. In this case, select **Install New Software** from the **Help** menu, enter the URL `http://download.eclipse.org/datatools/updates/1.12`, select the following package, and repeat the installation of the AWS plugin, as shown in the following screenshot:

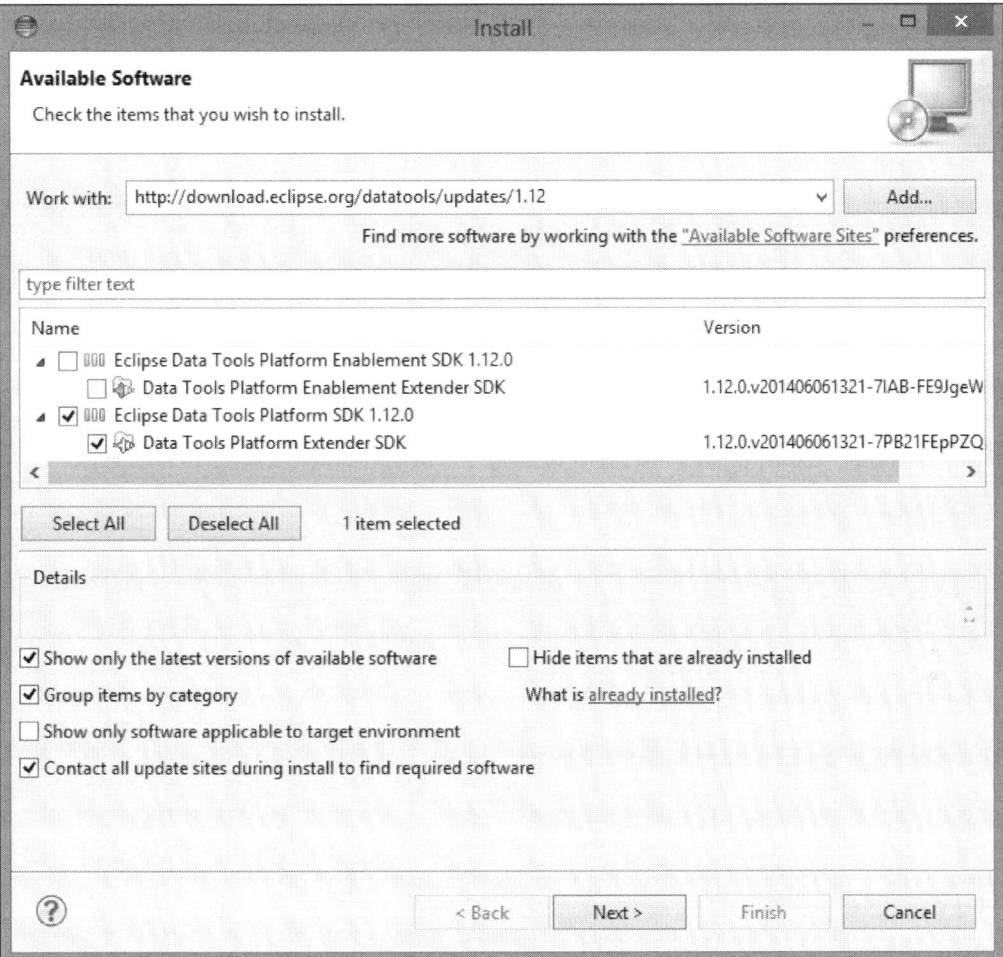

7. There's a possibility that you might see the following security warning. Make sure that you're installing from AWS and not from any third party. Once you know that the source is safe, only then proceed by clicking on **OK**.

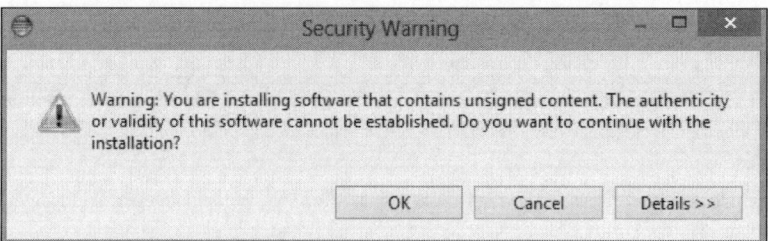

8. The same security warning will be shown, and if you wish, you can trust Amazon and add it to your safe list. This can be done by checking the following option:

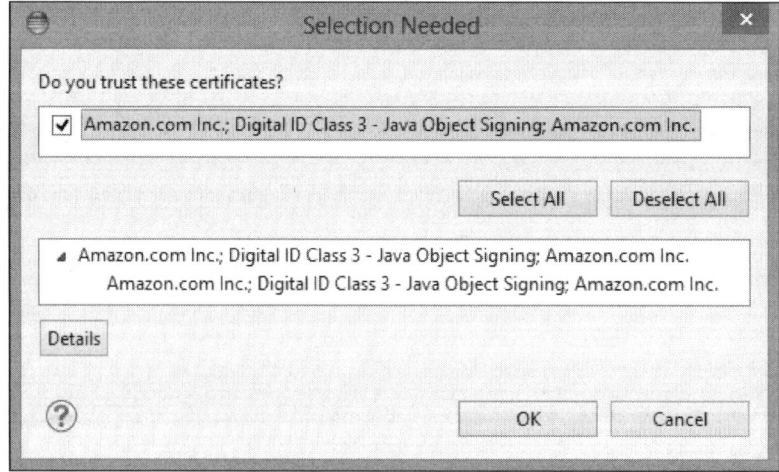

9. After successful installation, Eclipse will ask you to restart for the changes to take effect, as shown in the following screenshot:

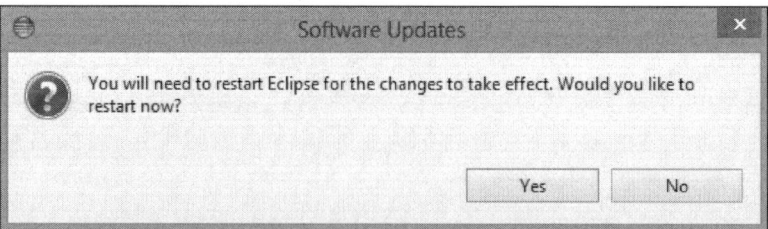

10. After restarting Eclipse, you will see a new icon called AWS toolkit, and the default Eclipse perspective will be Java. To open the perspective to work with AWS, select the **Open Perspective** option from the **Window** menu. It will show the first two perspectives.

11. Double-click on **AWS Management** to begin your work, as shown in the following screenshot:

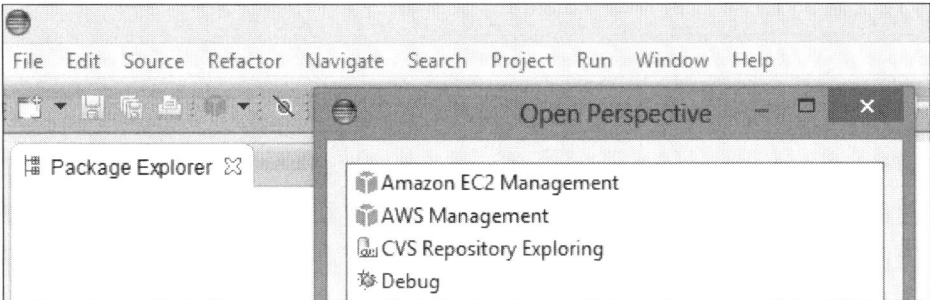

12. While working with the Management Console, you must log in with your AWS username and password. However, in the case of the Eclipse plugin, you need to specify a few more attributes for authentication. You can specify your account details by clicking on the AWS toolkit for the Eclipse icon, and select the **Preferences** option, as shown in the following screenshot:

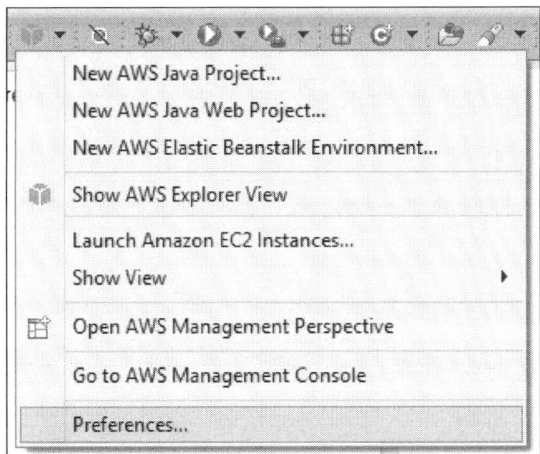

13. The following pop-up window will ask you for details, which you can fetch from the **Security** page in the Management Console:

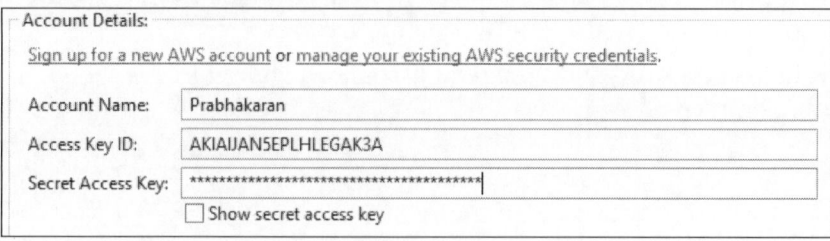

14. Once the configuration is successful, all the AWS components will be loaded. You can right-click on the corresponding service and select **Refresh** to get the latest data. The icon in the top-right corner (with the US flag) is the region that we selected, as shown in the following screenshot:

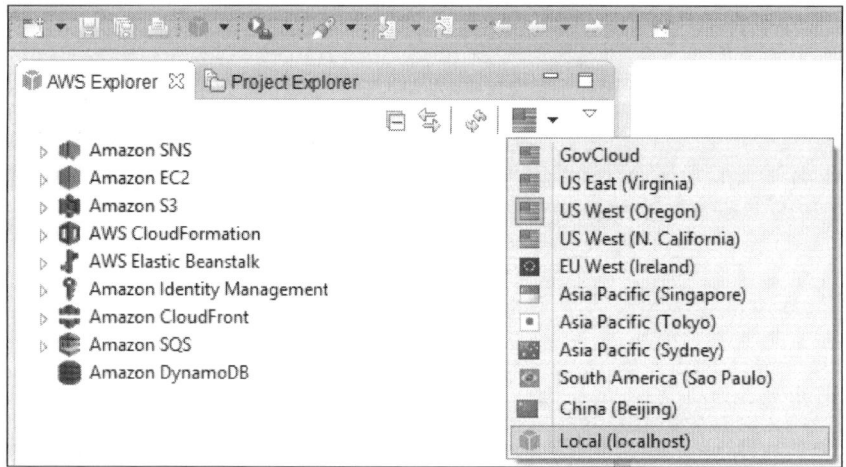

15. To change the region, click on the flag icon in the top-right corner of the page, and then select the region from the drop-down menu.

Downloading the example code

You can download the example code files for all Packt books you have purchased from your account at http://www.packtpub.com. If you purchased this book elsewhere, you can visit http://www.packtpub.com/support and register to have the files e-mailed directly to you.

The SDK tool

Working with AWS using the **Software Development Kit** (**SDK**) is a bit difficult compared to the Eclipse IDE. Even though both perform the same operation, the complexity is a little higher with SDK because of the SDK configuration. The SDK can be downloaded in a ZIP format from `http://sdk-for-java.` `amazonwebservices.com/latest/aws-java-sdk.zip`.

You can extract the downloaded ZIP file to any location of your choice. After this, in the case of Windows OS, you need to create a file named credentials at the `C:\Users\<USERNAME>\.aws\` location. The file should have the following details:

```
[Prabhakar]
aws_access_key_id=AKIMODIFIEDAK3A
aws_secret_access_key=5W6jveTZ7PrabhakarHasModifiedwHpzM+hzOo
```

This file was created while configuring the Eclipse plugin. If this file or directory is not available, you need to create it and fill it with the access key ID and secret access key value. Apart from this, almost everything else is specific to the individual service. You will learn about this in detail in the upcoming chapters.

Summary

In this chapter, you learned the AWS Management Console and its commonly used SDKs and IDEs. You also learned how AWS secures your data. Then, you looked at the AWS plugin configuration on the Eclipse IDE.

The first section made the user familiar with the AWS Management Console. After that, you explored a few of the important security aspects of AWS and learned how AWS handles it. Finally, you learned about the different AWS tools available to the programmer to make his development work easier. In this last section, you examined the common SDKs and IDE tools of AWS. The service-specific SDK and IDE will be discussed separately in the upcoming chapters.

In the next chapter, you will learn about how to store and manage your data on AWS using **Elastic Block Storage** (**EBS**) and **Simple Storage Service** (**S3**).

2
Working with AWS Storage Services

AWS offers high durability and availability for its storage services at a low cost. With a pay-as-you-go pricing model, AWS provides flexibility and agility in its storage services and processes within a highly secured environment. AWS provides storage solutions and services for backup, archive, disaster recovery, and much more. It also supports block, file, and object types of storage with a highly available and flexible infrastructure. The major characteristics of storage include:

- Cost-effective and high-scale storage
- Data protection and data management
- Storage gateway
- Choice of instance storage options

AWS provides us with a lot of storage options depending on the expected quality. Some users might want faster, elastic, and Plug and Play type of storage, such as a pen drive. On the other hand, some users might need the storage available to them in the form of files and folders, similar to an operating system such as Windows. We will discuss what is possible and the best storage scenarios and options in this chapter. Our discussion will cover the following topics:

- AWS storage options
- Amazon EBS
- Amazon S3 bucket and objects

AWS storage options

There are various storage options available on AWS from which you can choose the best suitable option. You can divide the storage options into the following two categories:

- Ephemeral storage (instance storage)
- Persistent storage (Elastic Block Storage)

While launching an instance from the AWS EC2 dashboard, a user can select an instance type and its size, which will be discussed in the upcoming chapters. The instance types start from the `m1.small` type. Any extra storage will be added for this instance automatically without attaching an external storage after launching the instance. The storage is more noticeable in larger instances, such as `m1.medium`, and will come with a larger disk in the `/mnt` directory of your Linux system. Also, it's free. The user won't incur any additional charges for using it to either read or write. To identify the storage functionalities, it is necessary to learn the major types of storage. Let's start with the first storage type, that is, ephemeral storage.

Working with ephemeral storage

An ephemeral disk is a temporary storage option that is automatically added to your instance, and its size depends on your instance type. The ephemeral disk size of an instance ranges from 150 GiB to 48 TiB and varies by a particular instance type. There are several instance types available on the AWS EC2 launching wizard. For certain instance types such as `c1.medium` and `m1.small`, they practice instance storage repeatedly as swap as they have limited memory, whereas several are habitually structured and mounted in the `/mnt` directory.

 More information about instance types is available in *table 2.0*, in the *Persistent storage (EBS)* section.

Ephemeral storage is temporary in nature. For this kind of storage, one should not depend on these disks to keep long-term production data or other important data. Let's take an example such as stopping and starting an instance on a failure of the underlying hardware of EC2 while terminating the instance. For these scenarios, the user should consider EBS/S3 or any other instant storage to be the best solution. Let's take an example of losing the ephemeral disk data while starting and stopping the instance.

The following are the steps to test this operation practically:

1. Launch an instance that has an ephemeral disk, as shown in the following screenshot:

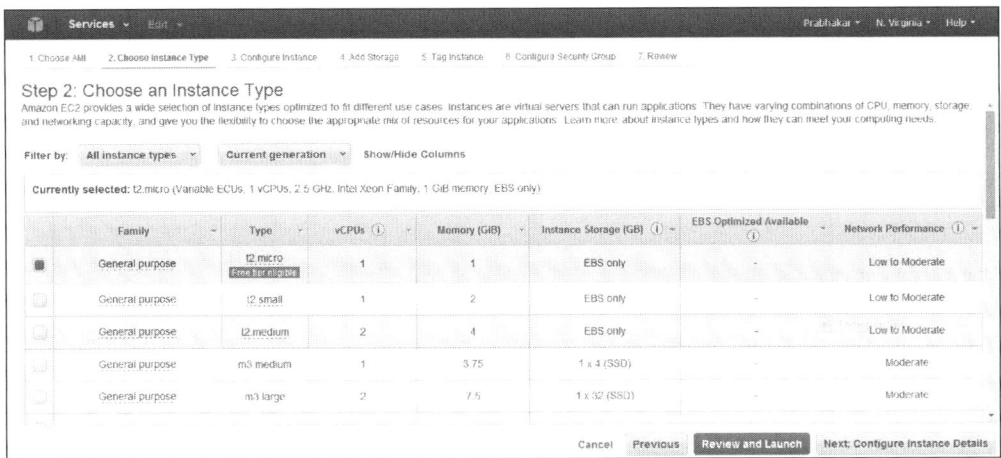

2. Log in with the instance and navigate to the /mnt or /media directory after checking the ephemeral storage using the # df -h command, as shown here:

```
[root@ip-172-31-19-132 ec2-user]# df -h
Filesystem      Size  Used Avail Use% Mounted on
/dev/xvda1      7.8G  1.1G  6.7G  14% /
devtmpfs        813M   20K  813M   1% /dev
tmpfs           828M     0  828M   0% /dev/shm
/dev/xvdb       147G  188M  140G   1% /media/ephemeral0
[root@ip-172-31-19-132 ec2-user]#
```

3. Create any directory or file in the /media directory as per the example:

```
[root@ip-172-31-25-73 ephemeral10]# mkdir prabhakar
[root@ip-172-31-25-73 ephemeral10]# ls
prabhakar
[root@ip-172-31-25-73 ephemeral10]#
```

4. Now, stop the instance and start it again. After starting the instance, check the /media directory with your content, as shown in the following screenshot. You won't be able to see your content as you have performed the stop and start operation with the instance.

```
login as: ec2-user
Authenticating with public key "imported-openssh-key"
Last login: Thu May  1 16:41:40 2014 from 49.200.119.200

       _|  _|_  )
      _|  (     /    Amazon Linux AMI
        _|\___|___|

https://aws.amazon.com/amazon-linux-ami/2014.03-release-notes/
1 package(s) needed for security, out of 18 available
Run "sudo yum update" to apply all updates.
[ec2-user@ip-172-31-19-132 ~]$ sudo -s
[root@ip-172-31-19-132 ec2-user]# cd /media/
[root@ip-172-31-19-132 media]# ls
ephemeral0
[root@ip-172-31-19-132 media]# cd ephemeral0/
[root@ip-172-31-19-132 ephemeral0]# ls
lost+found
[root@ip-172-31-19-132 ephemeral0]#
```

5. Now, let's check the reboot operation after creating some content in the /media/ephemeral10 directory, as shown here:

```
login as: ec2-user
Authenticating with public key "imported-openssh-key"
Last login: Thu May  1 16:41:40 2014 from 49.200.119.200

       _|  _|_  )
      _|  (     /    Amazon Linux AMI
        _|\___|___|

https://aws.amazon.com/amazon-linux-ami/2014.03-release-notes/
1 package(s) needed for security, out of 18 available
Run "sudo yum update" to apply all updates.
[ec2-user@ip-172-31-19-132 ~]$ sudo -s
[root@ip-172-31-19-132 ec2-user]# cd /media/
[root@ip-172-31-19-132 media]# ls
ephemeral0
[root@ip-172-31-19-132 media]# cd ephemeral0/
[root@ip-172-31-19-132 ephemeral0]# ls
lost+found
[root@ip-172-31-19-132 ephemeral0]# mkdir prabhakar
[root@ip-172-31-19-132 ephemeral0]# ls
lost+found  prabhakar
[root@ip-172-31-19-132 ephemeral0]#
```

6. Reboot your instance from the EC2 dashboard, as shown in the following screenshot. For more details, refer to *Chapter 3, Computing Services and Networking*.

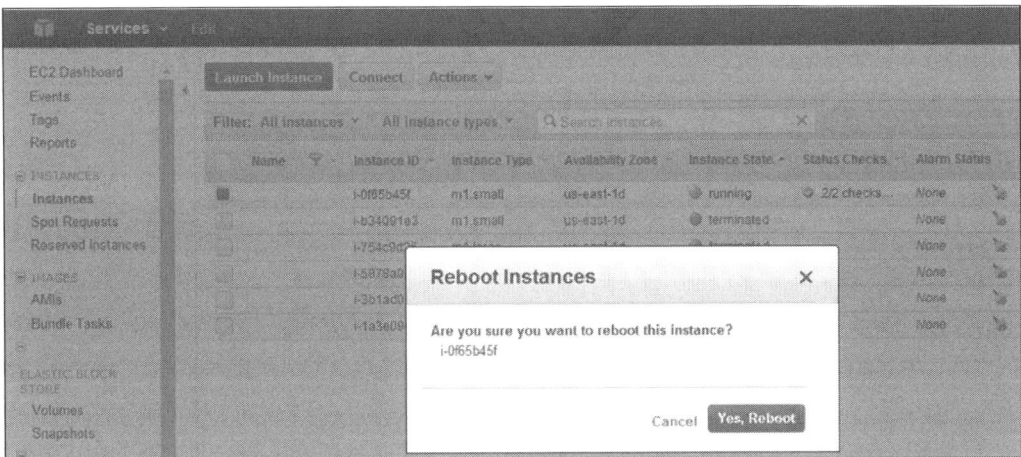

7. After rebooting the process, check the content as follows:

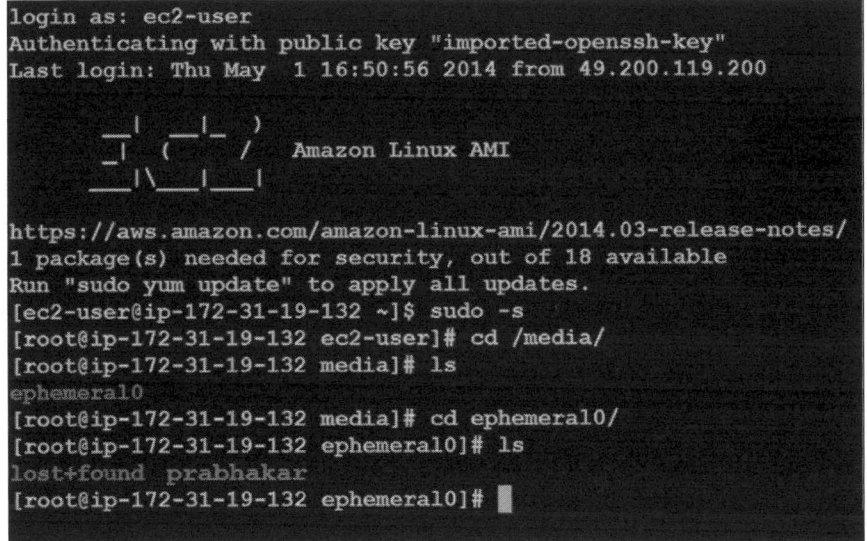

Persistent storage

EC2 instances that use Amazon **Elastic Block Storage (EBS)** for the root device do not, by default, have an instance store accessible at boot time. It is not possible to assign an instance to store volumes after the instance has been launched. Therefore, if a user wants their Amazon EBS-backed instance to use the instance to store volumes, they must postulate them using a block device mapping when creating the AMI or when launching an instance. For example, the block device mapping entries are /dev/sdb=ephemeral0 and /dev/sdc=ephemeral1.

The following table, table 2.0, lists the ephemeral storage size with respect to the instance type of EC2, which can be found on AWS official site (http://aws.amazon. com/ec2/instance-types/):

Instance type	Instance storage volume
c1.medium	1 x 350 GB†
c1.xlarge	4 x 420 GB (1680 GB)
c3.large	2 x 16 GB SSD (32 GB)
c3.xlarge	2 x 40 GB SSD (80 GB)
c3.2xlarge	2 x 80 GB SSD (160 GB)
c3.4xlarge	2 x 160 GB SSD (320 GB)
c3.8xlarge	2 x 320 GB SSD (640 GB)
cc2.8xlarge	4 x 840 GB (3360 GB)
cg1.4xlarge	2 x 840 GB (1680 GB)
cr1.8xlarge	2 x 120 GB SSD (240 GB)
hi1.4xlarge	2 x 1024 GB SSD (2048 GB)
hs1.8xlarge	24 x 2048 GB (49 TB)
i2.xlarge	1 x 800 GB SSD
i2.2xlarge	2 x 800 GB SSD (1600 GB)
i2.4xlarge	4 x 800 GB SSD (3200 GB)
i2.8xlarge	8 x 800 GB SSD (6400 GB)
m1.small	1 x 160 GB†
m1.medium	1 x 410 GB

Instance type	Instance storage volume
m1.large	2 x 420 GB (840 GB)
m1.xlarge	4 x 420 GB (1680 GB)
m2.xlarge	1 x 420 GB
m2.2xlarge	1 x 850 GB
m2.4xlarge	2 x 840 GB (1680 GB)
m3.medium	1 x 4 GB SSD
m3.large	1 x 32 GB SSD
m3.xlarge	2 x 40 GB SSD (80 GB)
m3.2xlarge	2 x 80 GB SSD (160 GB)
r3.large	1 x 32 GB
r3.xlarge	1 x 80 GB
r3.2xlarge	1 x 160 GB
r3.4xlarge	1 x 320 GB
r3.8xlarge	2 x 320 GB (640 GB)

There are lots of theories around instances backed with EBS or instance storages concerning performance, costs, and so on. In general, one can find the subsequent facts, as follows:

- An instance with store-backed storage is faster than EBS for the modest statistic that it is not persistent.

- You can't stop an instance to pay less. Nevertheless, if you do, you will simply lose everything. It is, therefore, necessary to create backup strategies.

- You can't advance an instance or scale vertically. It is necessary to create an **Amazon Machine Image** (**AMI**), which can be used to launch a bigger instance.

And, of course, there are numerous workarounds for this, but it is highly recommended that you use this type of storage only when your application is currently designed to not store anything locally. For data assurance and reliability, you can have an EBS volume attached to the instance. This is to make the application data safe, which in turn will serve backups or to store sensitive data that could be lost.

Working with Amazon EBS

Amazon EBS is a persistent storage provided by AWS. All the data stored on persistent storage is available even after instance shutdown and can be operated at a device level. When the instance is launched, the root device volume holds the image that is used to boot it. When AWS announced Amazon EC2, all AMIs were supported by the Amazon EC2 instance store. This means that the root device for an instance (where the OS is installed) launched from the AMI is an instance store volume formed from a template stored in Amazon's **Simple Storage Service (S3)**. After introducing EBS storages (EBS volumes) in late 2009, AWS presented AMIs that were backed by Amazon EBS. This means that the root device for an instance launched from the AMI will be an Amazon EBS volume created from an Amazon EBS snapshot itself. The user can either choose AMIs backed by the Amazon EC2 instance store or AMIs backed by Amazon EBS. Experts recommend that you use AMIs backed by Amazon EBS because they are launched faster and use persistent storage.

For example, a user can detach an EBS volume from one instance and attach it to another. However, EBS cannot be attached to more than one instance at the same time, but multiple EBSs can be assigned to one EC2 instance and can then be lined and/or emulated into a larger volume using **Redundant Array of Inexpensive Disks (RAID)**.

These two AMIs are based on type and reveal several differences, for example, in their life cycle, boot time, and data persistence characteristics, as shown in the following table:

Characteristic name	Amazon EBS backed	Instance (S3) store backed
Life cycle	Supports the stopping and restarting of an instance by saving a state to EBS.	An instance cannot be stopped; it can either be in the running state or terminated state.
Data persistence	Data continues in EBS on an instance failure or system restart. Data can also be configured to persist when the instance is terminated.	Instance storage does not continue on instance shutdown or failure. It is possible to attach the nonroot devices using EBS.
Boot time	Usually less than 1 minute.	Usually less than 5 minutes.

Using persistent storage with EC2

EBS is a mountable storage service; it can be mounted as a device (such as a Plug and Play USB pen drive) to an EC2 instance.

Let's take a look at an example to attach EBS (persistent storage) to your instance using the following steps:

1. Navigate to the Amazon EC2 console, as shown in the following screenshot:

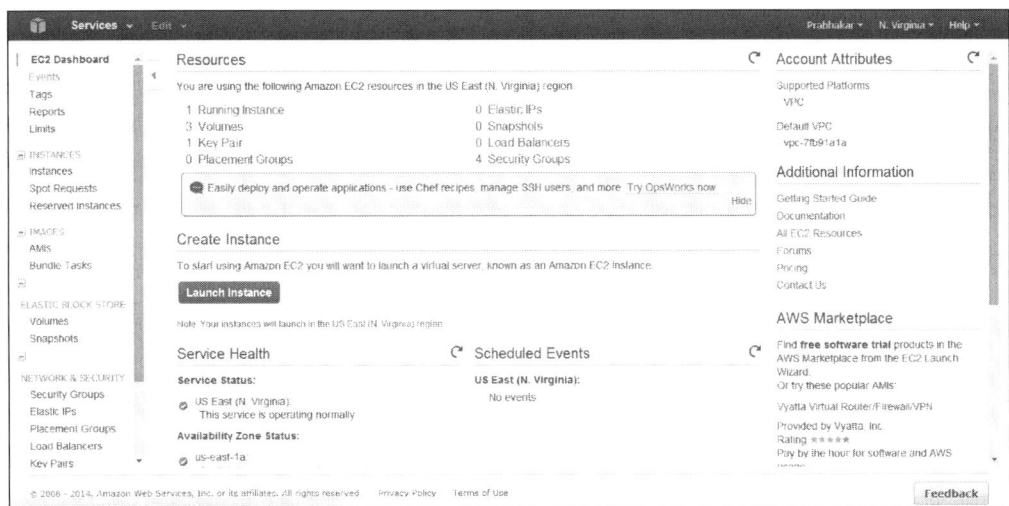

2. On the left-hand side, in the navigation pane, you will find the **ELASTIC BLOCK STORE** section; in this, click on **Volumes**, as shown here:

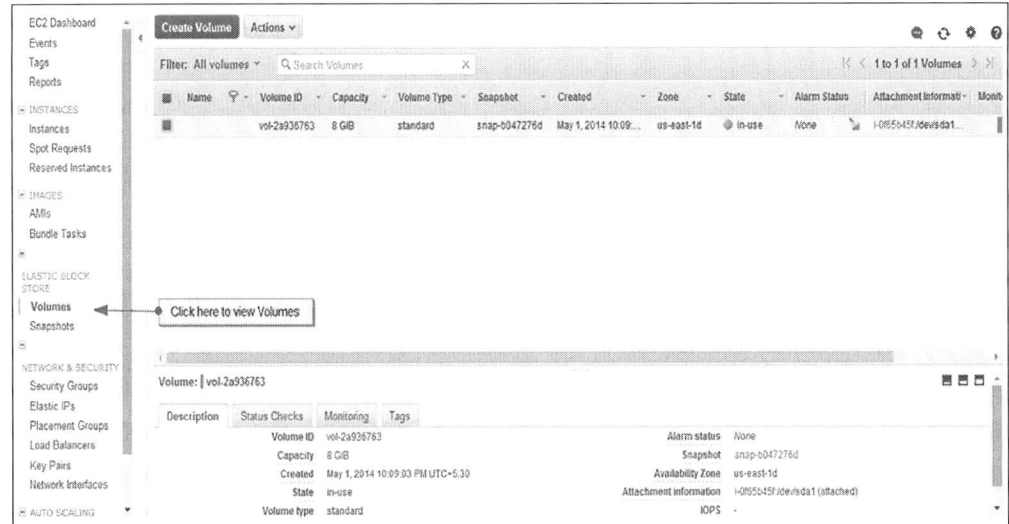

The console displays a list of the current volumes.

3. Select a volume and click on **Attach Volume**. Select the appropriate instance from the drop-down box. Only the instances in the same availability zone as the volume will be displayed, as shown in the following screenshot:

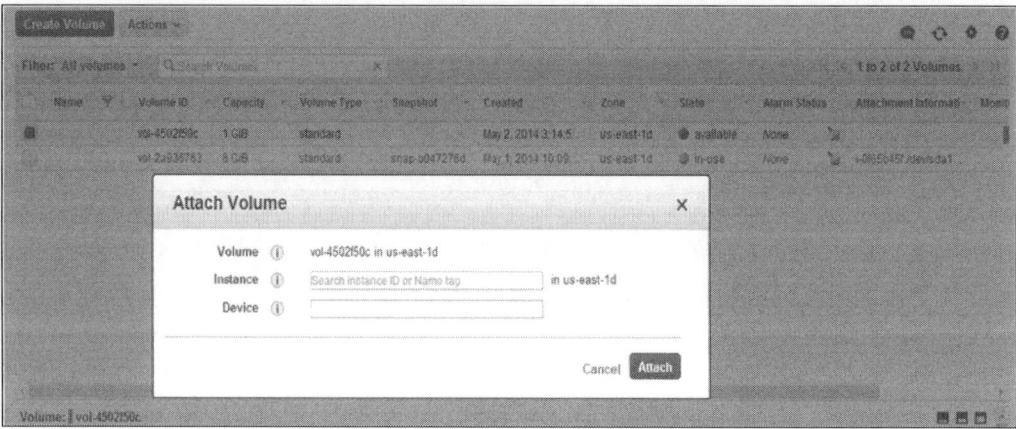

4. Fill the necessary details and click on the **Attach** button to attach the volume to the instance. The volume and the instance must be in the same availability zone.

 Instances with a Windows OS will be using either Red Hat or Citrix **paravirtual (PV)** drivers. If you have a Windows instance with Citrix PV drivers, you can attach a total of 25 EBS volumes; but Windows instances with Red Hat PV drivers are limited to 16 volumes only.

The following diagram summarizes the life cycles of both persistent and nonpersistent storages with S3 and EBS-backed EC2 instances:

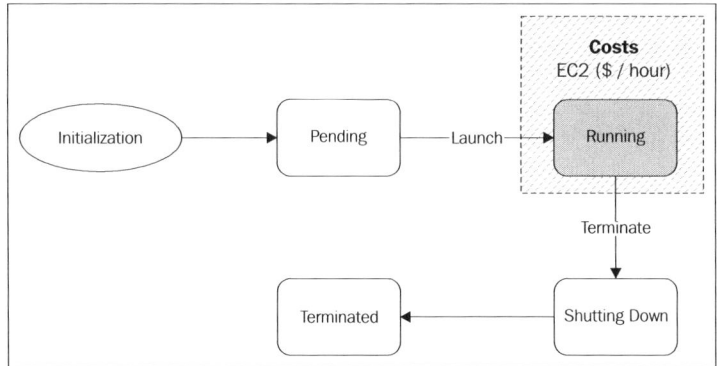

The EBS-backed EC2 instances present a new stopped state, which is currently not available in the S3-backed instances. It is essential to keep in mind that while an instance is in a stopped state, the user will not experience any EC2 running charges except the EBS storage charges that are related to the instance, as shown in the following diagram:

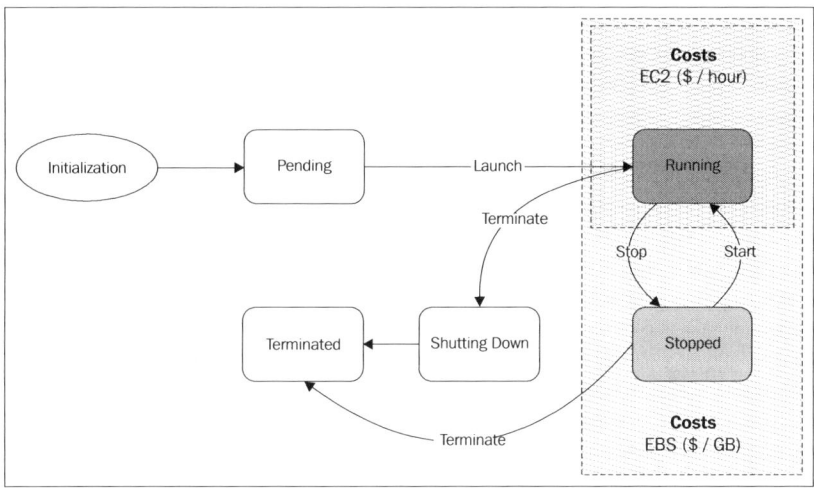

The other benefit of using EBS-backed instances over S3-backed instances is that a stopped instance can be started at a later time while still preserving its core state.

Working with AWS

To store an object in Amazon S3, the user can upload a file to a bucket. When uploading the file, a user can set permissions on the object as well as on the additional metadata.

Buckets are the containers for objects, and a user can have one or more buckets. For each bucket, the user can control user access (who can create, delete, and list objects in the bucket), view access logs for it and its objects, and choose the geographical region where Amazon S3 will store the bucket and its contents.

Creating the S3 bucket

An object can be a file and might contain metadata that describes the file. The following screenshot illustrates the AWS S3 dashboard in detail:

To create an S3 bucket, perform the following steps:

1. By selecting S3, you will be taken to the S3 dashboard, as shown in the following screenshot:

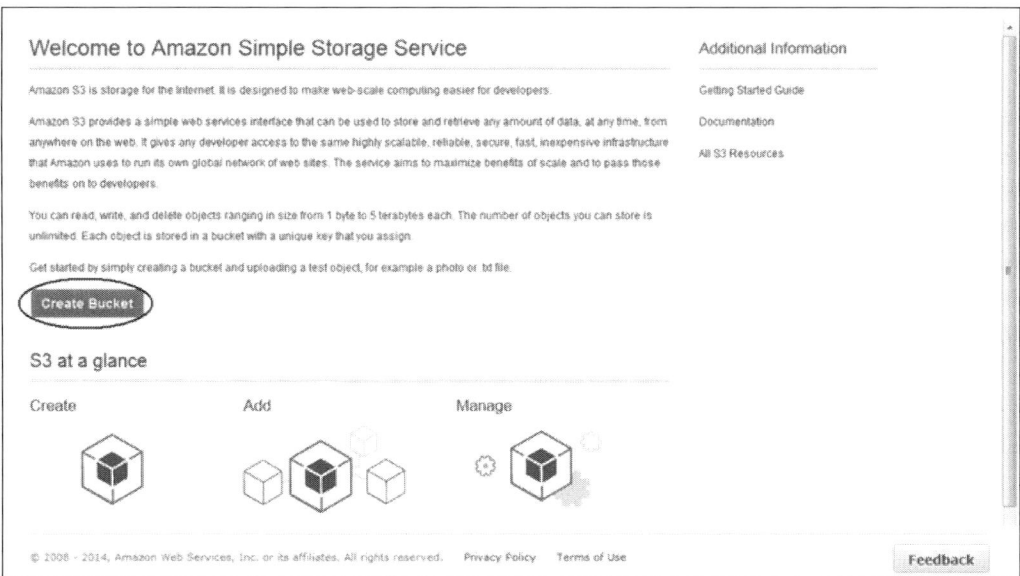

2. Click on the **Create Bucket** button and you will be prompted by a pop-up box to create your first bucket. Supply a region name to see the following bucket creation dashboard that demonstrates the power of AWS S3 and its configurations:

3. The bucket name must be unique worldwide; otherwise, AWS won't allow you to create a bucket with that name. After the creation of the bucket, you will see the following page:

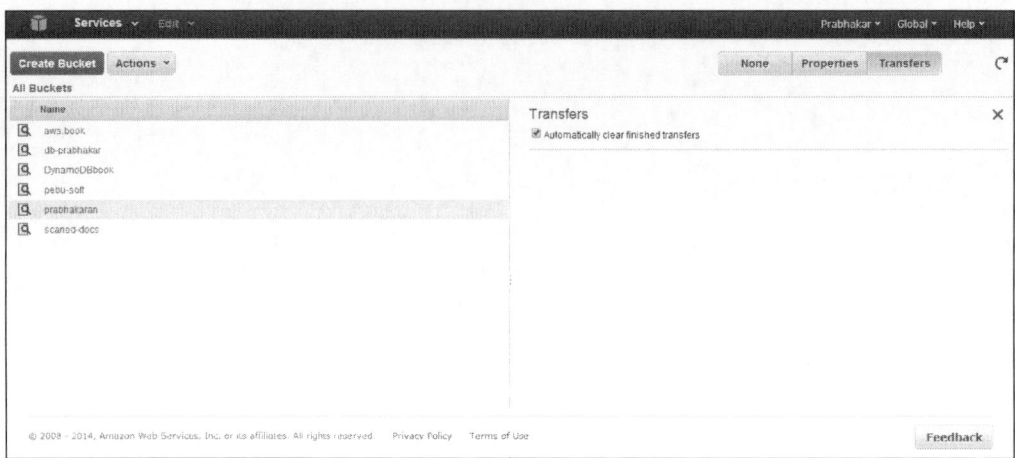

Bucket-related operations can be executed via the CLI, API, or from the dashboard directly. This chapter will detail various bucket operations and configurations from CLI. To start with CLI, the user will require the Amazon Web Service SDK and an AWS account with an access key and a private key to connect to Amazon S3 (as configured in *Chapter 1, An Introduction to AWS*). The object controls all the actions by which you can interact with the AWS S3 instance, as shown here:

```
const string AWS_ACCESS_KEY = "your_AWS_access_key";
const string AWS_SECRET_KEY = "your_AWS_secret_key";
AwsS3 client = newAwsS3(AWS_ACCESS_KEY, AWS_SECRET_KEY)
```

Normally, these keys are stored in the `web.config` file and are accessed by the code in web-based applications, as follows:

```
// In your application config file, set this
<appSettings>
<add key="AWSAccessKey" value="AWS_access_key"/>
<add key="AWSSecretKey" value="AWS_secret_key"/>
<appSettings>
```

It is now necessary to create a function to access the S3 credentials, as follows:

```
// Function to get it
public static AwsS3 GetS3Client()
{
```

```
NameValueCollection appConfig = ConfigurationManager.AppSettings;

    AwsS3 s3Client = AWSClientFactory.CreateAmazonS3Client(
appConfig["AWSAccessKey"],
appConfig["AWSSecretKey"]
            );
return s3Client;
}
```

A user can now start working with AWS S3. In the following example, you will see how to upload and retrieve content from the S3 bucket. If you want to store data in S3, you need to create a bucket. It is similar to the `root` folder in Windows. In Amazon S3, the maximum number of buckets is 100 and the names of buckets are unique globally.

You are allowed to create a maximum of 100 buckets per account, and these bucket names must be unique around the globe. Using the following code, you can create a sample bucket on AWS S3:

```
AWSCredentials credentials = new
    ProfileCredentialsProvider().getCredentials();
AmazonS3 s3 = new AmazonS3Client(credentials);
Region usEast = Region.getRegion(Regions.US_EAST_1);
s3.setRegion(usEast);
String bucketName = "prabhakaran";
s3.createBucket(bucketName);
```

After the successful execution of the preceding code, you will be able to see a new bucket named **prabhakaran** on the AWS S3 dashboard, as shown in the following screenshot:

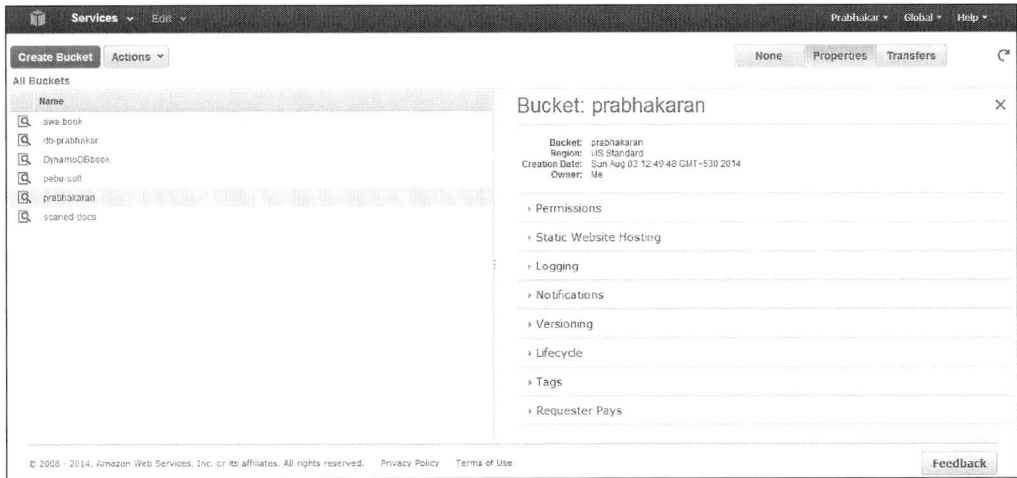

There are various ways to create a new file in the S3 bucket, but we will introduce you to some of the generic/simplest ways. In the first method, a user needs a FileKey, which will be unique with a full path and a content body that contains information. To create a directory, use the FileKey with the special character (/) at the end to show that you want to create a specified directory, as shown in the following code:

```
String folder_KEY = "Demo Create folder/";
PutObjectRequest request = new PutObjectRequest();
request.WithBucketName(BUCKET_NAME);
request.WithKey(folder_KEY);
request.WithContentBody("");
client.PutObject(request);
```

The following screenshot shows how the new directory that will be created will look:

To create a new file, there is a minor change in the directory creation code, shown as follows:

```
String S3_KEY = "Demo Create File.txt";
PutObjectRequest request = new PutObjectRequest();
request.WithBucketName(BUCKET_NAME);
request.WithKey(s3_KEY);
request.WithContentBody("This is content of S3 object in Demo file.");
client.PutObject(request);
```

After the successful execution of the preceding code, the file will be created in the bucket, as follows:

To create a file within the directory, it is necessary to change the FileKey to include the directory name, as shown here:

```
String S3_KEY = "Demo Create folder/" + "Demo Create File.txt";
PutObjectRequest request = new PutObjectRequest();
request.WithBucketName(BUCKET_NAME);
request.WithKey(s3_KEY);
request.WithContentBody("This is content of S3 object in Demo file.");
client.PutObject(request);
```

After the successful execution of the preceding code, the file will be created in the defined directory within the bucket. You will now see how to upload files from a local machine to an S3 bucket with an absolute path, as follows:

```
//s3_KEY is name of file we want to upload
PutObjectRequest request = new PutObjectRequest();
request.WithBucketName(BUCKET_NAME);
request.WithKey(s3_KEY);
request.WithFilePath(pathToFile)
client.PutObject(request);
```

Amazon S3 has many useful features that are useful to developers who want to create a web app that needs to store data online.

Similar operations can be performed using the following code:

```
public class S3 {
    public static void main(String[] args) {
            AWSCredentials credentials = new
                ProfileCredentialsProvider().getCredentials();
            AmazonS3 s3 = new AmazonS3Client(credentials);
            Region usEast = Region.getRegion(Regions.US_EAST_1);
            s3.setRegion(usEast);
            String bucketName = "prabhakaran";
            //s3.createBucket(bucketName);
            String key = "folder2/sampleFile.txt";
            s3.putObject(new PutObjectRequest(bucketName, key,
                getFileToBeUploaded()));
    }

    private static File getFileToBeUploaded() {
            File file = null;
            try {
                    file = File.createTempFile("localFile", ".txt");
                    file.deleteOnExit();
```

```
                    Writer writer = new OutputStreamWriter(new
                        FileOutputStream(file));
                    writer.write("Sample content through Java SDK");
                    writer.close();              } catch (IOException e) {
                    e.printStackTrace();
            }
        return file;
    }

}
```

The preceding code will create a folder named `folder2` inside the bucket `prabhakaran`. After this, it will create a file named `sampleFile.txt` inside `folder2`. Then, the file will be written with the `Sample` content through the Java SDK.

> The private function, `getFileToBeUploaded`, will create a temporary file named `localFile.txt`, which is used to write the content to S3. This local file will be deleted once the content is written to S3.

AWS Glacier

AWS Glacier is a storage solution to archive and back up data at a very low cost and with rich security features. Using the AWS Glacier solution, customers can store their data as long as they want, and it allows you to offload administrative tasks, such as scaling and operations, on AWS. By using the AWS Glacier service for storage, the user doesn't need to worry about data security, data replication, and time-consuming data/hardware migrations.

AWS Glacier is a REST-based web service having data model core concepts, including vaults and archives. Moreover, its data model includes job and notification configuration complementary resources to the core resources. The user can have up to 1,000 vaults per region in their AWS account. AWS Glacier is designed to provide an average annual durability of 99.999999999 percent per archive. To start with AWS Glacier, follow these steps:

1. Download the proper AWS SDK tools for Java:
   - If you are using Eclipse, you can download and install the tools from `http://aws.amazon.com/eclipse/`

° For other SDK users, you can download the tools from
`http://aws.amazon.com/sdkforjava/`

2. Create a vault by performing the following steps:

1. Create a vault from the Amazon Glacier console by clicking on
Create Vault, as shown in the following screenshot:

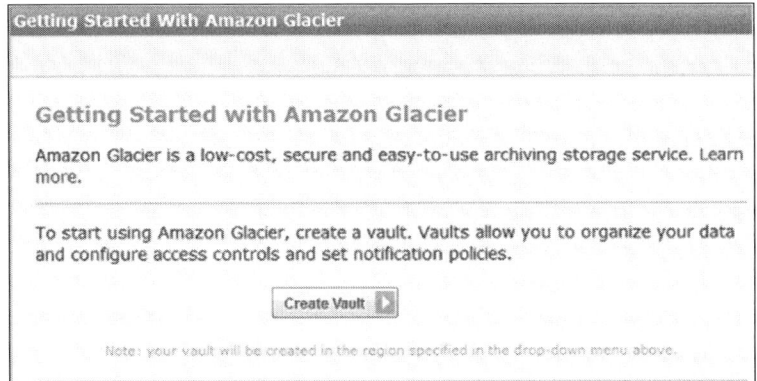

2. Provide the appropriate vault name by clicking on **Continue To
Notifications**, as shown here:

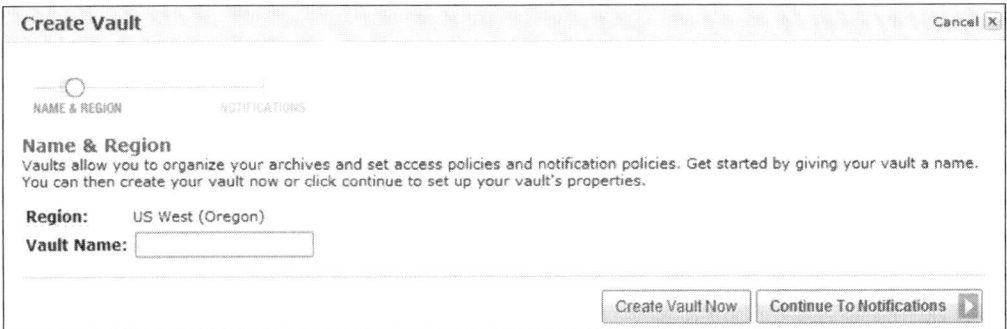

3. If you require notifications from SNS, configure it for your vault, as follows:

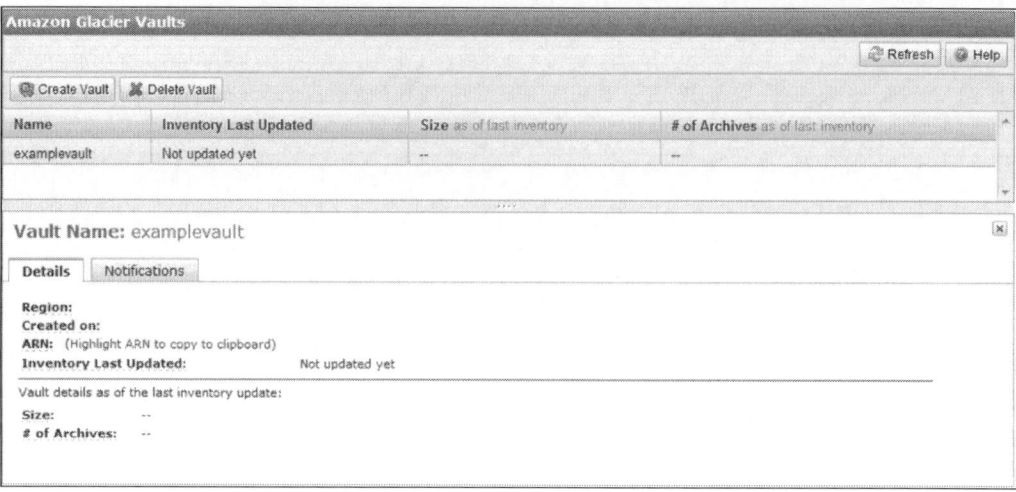

3. Upload your content through the Java SDK or the .NET SDK to your vault using the code in the next step. There are three ways to upload your content to the vault:

   ○ **Using the low-level API**: This provides basic methods, which are available via the REST API calls to AWS Glacier.

   ○ **Using the high-level API**: This provides a high level of abstraction for the low-level API methods.

   ○ **Using Eclipse**: This will install the AWS SDK toolkit for Eclipse and then you can use it via an API call. To use the low-level API, refer to the `AmazonGlacierClient` class, which provides each and every method that maps REST calls for Glacier. The user then creates an appropriate request and a response object from which the method can return the response.

4. The high-level API is explained now. Its method is pretty straightforward, so anybody can do this. To use the high-level API to upload content, use the following code snippet:

```
String vaultName = "exampleVault";
String archiveToUpload = "c:/folder/demoArchive.zip";

ArchiveTransferManager atm = new
  ArchiveTransferManager(client, credentials);
String archiveId = atm.upload(vaultName, "Result 2014
  documents", new File(archiveToUpload)).getArchiveId();
```

Usually, even when you upload a file to a vault, it will not be available instantaneously. It usually takes at least a day for the vault inventory to be updated. Only then will you be able to see the vault items.

5. Conversely, you can download your content from the Amazon vault using the Java SDK, as follows:

```java
importjava.io.File;
importjava.io.IOException;
importcom.amazonaws.auth.profile.ProfileCredentialsProvider
;
importcom.amazonaws.services.glacier.AmazonGlacierClient;
importcom.amazonaws.services.glacier.transfer.ArchiveTransf
erManager;
importcom.amazonaws.services.sns.AmazonSNSClient;
importcom.amazonaws.services.sqs.AmazonSQSClient;
public class AmazonGlacierDownloadArchive_GettingStarted {
public static String vaultName = "demovault";
public static String archiveId = "*** archive ID ***";
public static String downloadFilePath  = "location to
download archive ";
public static AmazonGlacierClient glacierClient;
public static AmazonSQSClient sqsClient;
public static AmazonSNSClient snsClient;
public static void main(String[] args) throws IOException {
    ProfileCredentialsProvider credentials = new
ProfileCredentialsProvider();

glacierClient = new AmazonGlacierClient(credentials);
sqsClient = new AmazonSQSClient(credentials);
snsClient = new AmazonSNSClient(credentials);

glacierClient.setEndpoint("glacier.us-west-
2.amazonaws.com");
sqsClient.setEndpoint("sqs.us-west-2.amazonaws.com");
snsClient.setEndpoint("sns.us-west-2.amazonaws.com");

try {
ArchiveTransferManager atm = new ArchiveTransferManager(glacierCli
ent, sqsClient,
snsClient);
```

```
atm.download(vaultName, archiveId, new
File(downloadFilePath));

        } catch (Exception e)
        {
System.err.println(e);
        }
    }
}
```

6. You cannot delete content from the vault directly; it should be done via the SDK or API. Use the following code snippet to delete content from the vault:

```
importjava.io.IOException;

importcom.amazonaws.auth.profile.ProfileCredentialsProvider
;
importcom.amazonaws.services.glacier.AmazonGlacierClient;
importcom.amazonaws.services.glacier.model.DeleteArchiveReq
uest;
public class AmazonGlacierDeleteArchive_GettingStarted {

public static String vaultName = "demovault";
public static String archiveId = " archive ID";
public static AmazonGlacierClient client;
public static void main(String[] args) throws IOException {
        ProfileCredentialsProvider credentials = new
  ProfileCredentialsProvider();

client = new AmazonGlacierClient(credentials);
client.setEndpoint("https://glacier.us-west-
2.amazonaws.com/");
try {
        // Delete the archive.
client.deleteArchive(new DeleteArchiveRequest()
            .withVaultName(vaultName)
            .withArchiveId(archiveId));

System.out.println("Deleted successfully.");

        } catch (Exception e) {
System.err.println("Archive not deleted due to some
error");
System.err.println(e);
        }
    }
}
```

7. To delete the vault, click on the **Delete Vault** button and you are done, as shown in the following screenshot:

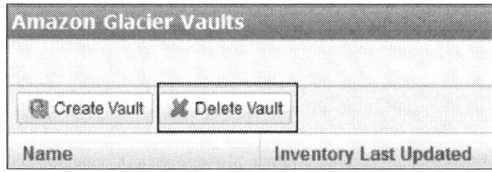

Amazon Glacier is a very useful and easy-to-operate service if you want to store your long-term data at a very cheap storage rate on AWS.

Summary

In this chapter, we have seen the major storage concepts such as ephemeral storage and persistent storage, which are useful for startups and new users. Later, EBS storage systems were discussed and their usage with EC2. Using the S3 service, we illustrated how a user can leverage the benefits of object storage on the AWS platform.

In the next chapter, you will learn about AWS Compute and Networking services, for example, learning to create instances with other effective services. Finally, the chapter will focus on creating virtual, private cloud fundamentals and methods of creation for VPC.

3
Computing and Networking Services

AWS offers a huge range of various cloud-based core computing services, including a variety of compute instances that can be autoscaled to justify the needs of your users and your application, a managed elastic load-balancing service, and fully-managed desktop resources on the way to cloud. AWS offers a wide set of networking services that enable you to create a logical, isolated network, which an architect can define, and create a private network connection to the AWS infrastructure, with a fault-tolerant, scalable, and highly available DNS service. AWS also offers delivery services for content to end users with very low latency and high data-transfer speed with an AWS CDN service.

AWS provides a diverse variety of computing services, which can be automatically scaled up/down depending on the requirements of the applications in real-time usage. Performance as well as minimal costs at certain demanding spike times can be ensured, which is very much suited for web applications with varied traffic patterns and load. AWS also provides load balancing services that automatically distribute the incoming application traffic across multiple instances, enabling greater levels of fault tolerance in multiple AZs and regions. It enables its customers to create a logically defined isolated network, establish a private connection to the cloud, and use the highly reliable yet scalable DNS service called **Route 53**. Amazon VPC, Amazon Route 53, AWS Direct Connect, and so on are a few network-related services. Amazon EC2 is one of the computing services that enables resizable computing capacity in the Amazon Cloud. It makes web-scale computing easier and scalable. As a part of the discussion, we will learn the following topics:

- Working with EC2
- Tools available to access EC2
- Best practices for EC2
- Create, secure, and access your own VPC

Amazon Elastic Compute Cloud

Amazon **Elastic Compute Cloud (EC2)** is a web service from AWS, which provides a resizable compute capacity in the cloud using its simple interface designed for an easier web-scaling experience. It allows complete control over the computing resources. Amazon EC2 provides the following benefits:

- **Flexible scaling**: Amazon EC2 enables you to scale resources up/down within minimal timelines via the web service that the API calls depending on the application requirements.

- **Full control**: Root access to each and every instance enables you to have complete control over them.

- **Flexible hosting**: Amazon EC2 allows you to choose your configurations (in terms of memory, CPU, and so on) so that are optimal to your operating system. You can pick from a wide range of instance types, operating systems, and software packages.

- **Compatible with other AWS**: Amazon EC2 in conjunction with other AWS such as S3 or RDS, or any other AWS, will shape up a complete computing solution around different areas.

- **Reliable**: The environments are highly reliable with 99.95 percent availability commitment.

- **Secure**: The environments are highly secure and robust. The inbound/outbound network access is controllable via the network ACLs and security groups. Let's discuss this topic in detail in a later chapter on security.

- **Cost-effectiveness**: Amazon EC2 allows you to pay as you go, thereby reducing upfront investments.

- **Ease**: The launch of the one-click EC2 console enables customers to deploy their apps easily.

Amazon EC2 operates with a few basic elements such as instances, AMIs, and others. Let's take a broader view of these basics in the next few sections.

Getting started with EC2 instances

EC2 instances are simply virtual computing environments/resources that can be completely controlled just as in the case of traditional hosting systems. The hardware of the host machine is the key for different instance types, which offers varied combinations of compute as well as memory capabilities and storage.

Images that are used to boot the instances are stored at root device volumes. The local storage volumes of instances are known as Instance store volumes, which can be configured at launch time with block device mapping. These volumes are mostly used for temporary data storage because when an instance is terminated or fails, the data on these volumes gets lost; so, it is called ephemeral storage.

Root device volume of Amazon EC2

During the launch of the EC2 Instance, the image (called AMI) required to boot an instance will be located at the root device volume. AWS AMIs are differentiated depending on the storage by which the instances are backed by the EBS or Instance store.

- **AMIs backed by Amazon EBS**: The instance launched by this AMI will contain the Amazon EBS volume as its root device
- **AMIs backed by Instance store**: The instance launched by this AMI will contain an instance store volume created from a template stored in Amazon S3 as its root device

Initially, when Amazon EC2 was introduced, all the AMIs were backed by the Amazon EC2 instance store. However, in the later stages, the concept of AMIs backed by EBS volumes came into the picture when Amazon EBS was published. In general, AMIs backed by Amazon EBS are preferred, as they use persistent storage and launch faster.

Working with Amazon EC2

Amazon EC2 allows you to launch your instances via web services with varieties of OSes, load them with custom web application environments, manage the authentication and access, and run your AMI on the required number of virtual hardware systems.

Perform the following steps to use Amazon EC2:

1. Select an AMI that enables you to get up and running.
2. Security and network configurations are adjusted on the instances.
3. Select the instance type and then manage them accordingly.
4. Determine the requirement for multilocation.
5. Utilize static IP endpoints.
6. Pay for the resources that you consume.

Currently, Amazon EC2 supports the following operating systems:

- CentOS
- Debian
- SUSE Linux Enterprise
- Amazon Linux
- Oracle Enterprise Linux
- Ubuntu
- Red Hat Enterprise Linux
- Windows Server

AWS AMIs come preconfigured with most of the operating systems, and you can also upload your own OS using the corresponding tools. Extensive support for wide varieties of free/commercial software is provided, for example:

- MicroStrategy
- Django
- MongoDB
- Ruby on Rails

 For more information visit `https://aws.amazon.com/marketplace/ref=mkt_ste_ec2`.

Best practices

Let's take an overview of a few best practices for the AWS EC2 service:

- It is wise to manage access to AWS APIs and resources via the **Identity and Access Management (IAM)** web service
- Instances should be launched into a VPC rather than in the EC2 Classic
- **Security Groups (SG)** should have at least permissive rules
- The root device's storage implications should be well-studied
- Dynamic IPs should be preferred on the restart of an instance
- Regular backups should be in place
- Events have to be monitored and responded to optimally
- Metadata should be used to track your AWS resources
- Critical components should be replicated and deployed across multiple availability zones

When you sign up with AWS, you will get all the services automatically and view them in your dashboard, but you only have to pay for the services that you really use. In the AWS free tier environments, customers will be able to use only micro instances. It provides the following services:

- Regional data transfer is limited to 1 GB
- An EBS standard storage volume of 30 GB
- 1 GB snapshot storage
- 750 hours of **Elastic Load Balancing (ELB)**
- 15 GB of data processing
- 750 hours of EC2 running Windows/Linux/Unix micro instance usage.

 More detailed pricing options can be found at
`http://aws.amazon.com/ec2/pricing`.

Tools

AWS provides a variety of tools to develop and manage applications on the cloud platform. They fall into one of the following categories:

- SDKs
- IDEs
- CLIs

Getting started

Let's take a hands-on tour of the generic steps to use the Amazon EC2 platform.

Sign up to the AWS. When you create your account on AWS, all the services are automatically enabled for your account, but you will be required to pay only for the service that you use. The procedure to create an account and sign up for AWS is as follows:

1. Create an IAM user from the IAM dashboard. IAM ensures secured access to your AWS and your resources.

2. Create a key pair for the EC2 Instance. It is used to secure the login details of your instances.

3. Create a security group to secure your instances. These act as firewalls, controlling both the inbound and outbound traffic at the instance level.

Let's start with the procedure to create an account and sign up with AWS. Visit `http://aws.amazon.com/` and create your account by following the on-screen instructions. The following screenshot shows the interface of the screen:

Let's proceed further by taking a look at how we can get started with Linux and Windows instances in detail.

Windows instances

Consider that the instances (which are virtual servers in the AWS cloud environment) have a root volume as an Amazon EBS running a Windows Server and are secured with the corresponding key pair along with a security group, as shown in the following diagram. Let's take a look at the step-by-step procedure. You should use the private key while connecting to your instance.

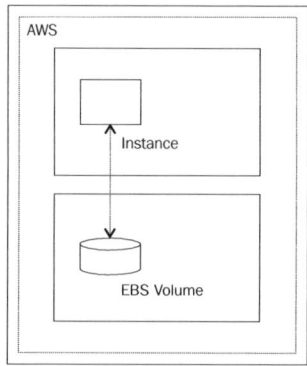

The steps to launch and connect to a Windows instance are as follows:

1. Launch the instance.
2. Connect to the instance.
3. Follow the optional steps to create a monitoring alarm.

Let's go through the preceding steps in detail:

1. Let's start by launching the instance from the dashboard:

    1. Sign in to **AWS management console** and navigate to **Amazon EC2**.
    2. Choose the **Region** for your instance from the **Navigation** bar.
    3. Click on **Launch Instance**.
    4. Choose the appropriate Windows version (if the free tier is eligible) from the **choose an AMI** page; this will serve as a template for your EC2 instance.
    5. Choose the appropriate hardware configuration for your instance on the **choose an instance type** page.
    6. Click on **Review & launch** (this enables the wizard to complete the settings/configurations to get you started).
    7. Review your instance settings on the **Review instance launch** page.
    8. Click on the **Launch** button.
    9. Create or select your key pair by visiting the **Select an existing key pair or create a new key pair** dialog box.
    10. You will receive a confirmation page. Close it and proceed further.
    11. Visit the **Instances** page and check the Public DNS.
    12. Review the security group's rules from the instance page details.

2. Now, let's move on to the next step of connecting to the instance.

 Remember that the Windows instance allows only two simultaneous remote connections at any point in time.

    1. Sign in to **AWS Management Console**, navigate to **Amazon EC2**, select the instance, and click on **Connect**.
    2. Visit the **Connect To Your Instance** dialog box and click on **Get password**.
    3. Click on **Browse** to select and copy your private key to the box available.

4. Select **Decrypt password**; this will display the default admin password, which you will require in order to connect to your instance. So make a note of it.

5. Click on **Download Remote Desktop File**. You can choose to either open or save the `.rdp` file. Once you are done, click on **Close**.

6. Connect to your instance by clicking on the **Connect** button.

7. Log in to the instance with your default admin password, which you noted earlier.

 Once every instance starts to boot, billing is done correspondingly even if the instance is idle.

3. Once any instance changes its state to shutting down or terminated, its corresponding billing will get halted. So, let's terminate our instance as follows:

    1. Sign in to **AWS Management Console**, navigate to **Amazon EC2**, select the instance, and locate the instance that you wish to terminate.

    2. Right-click on it and choose **terminate**.

    3. Confirm the termination by clicking on **Yes**.

Linux instances

Consider that the EC2 instances (which are virtual servers in the cloud environment) have a root volume as an Amazon EBS running a Linux server and are secured with the corresponding key pair along with the security group, as shown in the following diagram. Let's now take a look into the step-by-step procedure. You should use the private key while connecting to your instance.

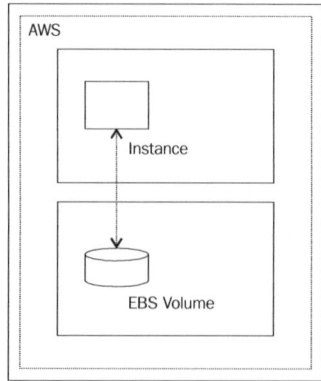

The steps to launch and connect to a Linux instance are as follows:

1. Launch the instance.
2. Connect to the instance.
3. Clean up.

Let's go through the preceding steps in detail:

1. Launch the instance in the same manner as how we launched for the Windows instance.

2. Now, let's move on to the next step of connecting to the instance. There are multiple ways to do this:

    ○ Connect using your browser
    ○ Connect from Windows using PuTTY
    ○ Connect from Mac or Linux using an SSH client

3. Let's take a look at the option of connecting via a browser. The prerequisite for this is to have Java installed and enabled.

    1. Sign in to **AWS Management Console** and navigate to **Amazon EC2**, select the instance, and click on **Connect**.

    2. Click on **A Java SSH client** directly from the browser.

    3. The public DNS name is automatically detected and populated while detecting the corresponding key pair as well. Then type the Linux default username in the **Username** field.

 For Amazon Linux, the default username is ec2-user.
For RHEL5, the username is often root but it might be ec2-user.
For Ubuntu, the username is Ubuntu. For SUSE Linux, the username is root. Otherwise, check with your AMI provider.

    4. Enter your private key file path in the **Private key path** field. Click on **Store** in **Browser cache** to store the location of the private key in your browser cache.

    5. Click on **No** when you are prompted to add a host to your set of known hosts.

    6. Click on **Run** for certificate and accept the license agreements.

    7. A new window opens, connecting you to your instance.

Let's move ahead with the cleanup procedure. Initially, terminate the instance (which is nothing but deleting it), which enables the detachment of the volume (if you have added any extra volume) from the instance, and then go ahead and delete the volumes.

So, terminate your instance as given in the previous Windows instances section.

Amazon VPC

Actually, Amazon VPC is a combination of two key points:

- This is a private, isolated section of the AWS Cloud where you can launch the AWS resources in a virtual network that you control. If you also want hardware isolation, there is an option known as **Dedicated Instances** in AWS.

- It provides complete control over your resources, including subnets, route tables, ACLs, and IP addresses.

Amazon VPC supports both hardware and software VPN tunnels at the datacenter level, and also supports client-based tunnels via software packages such as OpenVPN.

Creating an AWS VPC

VPC provides complete control over layers of security. Let's get started with creating your first VPC environment. Follow these steps to proceed:

1. Log in to the AWS console and select the **VPC** service.

2. Click on the **Start VPC Wizard** button to start with VPC, as shown in the following screenshot:

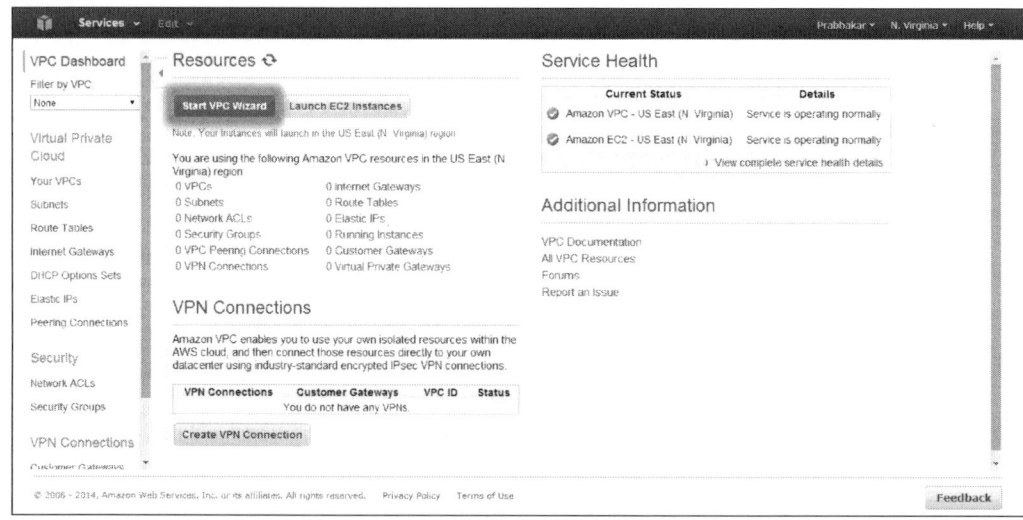

Once you click on the AWS VPC, you will see four options showing the different types of VPC.

Creating a public subnet within VPC

In this chapter, you'll create a VPC with a single, public subnet. To do this, follow these steps:

1. Choose the first wizard option, **VPC with a Single Public Subnet**, and then click on **Select**, as shown here:

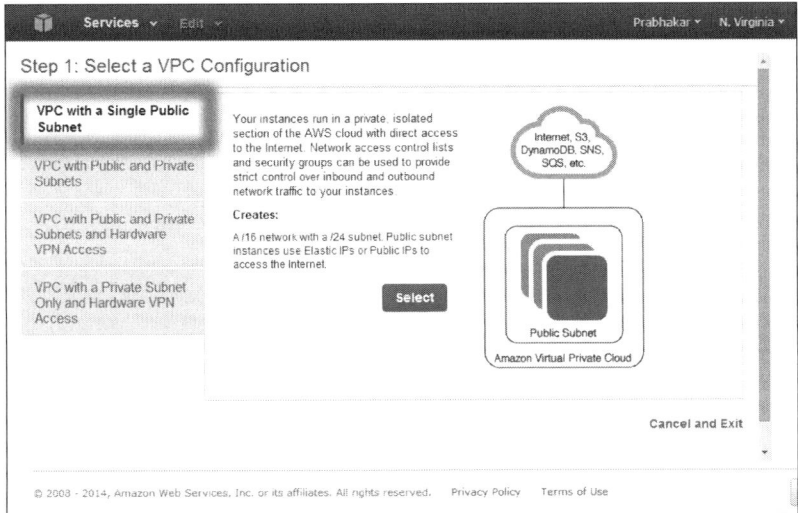

2. Review your configuration. The public subnet will have a default IP address range of **10.0.0.0/16**, which cannot be routed on the Internet.

3. Click on **Create VPC**, as shown in the following screenshot:

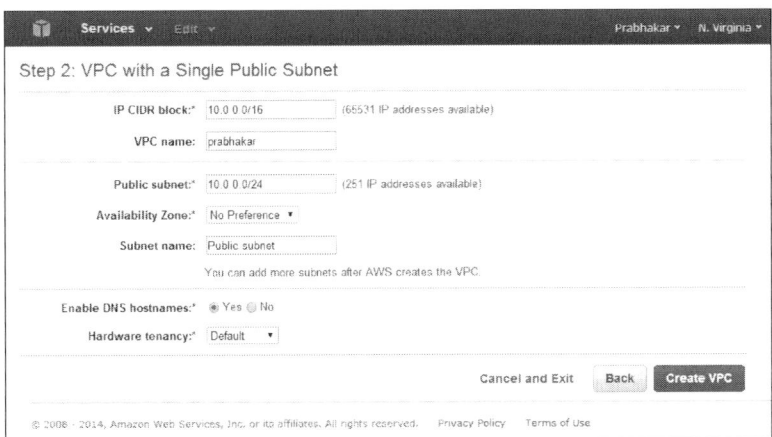

4. The wizard will take some time to finish its job. Once it is completed, you will see the following screenshot:

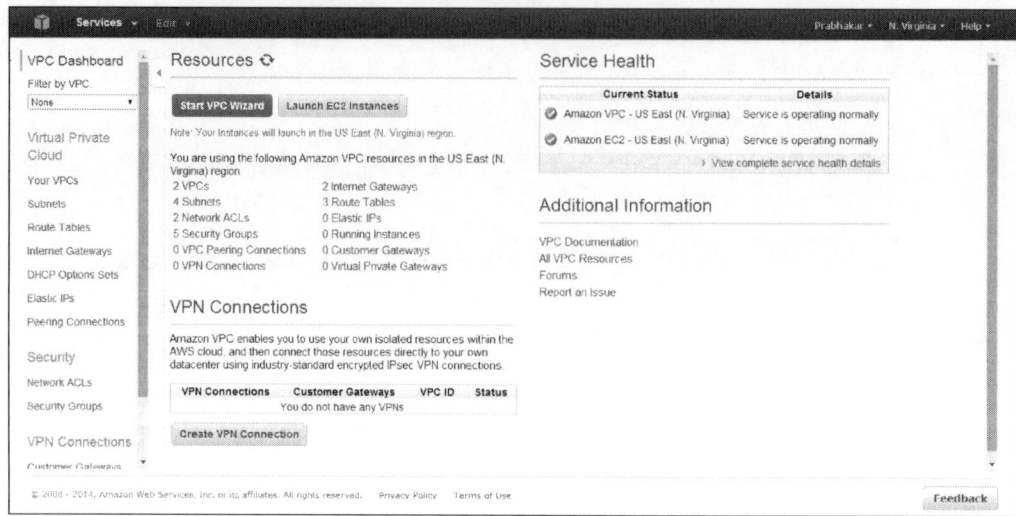

5. Click on the **Subnets** link and check your **Availability Zone**, which the wizard has picked, as shown here:

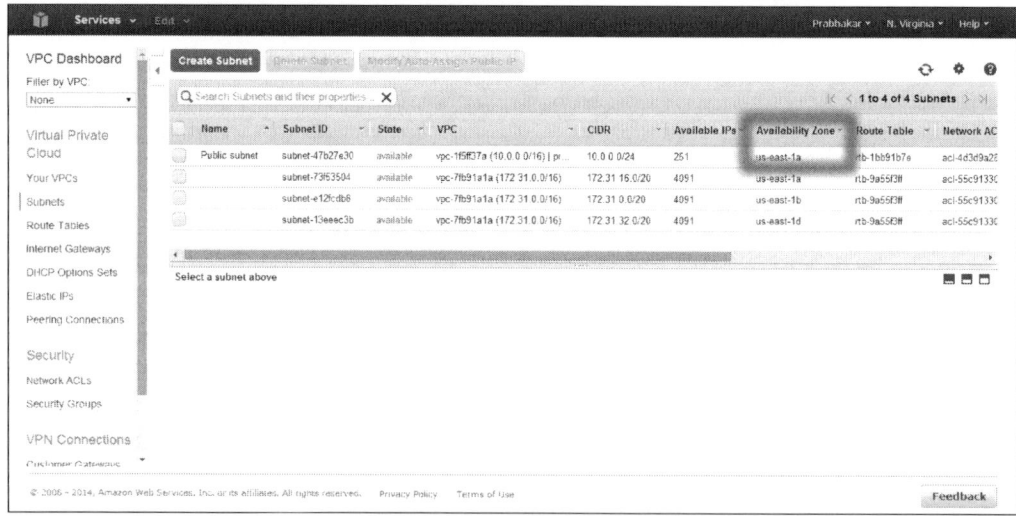

6. From the VPC dashboard, click on the **Launch EC2 Instances** button and start the EC2 Instance by clicking on **Launch Instance**, as shown in the following screenshot:

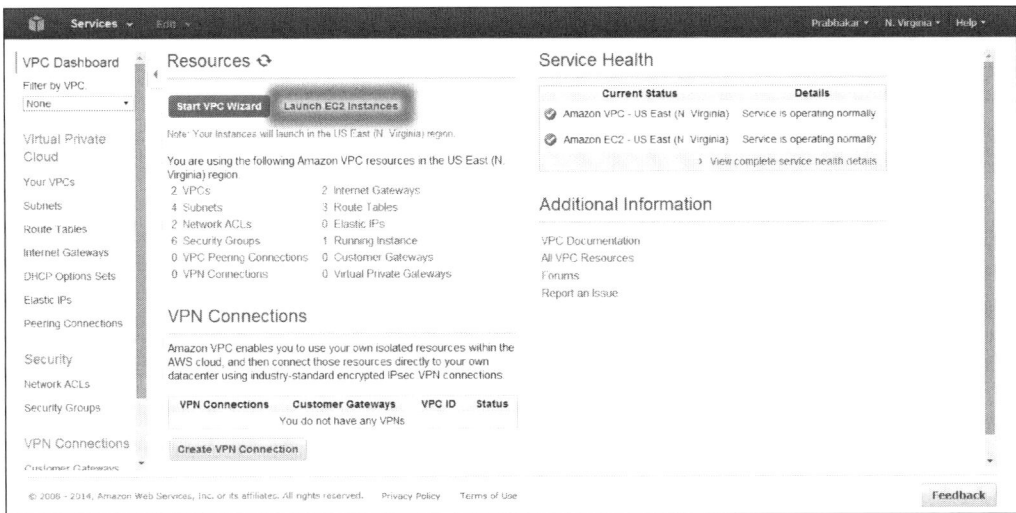

7. Select any option for the AMI (a basic 64-bit Amazon Linux AMI), shown as follows:

8. Change the instance type to **small**, **micro**, or any other instance type supported in the Amazon VPC as per your requirement.

9. Click on the **Next: Configure Instance Details** button after you have selected the appropriate option, as shown here:

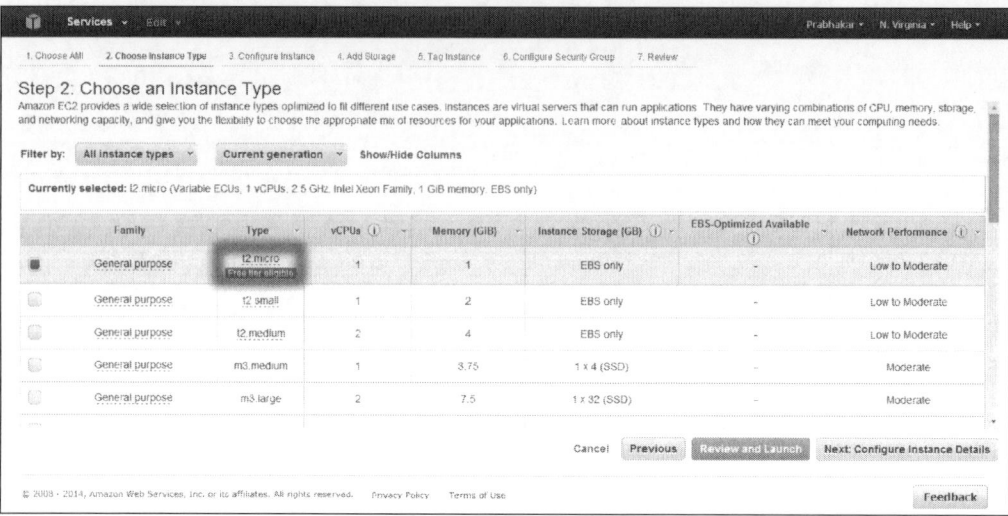

10. In the **Configure Instance** page, select **10.0.0.9** as the IP address for your instance, as shown in the following screenshot:

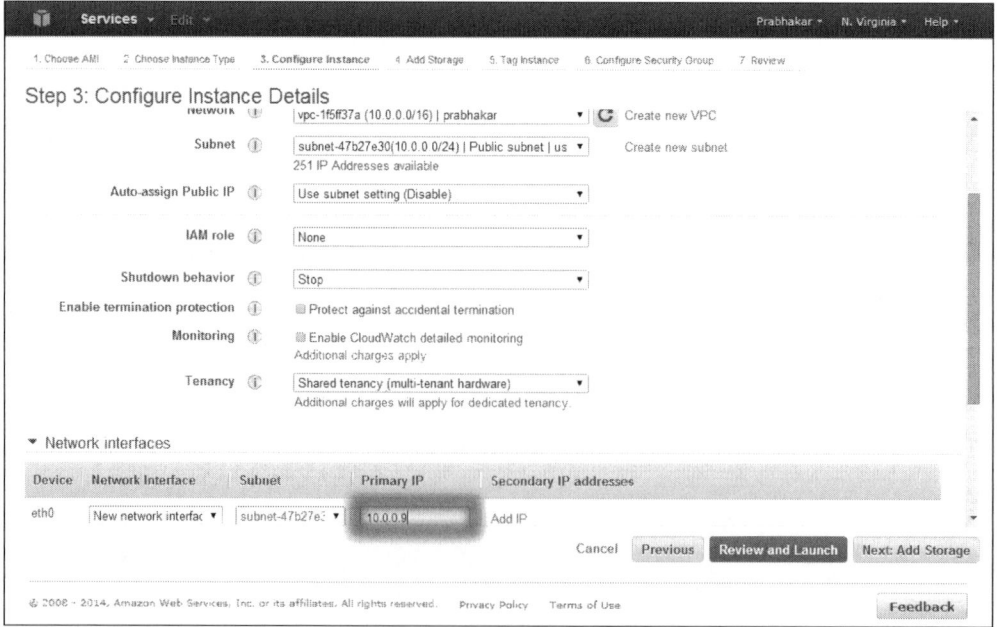

11. Click on the **Next: Add Storage** button to move to the following screen:

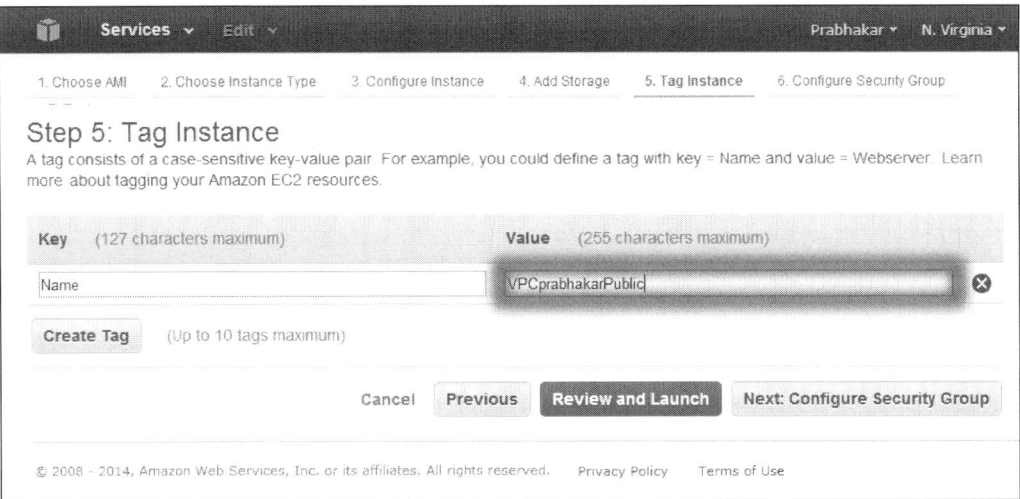

12. If you already have a key pair created previously, you can use it, or you can create a new one, as shown in the following screenshot:

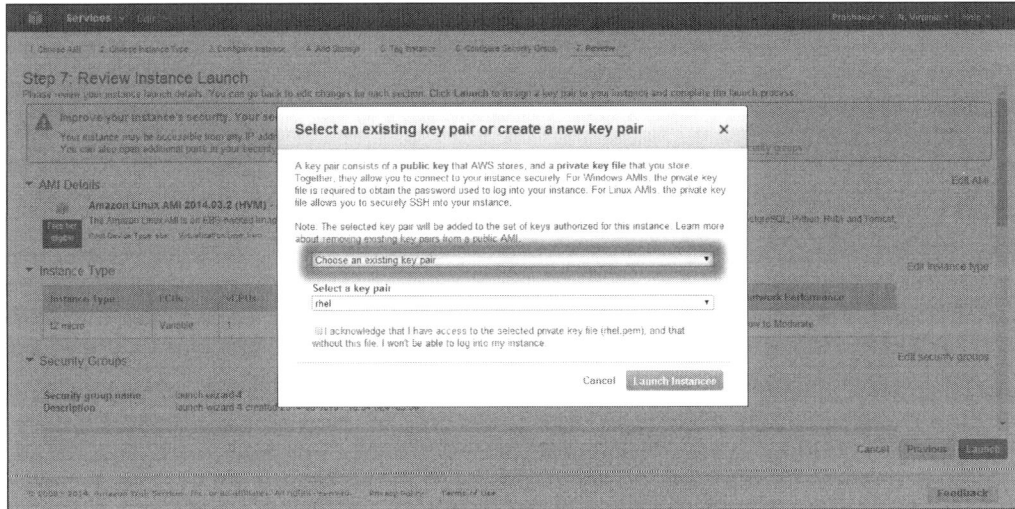

13. Create your new security group, which might be the default one or the customized one.

14. Add a rule for SSH (it should already be there) and also for all the ICMP protocols. Click on **Add Rule** to apply the changes.

15. Then, click on **Review and Launch**, as shown here:

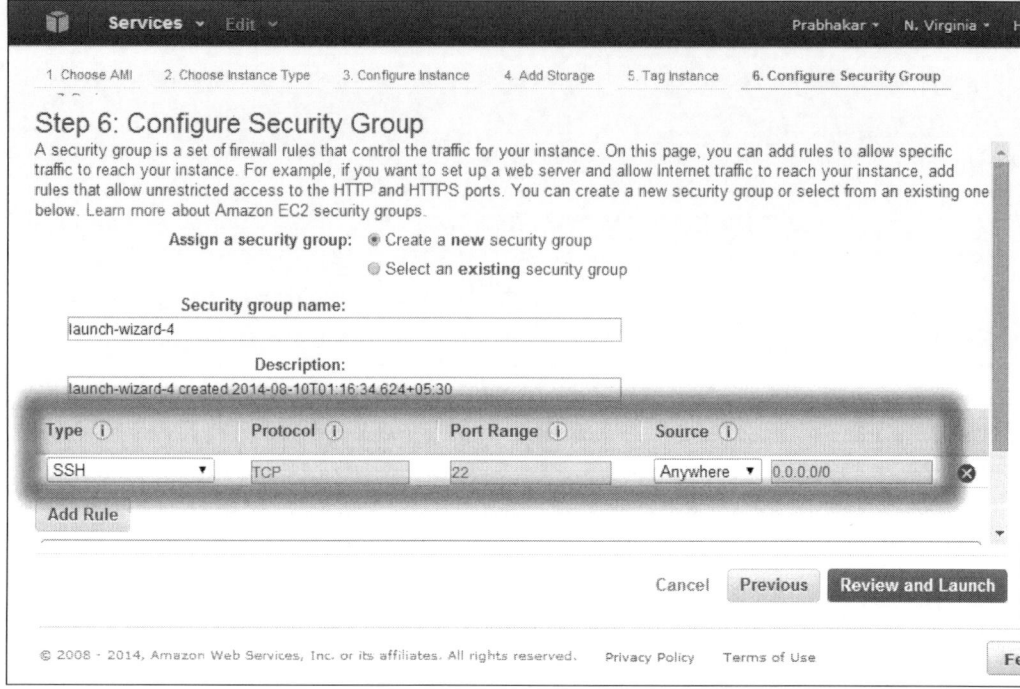

16. Review your settings and launch the instance to get the following page:

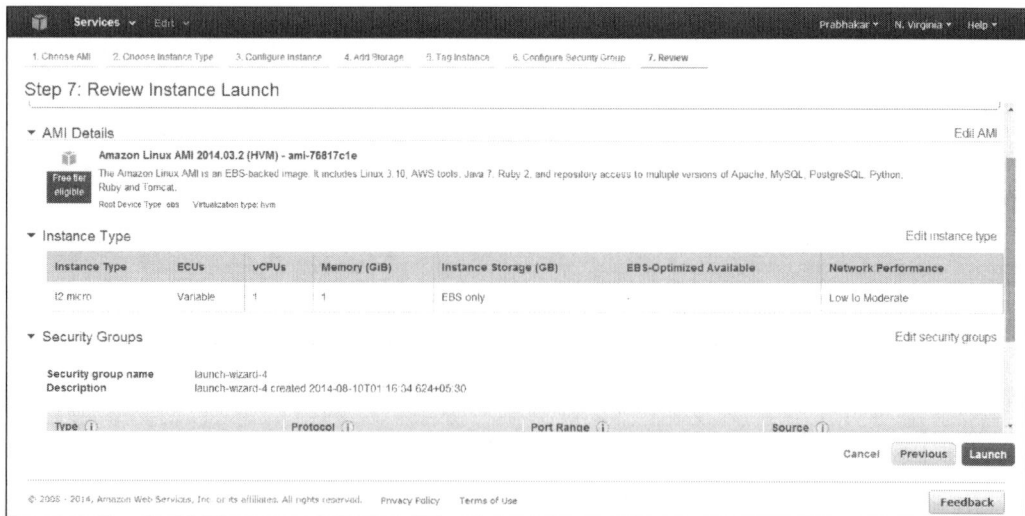

In order to access a publicly created instance over the Internet, you need a public IP address of this instance.

17. Go to the **Elastic IP** menu in the navigation pane on the left-hand side and click on the **Allocate New Address** button. Then select **VPC** and click on **Yes, Allocate**. That's all for now.

Creating a private subnet

Now you have to create a **10.0.1.0** subnet that is not directly connected to the public Internet. Note the *1* in the third octet, which is different from the *0* for the public subnet. In the **VPC** tab, click on **Subnets** and then click on **Create Subnet**. Enter `10.0.1.0/24` in the address tab. Technically, the **Availability Zone (AZ)** can be different from the previous one; however, using multiple AZs doesn't make much sense when you are simply separating the *public* from the *private*. In a fully developed implementation, you will most likely have a total of four subnets (two sets of public/private pairs, which are visible in the background of the following screenshot) distributed across multiple availability zones, as shown here:

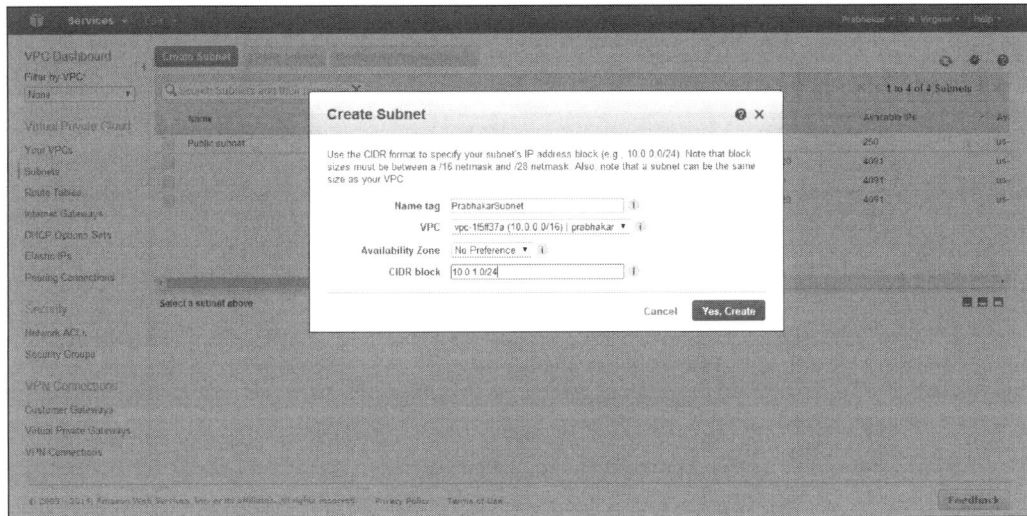

Now, you can launch instances into the public or private subnets, as follows:

- Add public-facing instances, such as web servers, into the public-facing subnet (**10.0.0.0/24**)

- Add backend instances that should not be reachable from the Internet, such as database servers, into the private subnet (**10.0.1.0/24**)

Launching a database server in the private subnet

Launch another Amazon Linux instance using the previous steps, but this time launch it into the private subnet category, which can be 10.0.1.0/24, and give it an IP address of 10.0.1.10, for example. Check the screenshots from the previous section to recollect what you did, if you require.

A quick question: can't you simply assign an Elastic IP address to the internal or to the instance having a private subnet, which can be reached from the Internet? While this seems to be a logical solution, it won't work. The reason is because the route table associated with this subnet does not pass traffic to the Internet or from it, as shown in the following screenshot:

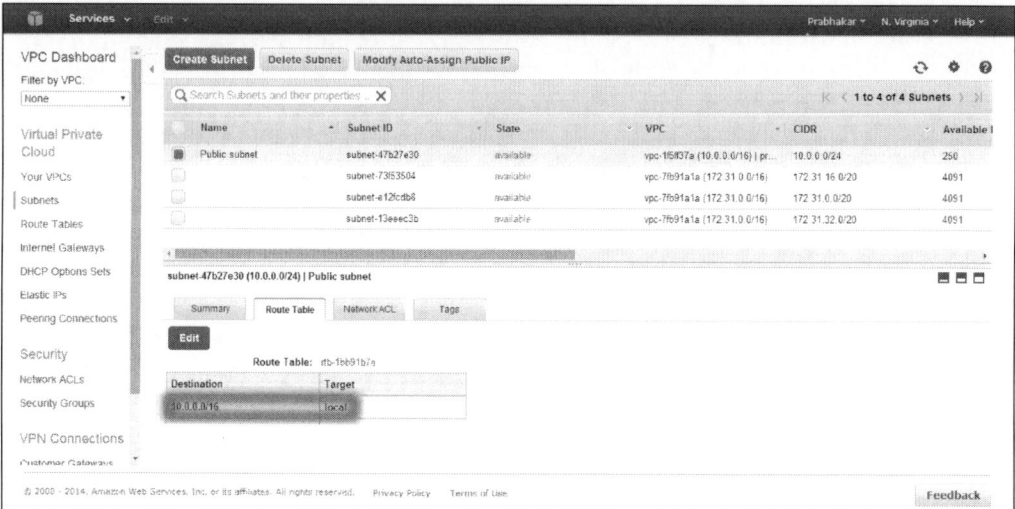

You can switch route tables, at which point the Elastic IP address will start to accept Internet traffic.

Launching an OpenVPN instance

We're going to build an OpenVPN appliance from an AMI image. To do this, follow these steps:

1. In the Amazon AMIs section, search for **openvpn**. In this case, you will find an image called `ami-id ami-76817c1e`. However, at the time when you do this, it might not be the latest version, so choose accordingly.

Make certain that you launch this AMI into the VPC using the public subnet, as shown here:

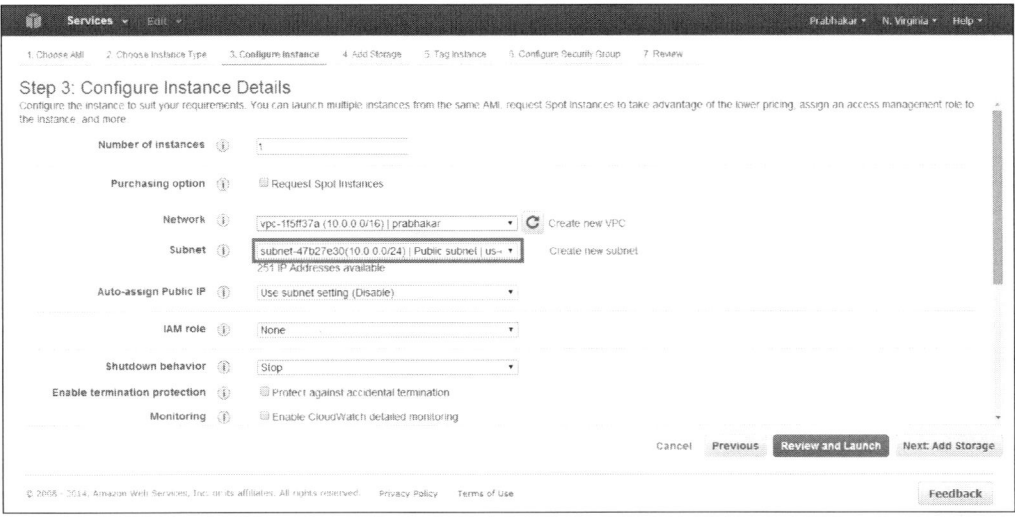

2. Use 10.0.0.99 as the static IP address and name it. Ensure that you have configured the security group with the recommended rules, as follows:

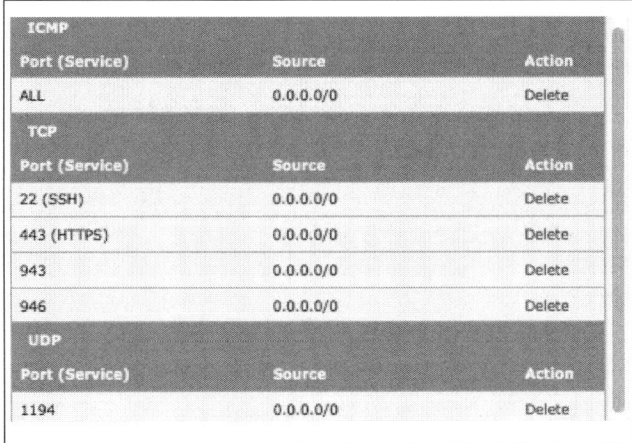

ICMP		
Port (Service)	Source	Action
ALL	0.0.0.0/0	Delete
TCP		
Port (Service)	Source	Action
22 (SSH)	0.0.0.0/0	Delete
443 (HTTPS)	0.0.0.0/0	Delete
943	0.0.0.0/0	Delete
946	0.0.0.0/0	Delete
UDP		
Port (Service)	Source	Action
1194	0.0.0.0/0	Delete

3. Review your configuration, accept the settings, and launch the instance.

4. To disable the source/destination, right-click on the OpenVPN instance and select the **Change Source/Dest. Check** option, as follows:

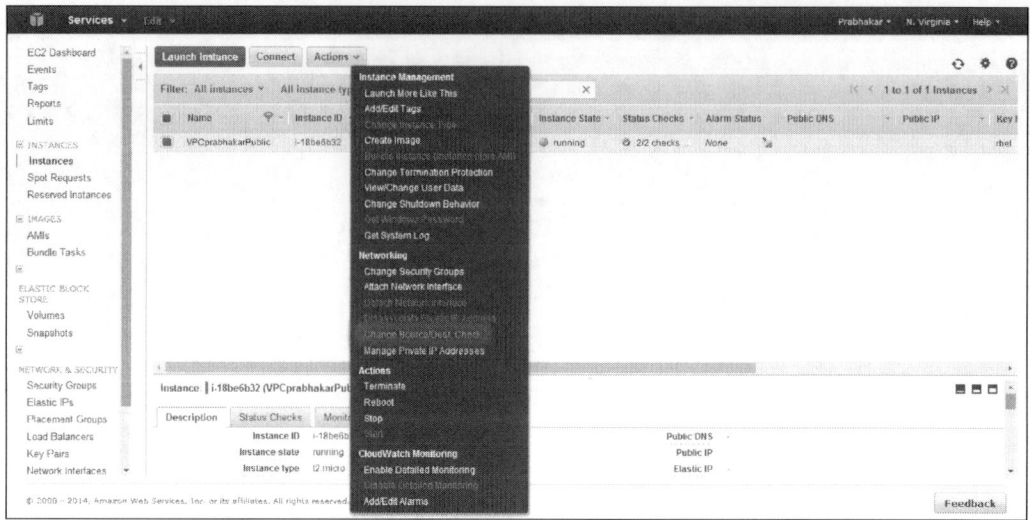

5. Click on the **Yes, Disable** button to confirm, as shown here:

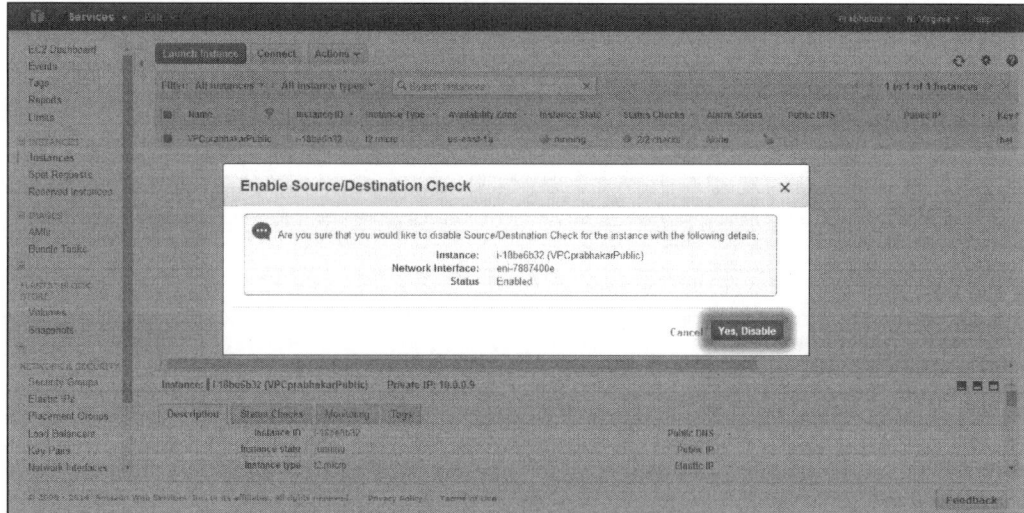

6. Allocate a new Elastic IP address to the OpenVPN server. Perform an SSH operation to confirm whether you can ping the OpenVPN instance and SSH into the OpenVPN server using the SSH client. Once it's completed, you need to create a password for the openvpn user using the following command.

```
PROMPT> passwd openvpn
```

7. Log in with the username, `openvpn`, and the appropriate password, as follows:

8. Download, install, and configure the client applicable to your platform, as shown in the following screenshot:

9. Try to connect to the OpenVPN server with an address such as `http://<Elastic IP>/admin`.

10. Accept the terms and conditions and then click on **Agree**. Click on **Server Network Settings** and enter your server's public IP address, as shown in the following screenshot:

11. Click on the **Update Running Server** button, as shown here:

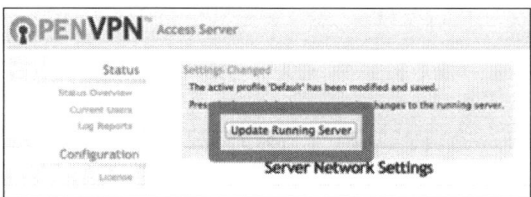

12. To allow access to the private subnet in the VPC, click on **VPN Settings**.

13. Add the private subnet to the **Routing** section, which will be **10.0.1.0/24** in your case, as shown in the following screenshot:

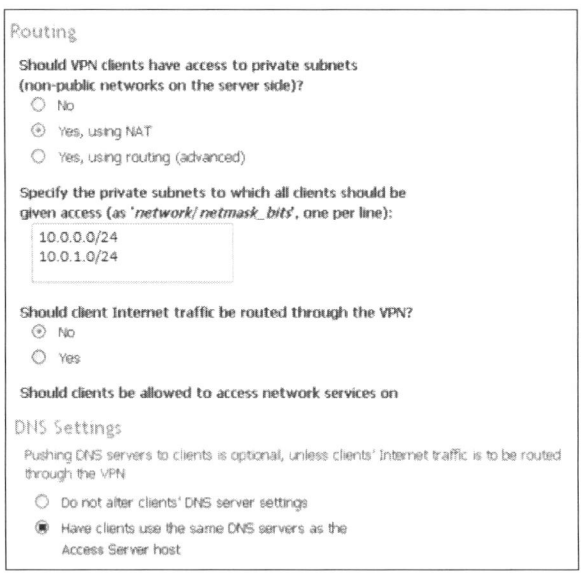

Until now, you have done with the configuration of VPC. Now, to access your VPC using VPN, you have to perform the ssh operation to your particular VPC-based instance, as follows:

```
$ ping 10.0.1.10
PING 10.0.1.10 (10.0.1.10): 56 data bytes
64 bytes from 10.0.1.10: icmp_seq=0 ttl=63 time=162.530 ms
64 bytes from 10.0.1.10: icmp_seq=1 ttl=63 time=163.819 ms
64 bytes from 10.0.1.10: icmp_seq=2 ttl=63 time=161.706 ms
^C
--- 10.0.1.10 ping statistics ---
3 packets transmitted, 3 packets received, 0.0% packet loss
round-trip min/avg/max/stddev = 161.706/162.685/163.819/0.870 ms
$ ssh -i ~/Downloads/ap-southeast-1-labkey.pem ec2-user@10
.0.1.10
The authenticity of host '10.0.1.10 (10.0.1.10)' can't be established.
RSA key fingerprint is 75:08:e3:3b:0c:90:fe:fe:14:aa:67:85:04:6a:fd:df.
Are you sure you want to continue connecting (yes/no)? yes
Warning: Permanently added '10.0.1.10' (RSA) to the list of known hosts.

       __|  __|_  )
       _|  (     /    Amazon Linux AMI
      ___|\___|___|
```

Computing and networking tools and libraries

A software development kit (SDK or *devkit*) is typically a set of software development tools that allow the creation of applications for a certain software package, software framework, hardware platform, computer system, video game console, operating system, or a similar development platform.

It might be something as simple as the implementation of one or more application programming interfaces (APIs) in the form of some libraries in order to interface to a particular programming or to include sophisticated hardware that can commune with a meticulous embedded system. Common tools include debugging services and other utilities frequently offered in an **Integrated Development Environment (IDE)**. SDKs also frequently include sample code and supporting technical notes or other supporting documentation to help clarify points made by the primary reference material.

SDKs might have attached licenses, which make them unsuitable for building software intended to be developed under an incompatible license. For illustration, a proprietary SDK will perhaps be unsuited for free software development, whereas a GPL-licensed SDK can be unsuited with proprietary software development. LGPL SDKs are classically safe and sound for proprietary development.

As shown in the following screenshot, you will be able to see the AWS SDK for Java on the AWS website. By clicking on **SDK for Java**, you can download it.

Let's understand each folder and internal files one after the other:

- `Documentation`: This folder contains all the content needed for the reference. It has a syntax, package, structure, and description of each class/method. Using this documentation, we are able to understand the given underlying class/method, and we can use them in our own library.

- `Lib`: This folder contains the `.jar` files that are necessary to start the development of AWS using your Java code. It also contains other `.jar` files such as:

    ○ `aws-java-sdk-<version>.jar`: This contains all the classes required for AWS development, ex-AWS Authentication, and so on, which are commonly used to execute all command-level operations from the command prompt. It can only be executed once they are configured in the environment variables.

    ○ `aws-java-sdk-<version>-sources.jar`: While creating the code, if you want to attach source files for reference, you can only do that using this file. You will see this runtime with Eclipse to configure the source with the code.

    There is one `Javadoc.jar` file that keeps the documentation for all AWS classes. Since it is optional, it's upon developers whether they want to keep them for reference.

- `Samples`: This folder contains the sample programs for a quick understanding of the code and its nature. In general, it's not easy to adapt new classes without understanding their basic flow. This code will give you a hands-on exercise. The following basic available examples are included:

    ○ Amazon-DynamoDB
    ○ Amazon-EC2SpotInstances-GettingStarted
    ○ Amazon-EC2SpotInstances-Advance
    ○ Amazon-Kinesis
    ○ Amazon-Kinesis-Application
    ○ Amazon-s3
    ○ AmazonS3TransferProgress
    ○ AmazonSimpleEmailService
    ○ AmazonSimpleQueueService
    ○ AwsCloudFormation
    ○ AwsConsoleApp
    ○ AwsFlowFramework

- `Third-party`: This folder contains the following third-party AP that can be helpful while code structuring:

    ○ aspectj-1.6

    ○ commons-codec-1.3

    ○ commons-logging-1.1.1

    ○ freemarker-2.3.18

    ○ httpcomponents-client-4.2.3

    ○ jackson-annotations-2.1

    ○ jackson-core-2.1

    ○ jackson-databind-2.1

    ○ java-mail-1.4.3

    ○ joda-time-2.2

    ○ spring-3.0

    ○ stax-api-1.0.1

    ○ stax-ri-1.2.0

You can also add your own components, such as jQuery or others, for useful purposes and a strong adaptability. This was all about the AWS SDK structure. Later, while executing the examples, you will see its usage and will gain an in-depth understanding of the flow and its components. Let's discuss the various features of AWS:

- **The AWS toolkit**: This toolkit, for Eclipse, is an open source plugin for the Eclipse Java IDE, which makes it easier for developers and code integrators to develop, debug, integrate, migrate, and deploy Java-based applications that use the Amazon web services resources platform. There are some extraordinary functions/features that make the Amazon platform best suitable for developers, for example, the AWS Explorer.

- **The AWS Explorer**: This enables you to interrelate many of the AWS services from inside the Eclipse IDE. The AWS Explorer supports managed data services such as Amazon **Simple Storage Service (S3)**, Amazon SimpleDB, Amazon **Simple Notification Service** (SNS), and Amazon **Simple Queue Service (SQS)**. The explorer also provides the right to use the Amazon **Elastic Compute Cloud (EC2)** management and deployment functionality to AWS Elastic Beanstalk using the SDK or API. AWS Explorer supports multiple AWS accounts; you can easily change the resources displayed in it from one account to another. It also enables supporting functionality, such as the ability to create and manage key pairs and security groups.

The AWS Toolkit for Eclipse will install and configure the latest version of the AWS SDK for any platform you have selected. From Eclipse, you can easily manage, customize, build, and deploy any of the samples included in the SDK packages, as follows:

1. Go to `aws-amazon.com/sdk-for-java`.

2. As shown in the following screenshot, click on **AWS Toolkit for Eclipse**:

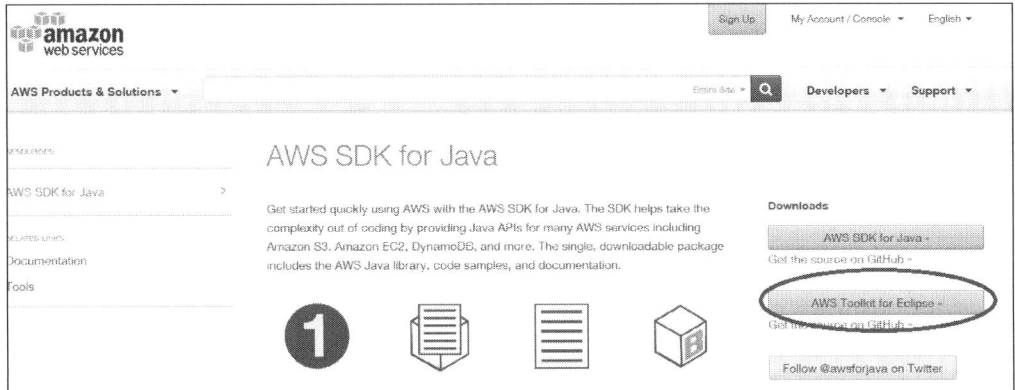

3. There is another alternative way to configure this. Download Eclipse Juno/Luna+ from `https://www.eclipse.org/downloads/`.

4. Start Eclipse.

5. Click on **Help** and then click on **Install New Software**.

6. In the **Work with** field, type `http://aws.amazon.com/eclipse` and then press the *Enter* key.

7. In the list that appears, expand **AWS Toolkit for Eclipse**.

8. Add a checkmark next to **AWS Toolkit for Eclipse** in order to download it.

9. Click on **Next**; the Eclipse wizard will, by default, take you through the installation procedure.

To admission AWS through the toolkit for Eclipse, you have to configure the Eclipse toolkit with your access key ID and secret access key, which should be available in your AWS account. In addition to allowing the toolkit for Eclipse to access your account, your access keys are used to sign requirements based on web services to AWS. By allowing web service requests, AWS ensures that only the approved programs can make such requests. Moreover, by associating access keys with each web service request, AWS will be able to track the service usage for billing purposes and monitoring.

The access keys will have a combination of an access key ID and a secret access key, which will be used to sign a programmatic logical request that you will compose from the application source code to AWS for accessing resources. If you don't have access keys, you can create their keys from the AWS Management Console too. For this, go to **Security Credentials** and select **Access Key ID** from the options available, as shown in the following screenshot:

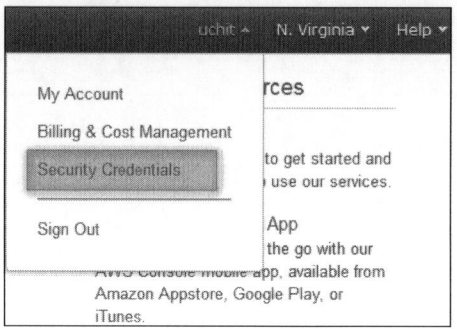

Keep it confidential in order to guard your account and don't e-mail it at all. Do not share it with a third person from your organization, even if any investigations come from AWS or from any other channel.

To deploy the web application, follow these steps:

1. In the Eclipse toolbar, click on the **AWS** icon, and then click on **AWS Java Web Project**, as shown in the following screenshot:

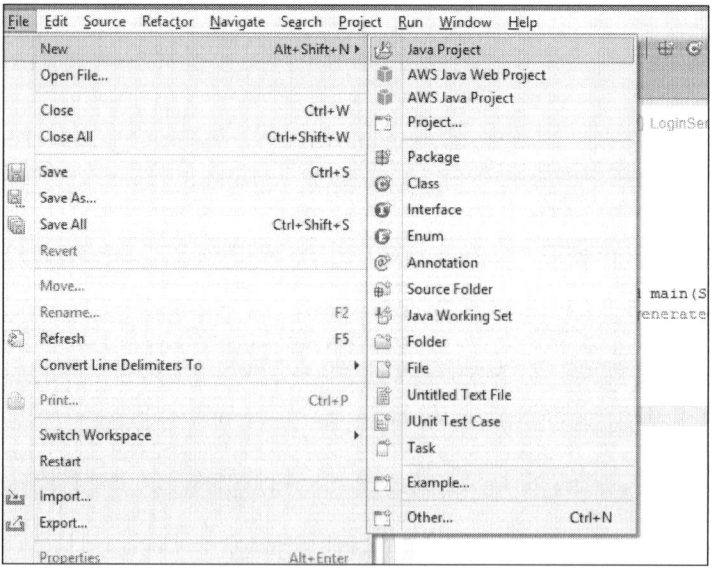

2. In the **New AWS Java Web Project** dialog box, at the top of the dialog box, select **AWS_Proj**, which is a sample Java web application, and enter the name `AWS_Proj` in the **Project name** box.

3. Click on the **Finish** button. The toolkit will create the project, and the project will be shown in **Project Explorer**.

   If **Project Explorer** is not visible in Eclipse, under the **Window** menu, click on **Show View** and select **Project Explorer**, as shown here:

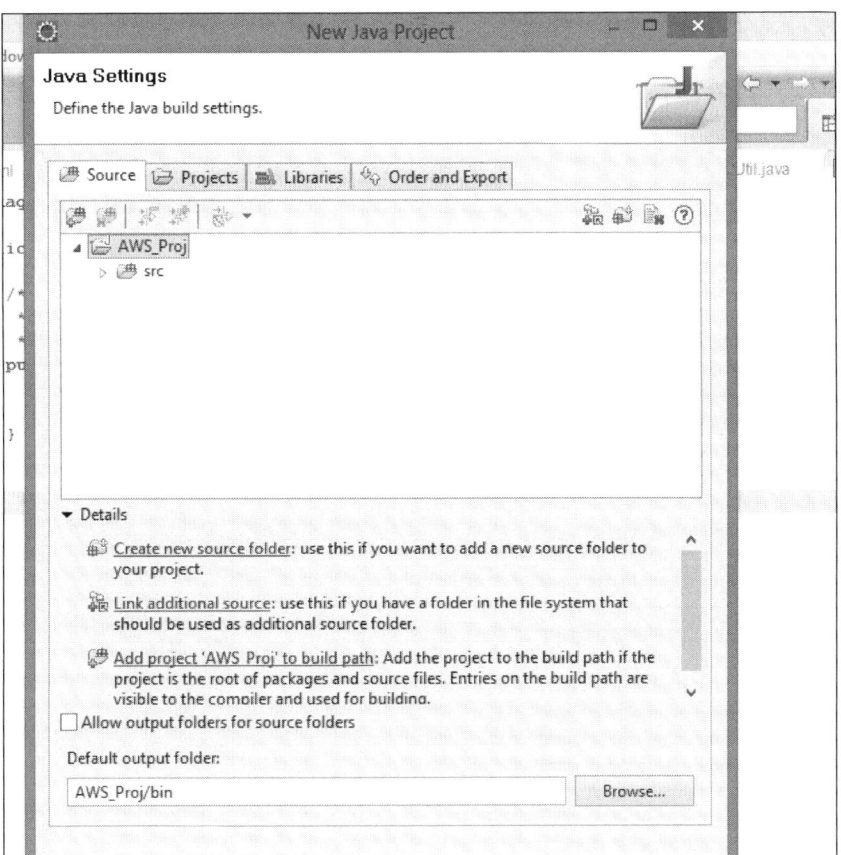

4. Now click on **Libraries** and then click on **Add External Jars**.

5. Select the path of `aws-java-sdk.jar`, as shown here:

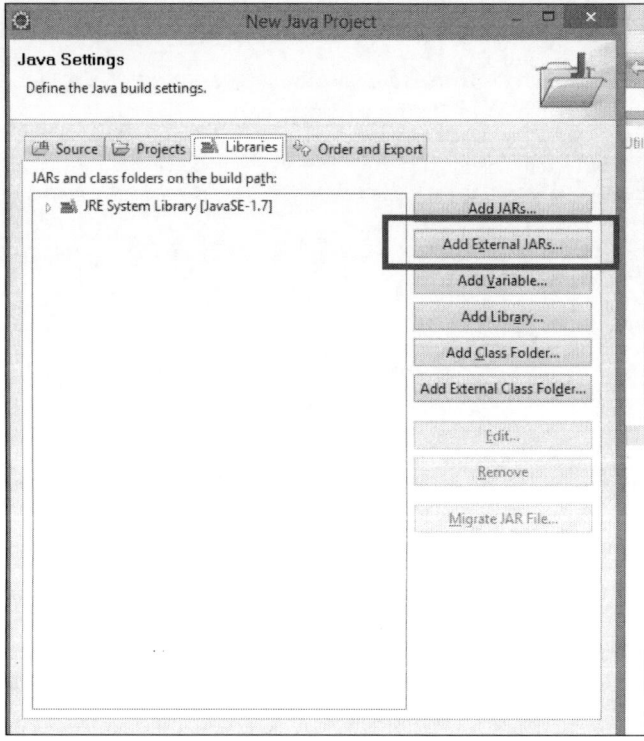

6. Select the `.jar` file, as follows:

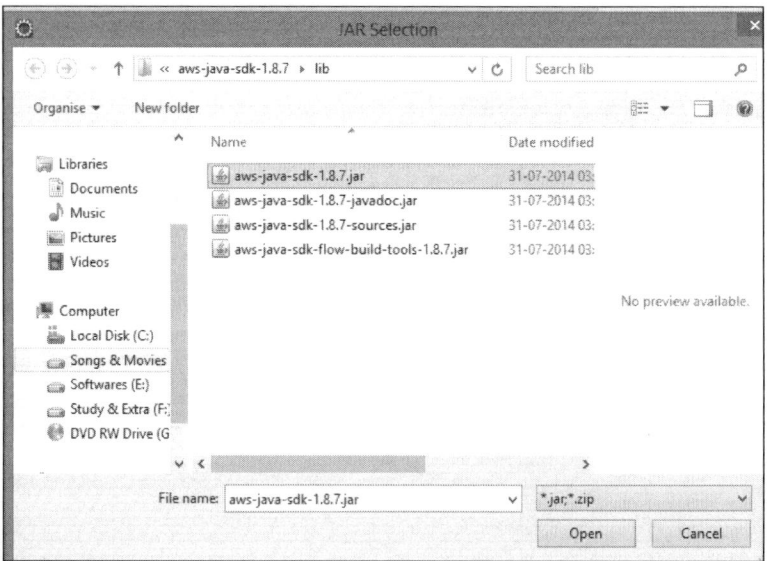

7. Now you will be able to access the AWS classes of your Java project.

8. Create a new class, `Hello`, in the package, `com.test`, as shown in the following screenshot:

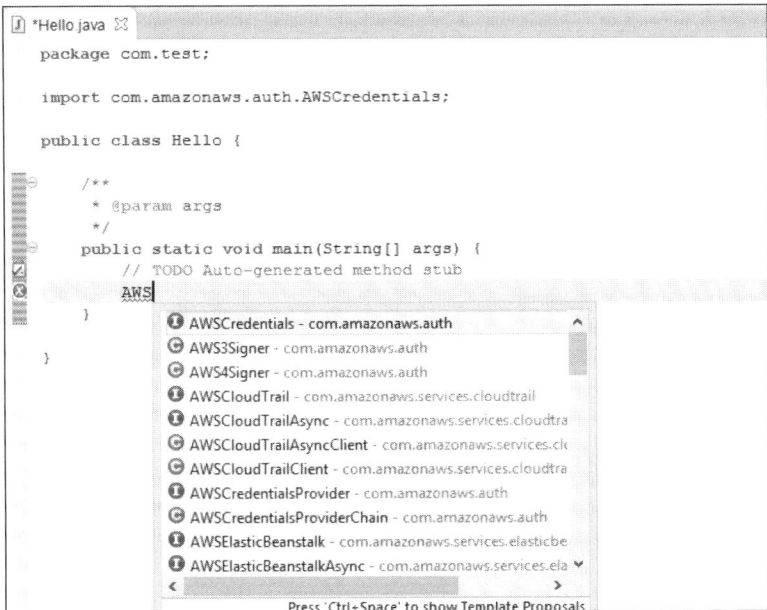

As you can see, you can now access the classes of AWS in our Java class and based on that, you can create your own examples. Let's try out one example here to start our instance programmatically:

1. Create a new class named `Main.java`, as follows:

```java
private Logger log = Logger.getInstance(Main.class);

private String accessKey = "YOUR ACCESS KEY";
private String secretKey = "YOUR SECRET KEY" ;
private AWSCredentials credentials;
private String endPoint ;
private Region region ;
private AmazonEC2Client ec2client ;

private String groupName = "uchitec2securitygroup";
private String groupDescription = "This is description";

private String sshIpRange = " IP/32";
private String sshprotocol = "tcp";
private int sshFromPort = 22;
```

```
private int sshToPort =22;

private String httpIpRange = "0.0.0.0/0";
private String httpProtocol = "tcp";
private int httpFromPort = 80;
private int httpToPort = 80;

private String httpsIpRange = "0.0.0.0/0";
private String httpsProtocol = "tcp";
private int httpsFromPort = 443;
private int httpsToProtocol = 443;

private String keyName = "uchitkeypair";
private String pemFilePath  = "PATH TO SAVE PEM FILE"; //
/Users/uchit/Desktop
private String pemFileName = "uchit_keypair.pem";


private String imageId =" ami-018c9568";
private String instanceType ="m1.small";
private String instanceName = "uchitm1small";
```

2. Initialize a method to create an object that will have the credentials `AmazonEC2Client`; also, you have to set an endpoint and a region for your `ec2client` using the following code:

    ```
    private void init(){
     credentials  = new BasicAWSCredentials(accessKey,
    secretKey);

    endPoint = "https://rds.ap-southeast-1.amazonaws.com";

     region = Region.getRegion(Regions.AP_SOUTHEAST_1);
     ec2client = new AmazonEC2Client(credentials);
     ec2client.setEndpoint(endPoint);
     ec2client.setRegion(region);
    }
    ```

3. Create a security group using the following code snippet:

    ```
    private void createEC2SecurityGroup(){
     try {
      log.Info("Create request for security group");
      CreateSecurityGroupRequest createSecurityGroupRequest =
    new CreateSecurityGroupRequest();
       createSecurityGroupRequest.withGroupName(groupName)
       .withDescription(groupDescription);
    ```

```
   createSecurityGroupRequest.setRequestCredentials(credential
s);
   CreateSecurityGroupResult csgr =
ec2client.createSecurityGroup(createSecurityGroupRequest);

   String groupid = csgr.getGroupId();
   log.Info("New Security Group Id : " + groupid);

   log.Info("Security Group Permission");
   Collection<IpPermission> ips = new ArrayList<IpPermission>();

   IpPermission ipssh = new IpPermission();
   ipssh.withIpRanges(sshIpRange).withIpProtocol(sshprotocol)
   .withFromPort(sshFromPort).withToPort(sshToPort);
   ips.add(ipssh);

   IpPermission iphttp = new IpPermission();
   iphttp.withIpRanges(httpIpRange).withIpProtocol(httpProtocol)
   .withFromPort(httpFromPort).withToPort(httpToPort);
   ips.add(iphttp);

   IpPermission iphttps = new IpPermission();
   iphttps.withIpRanges(httpsIpRange).withIpProtocol(httpsProtocol)
   .withFromPort(httpsFromPort).withToPort(httpsToProtocol);
   ips.add(iphttps);

   AuthorizeSecurityGroupIngressRequest
authorizeSecurityGroupIngressRequest = new
AuthorizeSecurityGroupIngressRequest();
   authorizeSecurityGroupIngressRequest
   .withGroupName(groupName).withIpPermissions(ips);
   ec2client.authorizeSecurityGroupIngress(authorizeSecurityGroupIn
gressRequest);

   } catch (Exception e) {
   e.printStackTrace();
   System.exit(0);
   }
 }
```

4. To create a key pair, use the following code:

```
private void createKeyPair(){
 try {
  CreateKeyPairRequest ckpr = new CreateKeyPairRequest();
```

```
  ckpr.withKeyName(keyName);

  CreateKeyPairResult ckpresult =
ec2client.createKeyPair(ckpr);
  KeyPair keypair = ckpresult.getKeyPair();
  String privateKey = keypair.getKeyMaterial();
  log.Info("KeyPair will be :" + privateKey);
  writePemFile(privateKey,pemFilePath,pemFileName);
 } catch (Exception e) {
  e.printStackTrace();
  System.exit(0);
 }
}
```

5. Create an on-demand instance using the following code snippet:

```
private void createEC2OnDemandInstance(){
 try {

  RunInstancesRequest uv = new RunInstancesRequest();
  uv.withImageId(imageId);
  uv.withInstanceType(instanceType);
  uv.withMinCount(1);
  uv.withMaxCount(1);
  uv.withKeyName(keyName);
  uv.withMonitoring(true);
  rir.withSecurityGroups(groupName);

  RunInstancesResult riresult = ec2client.runInstances(uv);
  log.Info(riresult.getReservation().getReservationId());

  String instanceId=null;
  DescribeInstancesResult result =
ec2client.describeInstances();
  Iterator<Reservation> i =
result.getReservations().iterator();
  while (i.hasNext()) {
   Reservation r = i.next();
   List<Instance> instances = r.getInstances();
   for (Instance ii : instances) {
     log.Info(ii.getImageId() + "t" + ii.getInstanceId()+
"t" + ii.getState().getName() + "t"+
ii.getPrivateDnsName());
     if (ii.getState().getName().equals("pending")) {
```

```
       instanceId = ii.getInstanceId();
      }
     }
    }

  log.Info("New Instance ID will be:" + instanceId);

  boolean isWaiting = true;
  while (isWaiting) {
   log.Info("we are Waiting");
   Thread.sleep(1010);
   DescribeInstancesResult r = ec2client.describeInstances();
   Iterator<Reservation> ir= r.getReservations().iterator();
   while(ir.hasNext()){
    Reservation rr = ir.next();
    List<Instance> instances = rr.getInstances();
    for(Instance ii : instances){
     log.Info(ii.getImageId() + "t" + ii.getInstanceId()+
"t" + ii.getState().getName() + "t"+ ii.getPrivateDnsName());
     if (ii.getState().getName().equals("running") &&
ii.getInstanceId().equals(instanceId) ) {
      log.Info(ii.getPublicDnsName());
      isWaiting=false;
     }
    }
   }
  }

  CreateTagsRequest crt = new CreateTagsRequest();
  ArrayList<Tag> arrTag = new ArrayList<Tag>();
  arrTag.add(new Tag().withKey("Name").withValue(instanceName));
  crt.setTags(arrTag);

  ArrayList<String> arrInstances = new ArrayList<String>();
  arrInstances.add(instanceId);
  crt.setResources(arrInstances);
  ec2client.createTags(crt);

 } catch (Exception e) {
  e.printStackTrace();
  System.exit(0);
 }
}
```

Summary

We started the chapter by discussing the basics of EC2 and how the Windows and Linux instances differ from each other. Then, we discussed the differences between an EBS backed instance and an instance store-backed instance. In the *Best Practices* section, we discussed the best practices and tools that can be used to access the EC2 instances. Then we dedicated the rest of the chapter to VPC. We started this section by creating a public VPN subnet and then we added an Amazon AMI instance to the VPC created by us. Then we assigned a static IP and set up a VPN client to access our VPC instances using openVPN. We concluded the chapter by connecting to our Amazon AMI instance created in our VPC. In the next chapter, you will learn about AWS-managed services and databases. You will get a basic understanding of how AWS manages the resources effectively and accurately. Later on, you will learn about the database services provided by AWS.

4
Managed Services and the Databases

A database is a critical part of any application. It is also a single point of failure; that is, if the database fails because of any hardware or network issues, then the application will become inaccessible. So, managing the database is a very big responsibility and small-scale or start-up companies will have to allocate a high-end server to host the database server. Database services offered by AWS are not only used by start-up companies but also by bigger organizations, as these databases are fully managed by Amazon. So Amazon will take care of the updating, patch installation, and backup of the database software. AWS offers four different kinds of databases. Out of these, two will be taken as part of the discussion in this chapter. First, you will learn about all the key aspects of DynamoDB—a NoSQL database fully managed by Amazon—and then move your focus to **Relational Database Service (RDS)**, which is used to create, run, and manage RDBMS servers on Amazon.

In this chapter, you will learn the following topics:

- The importance and usage of DynamoDB
- Understanding the key aspects of RDS
- Working with an RDS instance
- The usage of DynamoDB and RDS tools and libraries

Amazon DynamoDB

DynamoDB is a NoSQL database fully managed by Amazon, and it is available as a web service. It is available as a free tier and allows you to store up to 100 MB of data, five units of write capacity, and 10 units of read capacity (which counts up to 12 million writes and 24 million reads) per month. DynamoDB is well-suited as a backend for scalable applications which require fast-growing data from a database (hosting millions of tables with an increasing number of rows) to be accessed at a very high speed. Every table created by you can have different access speeds. In simple words, the user can decide to have one or more tables accessed at a very high speed and other tables to be accessed at a lower speed. There is a term called **provisioned throughput capacity**, which decides the data access speed of the table.

 The provisioned throughput capacity is a measure of how much speed you can expect from a DynamoDB table. This is usually measured in KBs per second. For example, if you set the read capacity unit (or the provisioned throughput capacity) as 5, it means that the table can respond to the scan or query operation at a speed of no less than 5 KB per second.

This throughput value can range from 1 to 10,000. However, a higher value means more speed and more cost. In order to make the retrieval faster, the table data will be partitioned (based on the Hash key value), and each partition might reside on a different (or the same) server to achieve the specified throughput capacity. This process of partitioning the table based on the Hash key value is called **sharding**. DynamoDB also provides a provision to read the data in two consistent (eventual and strong) ways.

Table operations

We can find the DynamoDB service in the **Database** section of the Management Console, as shown in the following screenshot; the highlighted section shows four services, out of which **DynamoDB** and **RDS** are going to be part of the discussion in this chapter:

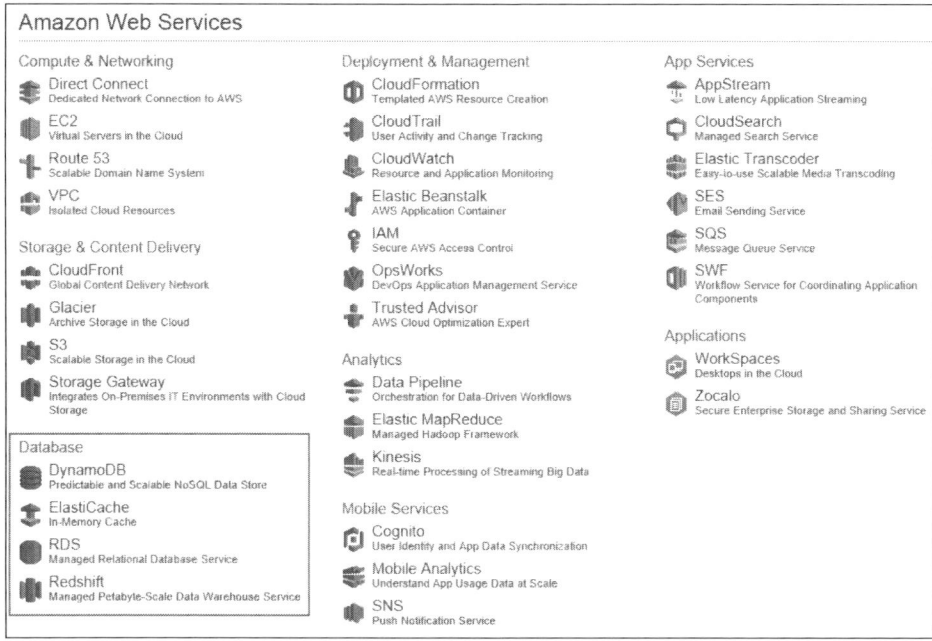

Clicking on the **DynamoDB** option (in the preceding screenshot) will take you to the following **Amazon DynamoDB Getting Started** screen. To the right-hand side of the account name (at the top), **Prabhakar**, you can select the region in which you need the table to be created, as shown in the following screenshot:

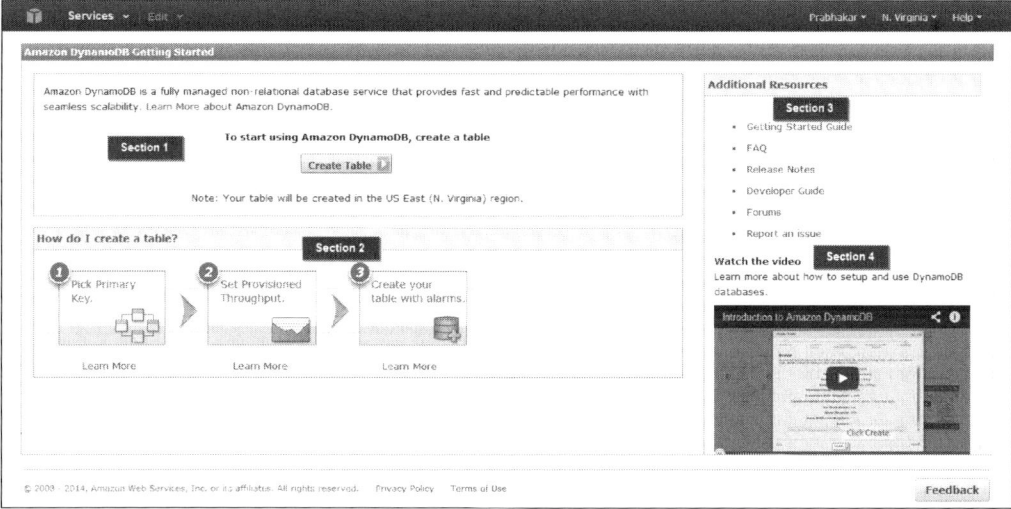

The preceding screenshot shows the following four sections:

- **Section 1**: This section, in the top-left corner, provides information such as where the tables will be created (this can be changed by clicking in the top-right corner of the page where **N. Virginia** is seen) and provides a button to create the DynamoDB table

- **Section 2**: This section, in the bottom-left corner, displays the steps involved in table creation

- **Section 3**: This section, on the right-hand side, provides additional useful links to get further information on DynamoDB

- **Section 4**: This section consists of a video that depicts the advantages of DynamoDB

You need to click on the **Create Table** button in **Section 1** to create your first DynamoDB table. Then you need to follow these five steps to configure your table that is being created:

1. Define a primary key for the table.
2. Add indexes (secondary) to the table.
3. Configure a provisioned throughput capacity for the table.
4. Set throughput alarms so that an e-mail or notification will be sent once your application requires or consumes more than 80 percent (this can be changed) of the throughput capacity.
5. Show the summary of the table.

If you feel that any value is not what you intended, you can click on **Back** and go back to the necessary step and make the changes. The following screenshot shows the final step:

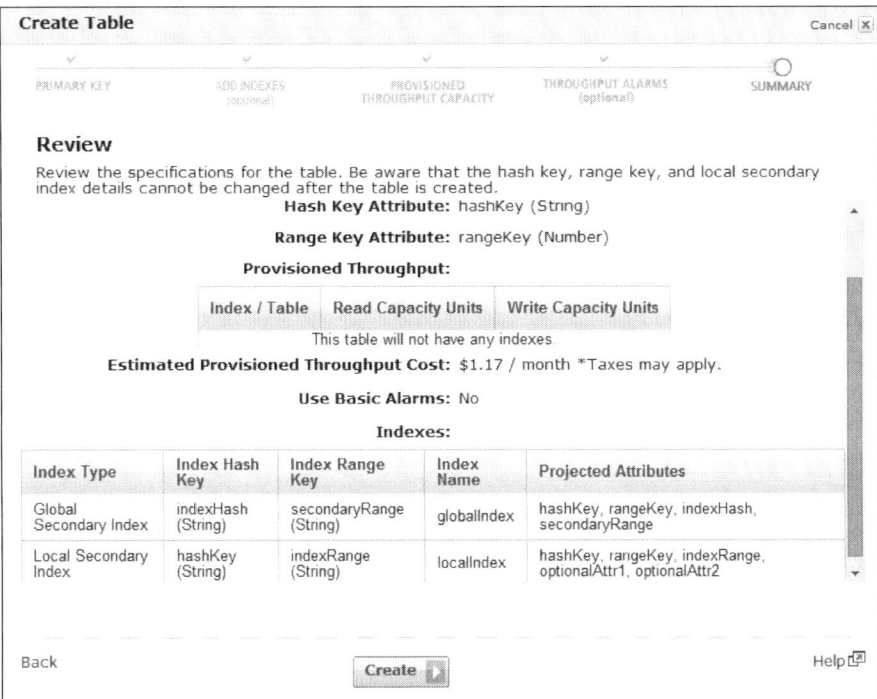

The preceding summary page shows you the following information; all the information is made available in this table:

Attribute	Data type	Attribute type	Table/index
hashKey	String	Hash key	The table's primary key attributes
rangeKey	Number	Range key	
indexHash	String	Hash key	Global index
secondaryRange	String	Range key	
indexRange	String	Range key	Local index
Other optional attributes			

Now it's time to discuss the primary key attributes. The Hash and Range keys are the two attribute types that act as the (compound) primary key. The Range key must be accompanied by the Hash key, but the Hash key can optionally be accompanied by the Range key. The Hash key is an attribute type that every table must have. The Hash key is an unordered collection of items; this means that the items with the same Hash key values will go to the same partition, but there won't be any ordering based on these Hash keys. Whereas, on the other hand, items will always be ordered on their Range key values (but grouped with the Hash key values).

Neither the Hash key nor the Range key can be of any complex type (the set type).

Once you review the table creation and click on the **Create** button, the following page will be displayed. This page will have three sections. **Section 2** shows information about the table schema, throughput values, and its status (you can see that the table is in the **CREATING** status). Once the table's status becomes **ACTIVE**, then you can perform I/O operations. **Section 1** has seven buttons to perform I/O operations on DynamoDB. **Section 3** provides additional information such as the read/write speed, alarm status, and so on.

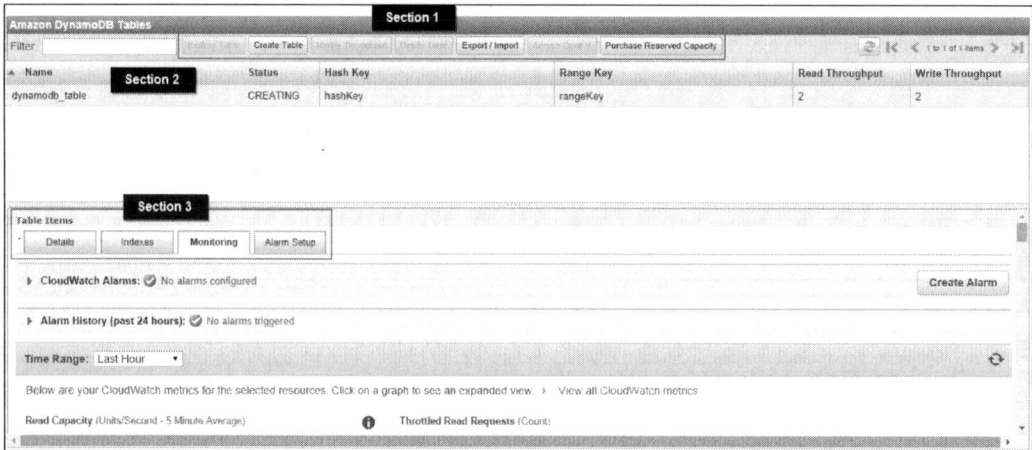

After a few minutes, the table will become **ACTIVE** (as shown in the following screenshot). Now it's time to discuss these seven buttons to perform I/O operations:

- **Explore Table**: This button opens a page (as shown in the following screenshot) that allows you to perform the query/scan operation or insert a new item in the table.

- **Create Table**: This button, as the name suggests, takes you through the five steps used to create a table (which we have already discussed).

- **Modify Throughput**: This button helps you to modify the throughput values for the selected table. This is the only feature of the table that you can modify at any point in time.

- **Delete Table**: This button deletes the selected table.

- **Export / Import**: This button allows you to read or write data to and from the S3 files or CSV files that are stored locally.

- **Access Control**: This button will restrict the user access to the table based on the IAM rules (for operations) specified for the user and for web applications such as Facebook.

- **Purchase Reserved Capacity**: This button is used to purchase the minimum provision capacity expected from Amazon DynamoDB for a period of 1 year or 3 years. Every month, irrespective of whether you use this capacity or not, the money will be deducted from your credit card. Even then, one advantage of this approach is the discount (from 53 percent to 76 percent) offered by Amazon.

The following screenshot displays all seven buttons:

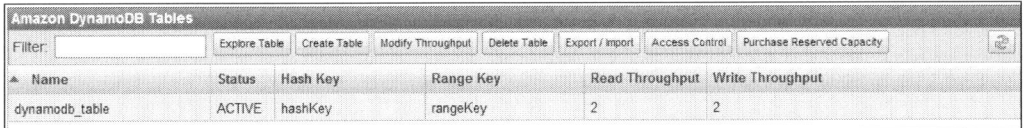

Item operations

After clicking on **Explore Table**, click on the **New Item** button to insert an item, as shown in the following screenshot:

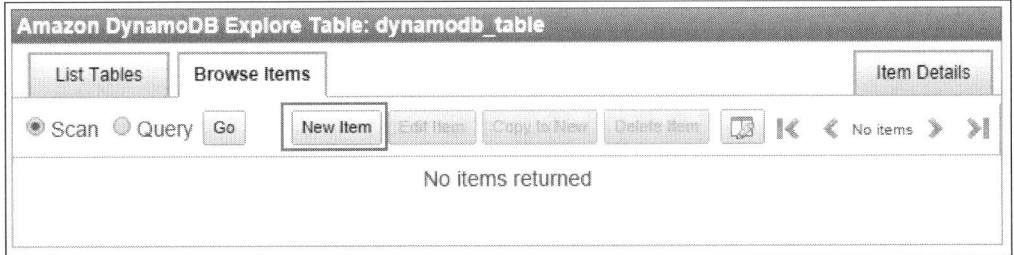

Clicking on the **New Item** button will open the following window:

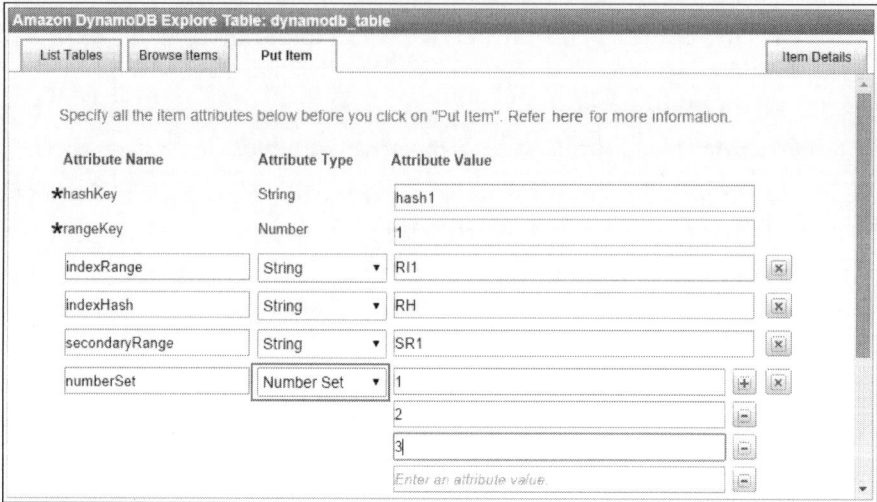

The mandatory attributes, **Name** and **Type**, will already be populated and you cannot change them. However, you can add the attribute values (which must be unique). In addition to this, you can simply click on the empty textboxes (below the Hash and Range key attribute names) to add an item-specific attribute name, type, and value. In the case of entering a set (NumberSet for the numberSet attribute), specify multiple numbers by clicking on the **+** symbol to the right-hand side of the value textbox. After entering all the attributes, click on the **PutItem** button, which will put this item in the table.

To view the inserted item, click on the **Browse Items** tab, select the **Scan** radio button, and then click on the **Go** button. Now you will be able to see the table's contents. In addition to this, you can perform four more item operations, which are highlighted in the following screenshot:

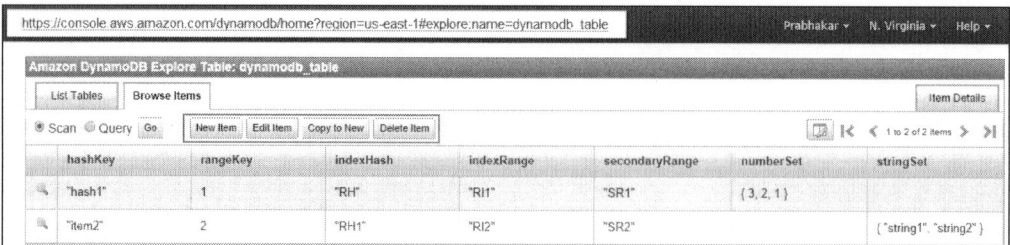

The scan operation will read the contents of the entire table's items. So, if the table has millions of items, then a single scan operation can cost you more capacity units (even though it returns a maximum of 1 MB of data at a time, it might scan all the non-returned items too). Always try to use a query operation instead of a scan.

In the **Explore Table** page, clicking on the **Query** radio button will open up the following options. If you recall, your table (**dynamodb_table**) has three indexes. The first index is the primary index created based on the primary key attributes, the second is the local secondary index, and the third is the global secondary index. Based on the type of index you choose, the **Hash Key** and **Range Key** dropdowns will be populated, as shown in the following screenshot. We can perform only the *equal to* operations on the Hash key and perform all kinds of *comparison* and *between* operations on the Range key.

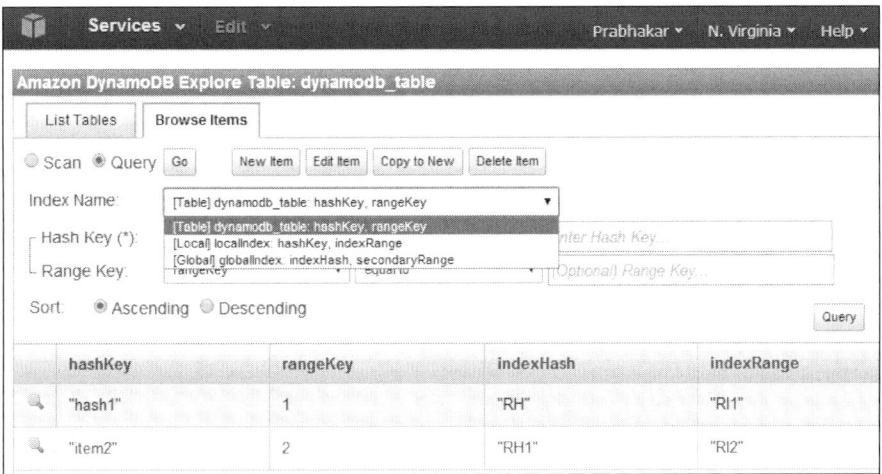

Once you are done with the table, you can delete it. This action will open up a window with the following options. The first checkbox is a must if you want to delete the table schema and its items. The second checkbox will delete all the alarms for the table, and the third checkbox will delete the data import/export pipelines for the table being deleted.

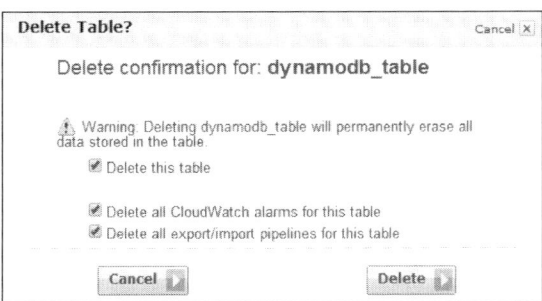

Best practices for DynamoDB

There are a lot more things to be done with DynamoDB, so you will see some of the best practices while using secondary indexes with DynamoDB. While deciding the attributes to be projected in the global secondary index, there are tradeoffs that you must consider between the provisioned throughput and storage costs. A few of them are listed as follows:

- If your application doesn't need to query a table so often and it performs frequent writes or updates against the data in the table, then you must consider projecting the KEYS_ONLY attributes. The global secondary index will be of a minimal size, but it will still be available when needed for the query activity.

- The smaller the index, the lesser the cost to store it, and your write costs will be less too. If you need to access only a few attributes with the lowest possible latency, then you must project only those (lesser) attributes in a global secondary index.

- If you need to access almost all the non-key attributes of the DynamoDB table on a frequent basis, you can project these attributes (even the entire table) to the global secondary index. This will give you the maximum flexibility with the tradeoff that your storage cost will increase or even double if you project the entire table's attributes into the index.

- The additional storage costs to store the global secondary index might equalize the cost of performing frequent table scans. If you frequently retrieve some non-key attributes, you must consider projecting them in the global secondary index.

There are four rules to be followed when creating the secondary index, so that your table will function without any hiccups. These rules are as follows:

- Distribute the load by choosing the correct Hash key attribute
- Make use of the sparse index
- Use the global secondary index for a quicker retrieval
- Creation of the read replica

Amazon RDS

As the name suggests, RDS helps you to configure, set up, operate, and scale a relational database in the Amazon Cloud. As of now, RDS supports MySQL, SQL Server, PostgreSQL, and Oracle. You can either use the open license provided by the vendor or, if you have your own license, you can use the same in RDS.

Amazon provides a wide range of server configurations in which you can run your RDS instance. Your instance can start with the db.t1.micro instance with 1 core, 0.613 GiB RAM and extend up to db.cr1.8xlarge with 32 core, 244 GiB RAM. You can also deploy your RDS instance replica across multiple zones. This is for disaster recovery. This read replica will act as a backup. RDS also provides hundreds of thousands of **I/O Operations Per Second (IOPS)**.

In RDS, whenever a new version of your database is available, you don't have to delete or migrate your database. This will be automatically done by Amazon. Another important feature with RDS is its ability to work with VPC. If you do so, then it will act as a two-level security that all the connections to the database must authenticate with the VPN gateway first and then with the database server. In addition to this, you can also allow a connection (inbound and outbound, separately) only through the specified ports.

Instance creation

Once you click on the **RDS** option in the Management Console, the following page will be displayed. It will have three important sections, which I have tagged as **Dashboard**, **Resources**, and **Information**. The **Dashboard** section has links that can be used to perform a few frequent RDS management operations. The **Resources** section gives you the information on the RDS resources that are used by you in the selected region. The **Information** section consists of links to the RDS documentation and a reference to perform frequent RDS operations. To create your first RDS DB instance, click on the **Launch a DB Instance** button.

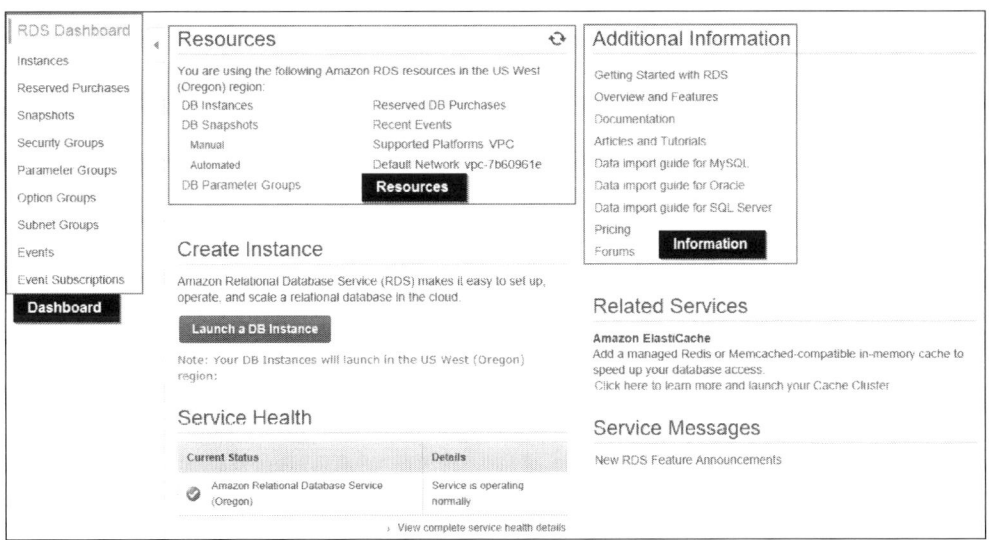

We will then be taken to the following **Select Engine** page, where you can choose the kind of relational database required from Amazon. We can choose any one of the four databases. Each of these will have several other distributions. For this discussion, select **MySQL** and click on the **Select** button, as shown in the following screenshot:

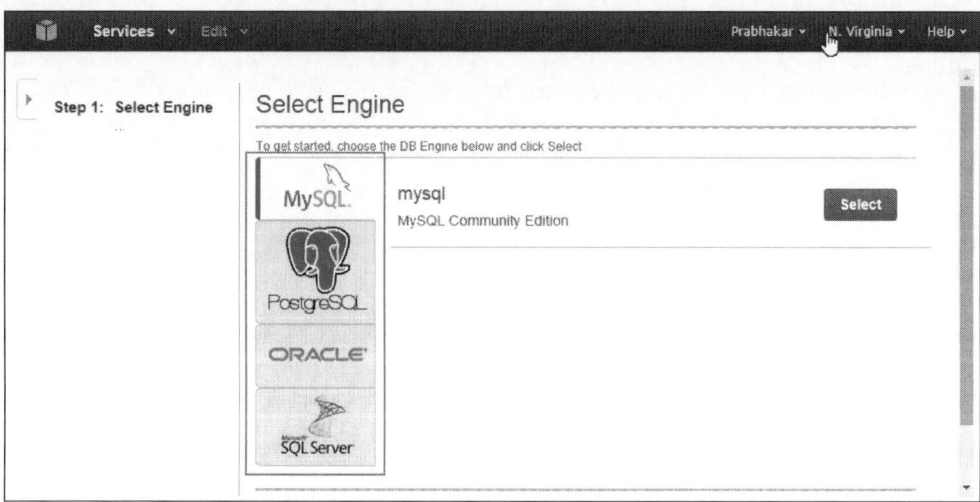

MySQL is simple and easy to configure; it has a lot of connectors available and one of the famous free database software that you will use in the primary discussion. The second step is called the **Deployment** step. Here, you can choose the first radio button if you want this RDS instance to be of production or deployment standards. If you choose this option, then your MySQL instance will be made available in multiple availability zones in order to make the instance highly available. One more advantage of using this option is the use of IOPS, which makes your database faster by sticking to the selected number of IOPS values, as shown in the following screenshot:

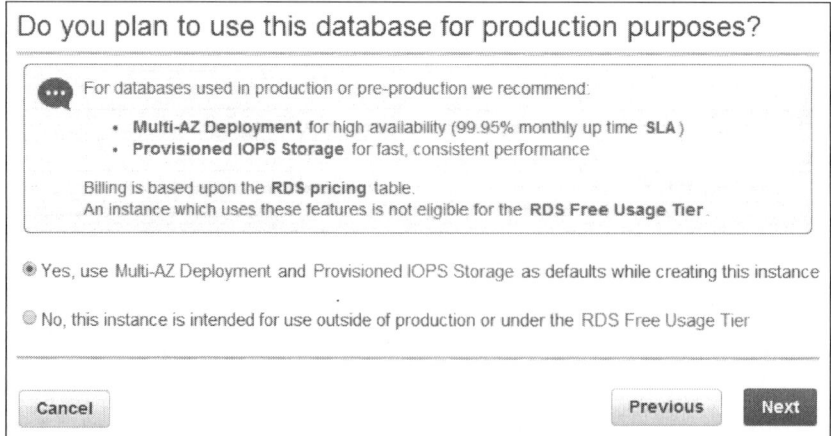

Selecting the second radio button will make the instance available in a normal environment. If you don't want to pay too much, then you must choose the second radio button (the tradeoff is the slowness, and sometimes the database might become unavailable) because the first option won't come under the free tier. Here, you can proceed by selecting the second option and continue by clicking on the **Next** button.

The third step is used to configure the MySQL instance version and its credentials. Here, select the **5.6.17** Version to be made available in the **db.t1.micro** instance type with a maximum storage capacity of **5 GB**. We have also specified the instance identifier (used to identify the instance in the Management Console), username, and password to access this instance, as shown here:

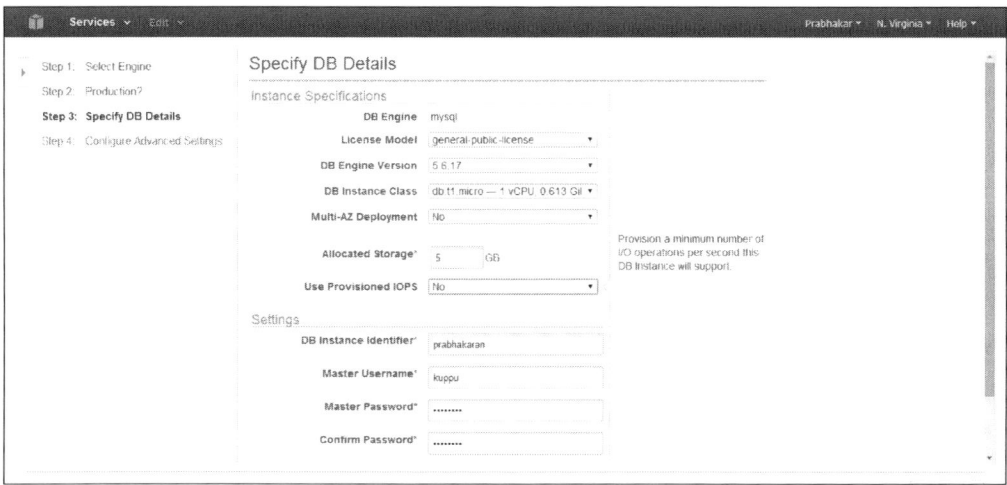

The next page will let you configure some of the advanced settings. This page has the following three sections:

- **Network & Security**: This section is used to select the VPC in which you want these MySQL instances to be hosted. We can also select the subnet (because a single VPC will have one or more subnets) and decide whether the instance should be available to the general public or not. If you select **No** in this dropdown, then you can access this instance only through the VPN gateway. It's secured to make this value **No**, but changing it to **Yes** will make it easily accessible. We can also specify the availability zone in which this instance has to be made available.

- **Database Options**: This section is used to create a database (here, you create a database named mysqlDB1) in the MySQL instance. You also need to specify the port in which you want the MySQL daemon to run. Then you can use the security group for this instance.

- **Backup and Maintenance**: This section is used to specify the maximum duration within which the instance modification (such as upgrading the MySQL instance version) should happen. The smaller the value, the better will be the instance available. Another operation that you can perform is setting up whether the MySQL version should be upgraded automatically.

Selecting the correct VPC is the key here. We can choose a VPC only if it has at least one subnet in all the availability zones. Otherwise, you cannot proceed with the DB instance creation. One more thing about the VPC Security Groups is that they should allow the incoming connection to (at least) the port 3306 or any other ports on which MySQL is running. A database port can be any port number. However, you need to make sure that the port is not preoccupied by the operating system, as shown here:

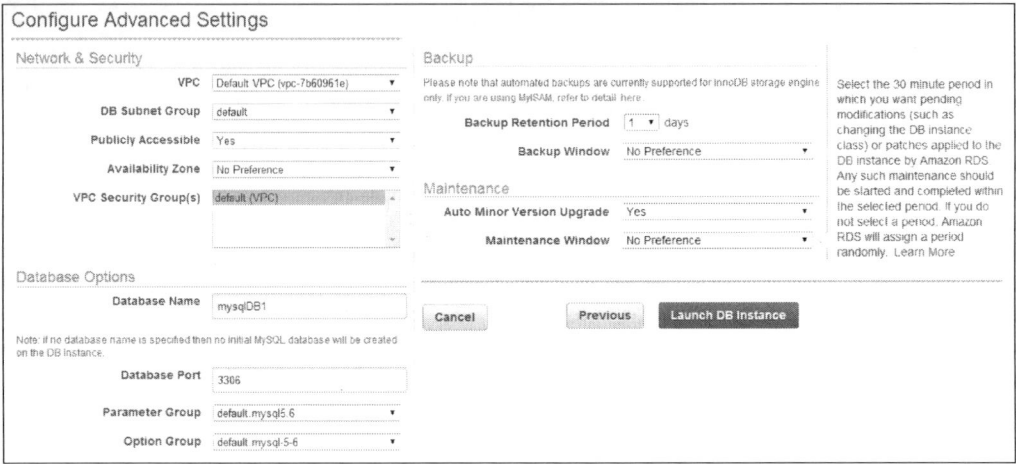

After setting the optimal values, you can proceed by clicking on the **Launch DB Instance** button, which will take you to the next page; this page will ask you to wait until the DB instance becomes available.

If there are some issues with the configuration then you won't be able to see the green tick mark. You can click on the link just below the green tick mark to look at all your DB instances.

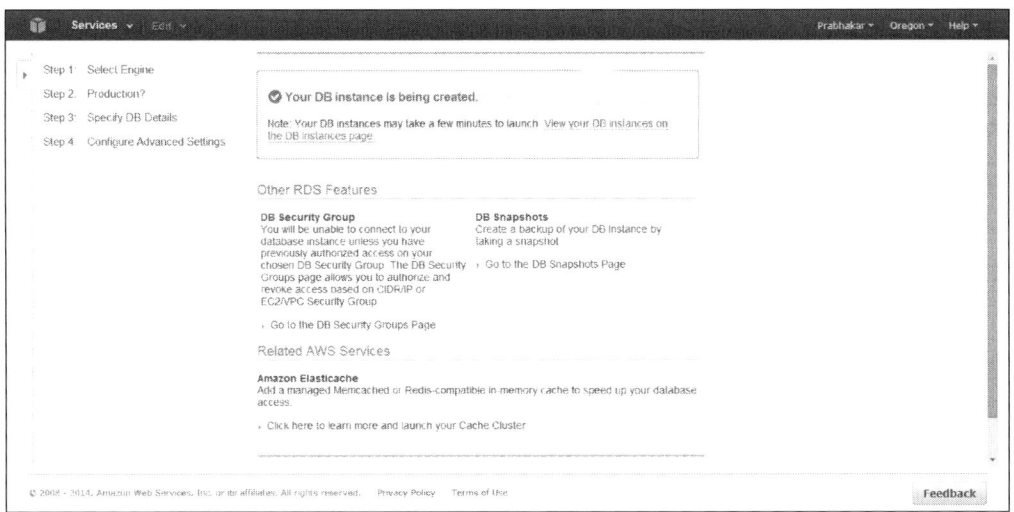

In the RDS dashboard, the **Instances** page will show you all the RDS instances that have been provisioned in this region, as you have requested for the MySQL instance with the identifier **Prabhakaran** on the **db.t1.micro** instance with **5 GB** of storage on the VPC, **vpc-7b60961e**, and with the **kuppu** database username. Initially, the status of the instance will be **creating**, as shown in the following screenshot. After a few minutes, the status will be updated to **available**.

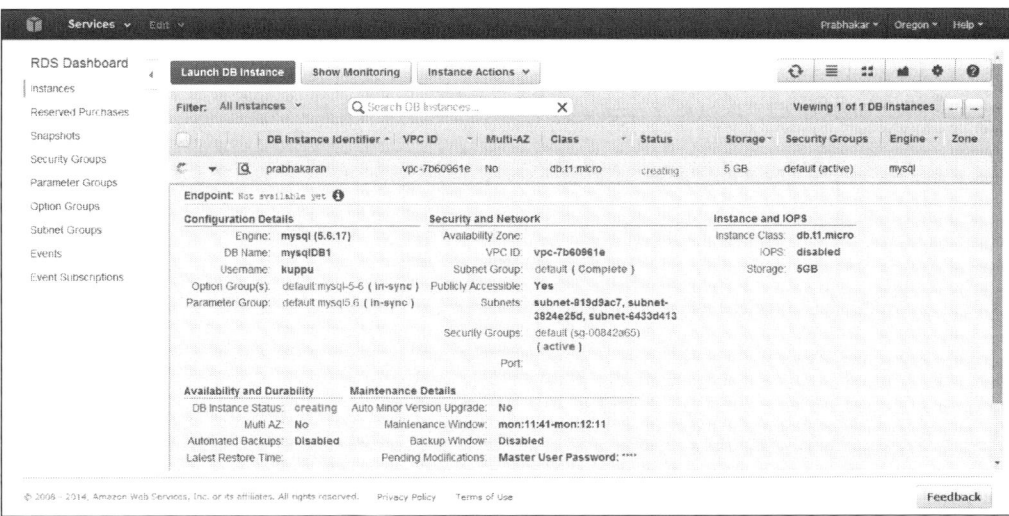

Also, at this point in time, the endpoint will not be available. It will only be available after the instance becomes available.

Once the instance becomes available, you will be able to see the MySQL DB instance's endpoint. Here, the instance's endpoint is **prabhakaran.cde8s5btscuk. us-west-2.rds.amazonaws.com:3306**, where **prabhakaran.cde8s5btscuk.us-west-2. rds.amazonaws.com** is the hostname and **3306** is the port through which you can communicate with the instance, as shown in the following screenshot:

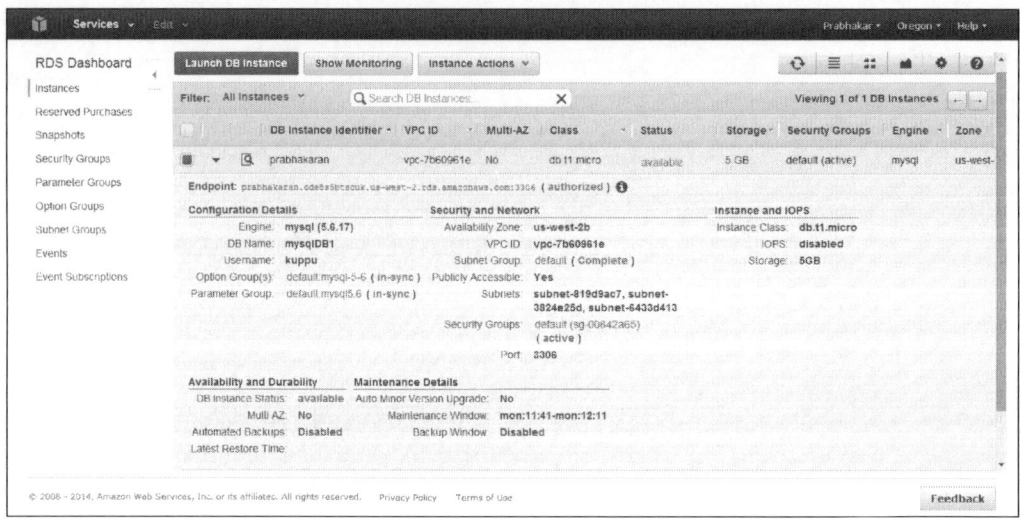

Connecting to the RDS DB instance

We are going to use MySQL Workbench 6.1 CE for the discussion. This can be downloaded from `http://cdn.mysql.com/Downloads/MySQLGUITools/ mysql-workbench-community-6.1.7-win32.msi`, and it is available as a freeware. After installation, proceed with the following steps:

1. Click on the **add connection** button to specify the connection parameters of your MySQL instance, as shown in the following screenshot:

2. Clicking on the **add connection** button will open **Setup New Connection**. Here, the **Connection Name** option can be anything (it is only for identification). The **Connection Method** field should be **Standard (TCP/IP)**. Then select the **Parameters** tab and specify the **Hostname** and **Port** fields, which you obtained from the RDS dashboard. The **Username** field must be the same as the one configured with the instance. To set **Password**, click on the **Store in Vault** button, which will open a window that allows you to enter and store it securely. Then, in the **Default Schema** textbox, you can either specify mysqlDB1 (which you created while creating this MySQL RDS instance) or you can leave it blank, as shown here:

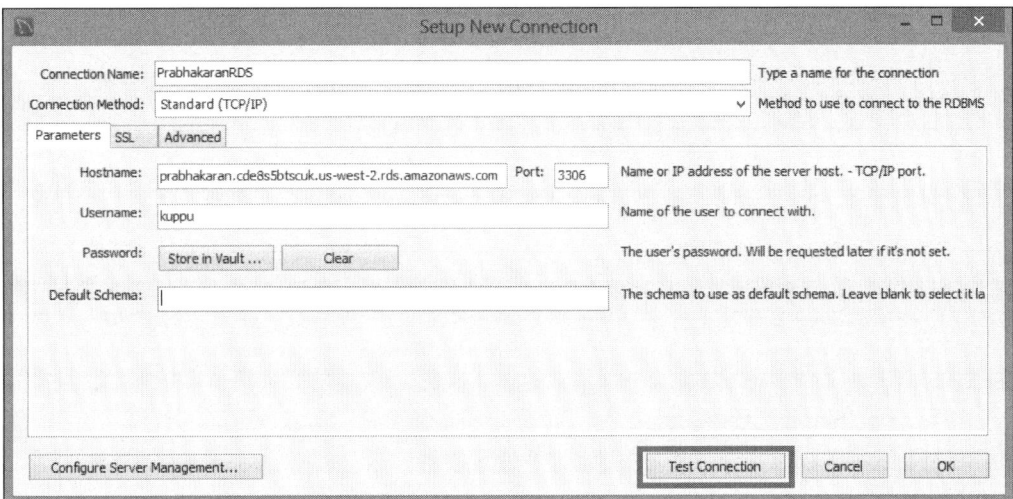

3. You can click on the **Test Connection** button to check whether your RDS instance is reachable. If the parameters are correct, then you will see the following response. Otherwise, you have to check either the connection parameters or the VPC subnet in which the RDS instance is made available, and an important thing is to check whether the instance is running.

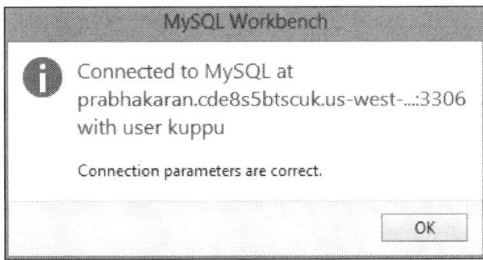

4. After testing the connection parameters, if you click on **OK**, these connection parameters will be added to your workbench home page (as shown in the following screenshot) with the name specified in the **Connection Name** field:

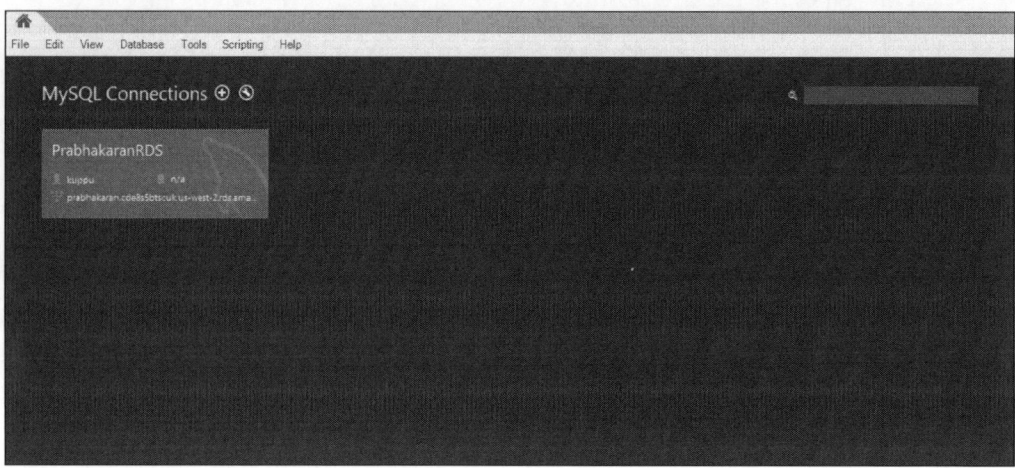

5. All you need to do is click on the shortcut created for your database connection. It will connect you to your DB instance and open the following page. Here, you can execute the query by writing it in the **Query 1** tab (where show databases is currently written) and clicking on the **execute query** button. Then, you will be able to see the output below (just below the **Query 1** tab where **mysqlDB1** is highlighted).

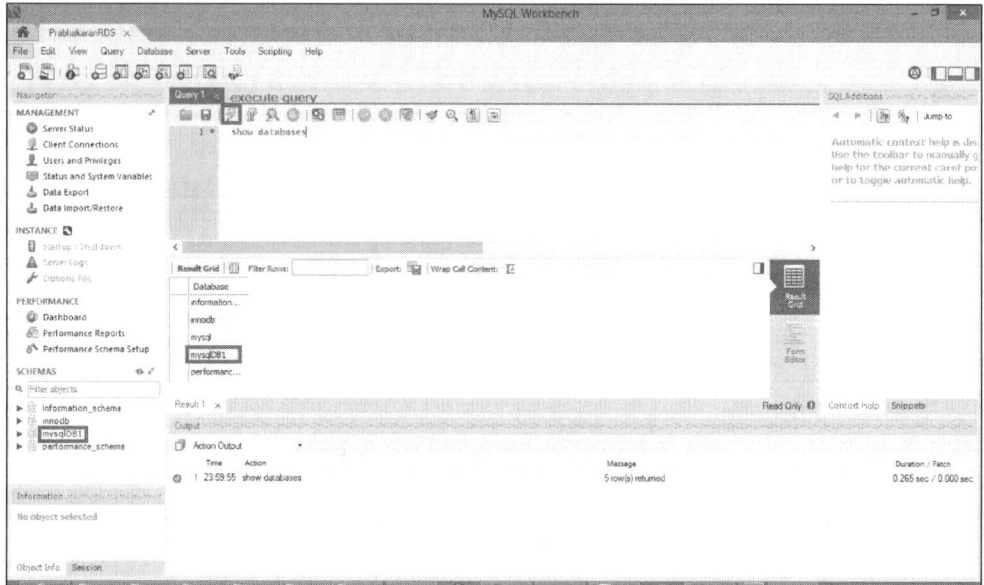

6. If you want to see the status of the MySQL DB instance, which you have borrowed from Amazon, then you can click on the **Server Status** link available in the **MANAGEMENT** section (on the top-left hand side). This will show you the following page:

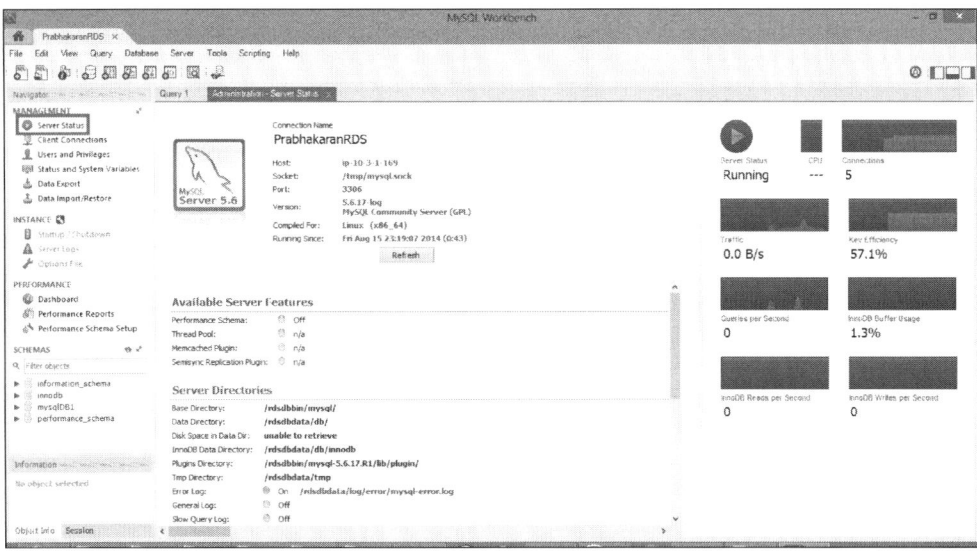

7. After making sure that everything is working perfectly, you can write some code to establish a connection to your MySQL RDS instance. The JDBC code will create a table named `RDStable` and insert three rows and queries for the number of rows in the table, as shown here:

```java
static final String JDBC_DRIVER = "com.mysql.jdbc.Driver";
static final String DB_URL = "jdbc:mysql://prabhakaran.has.removed.few.details.rds.amazonaws.com:3306/mysqlDB1";
static final String USER = "kuppu";
static final String PASS = "this.is.not.my.password";

public static void main(String[] args) throws SQLException {
    Connection connection = null;
    Statement statement = null;
    try {
        Class.forName("com.mysql.jdbc.Driver");
        connection = DriverManager.getConnection(DB_URL, USER, PASS);
        statement = connection.createStatement();
        String createTableQuery = "CREATE TABLE RDStable "
            + "(rowNumber INTEGER PRIMARY KEY, column1 INTEGER, "
            + "column2 VARCHAR(30), column3 VARCHAR(30))";
        statement.execute(createTableQuery);
        String insertQuery = "INSERT INTO RDStable "
            + "VALUES (1, 1111, 'element12', 'element13')";
        statement.executeUpdate(insertQuery);
        insertQuery = "INSERT INTO RDStable "
            + "VALUES (2, 2222, 'element22', 'element23')";
        statement.executeUpdate(insertQuery);
        insertQuery = "INSERT INTO RDStable "
            + "VALUES (3, 3333, 'element32', 'element33')";
        statement.executeUpdate(insertQuery);
        String query = "SELECT COUNT(*) FROM RDStable";
        ResultSet resultSet = statement.executeQuery(query);
        resultSet.next();
        System.out.println("Totally there are " + resultSet.getInt(1)
            + " elements in the table");
```

Problems Javadoc Declaration Console

`<terminated> RDSandMySQL [Java Application] C:\Program Files\Java\jre7\bin\javaw.exe (Aug 16, 2014, 12:36:42 AM)`
`Totally there are 3 elements in the table`

Therefore, the RDS instance created by you will function as an ideal MySQL server that is running and dedicated to you. The good news is that you can keep one RDS instance running continuously without paying a single dollar to Amazon (without using the Multi-AZ deployment, IOPS, and the low-end db.t1.micro instance).

Database tools and libraries

We have installed and configured the Eclipse plugin and the AWS SDK tools in *Chapter 1, An Introduction to AWS*. In the *Table operation* and *Item operation* section, you have performed DynamoDB operations using the Management Console. However, for advanced users to perform advanced operations, the Management Console is not enough. Therefore, in this section, you are going to learn about DynamoDB interactions through the Eclipse plugin and the AWS SDK tool. Along with the Management Console, DynamoDB supports lots of tools and libraries. Another important DynamoDB tool is DynamoDB local. We can easily create tables, indexes, attributes, and items with it. After doing all of these offline, you can commit or save to AWS DynamoDB. This is the usage of DynamoDB local.

In case you are developing a web application (let's say, a JSF application) and decide to use DynamoDB as the database, the biggest challenge will be to integrate DynamoDB with Java. This is where the SDK comes into the picture. By importing and including certain DynamoDB libraries, you can play with DynamoDB using a simple Java code.

Creating your first SDK project

If you have already installed the Eclipse plugin, as mentioned in *Chapter 1, An Introduction to AWS*, you will be able to see the credentials file created correctly and then you are ready to start using SDK. To do this, follow these steps:

1. Click on the AWS toolkit for the Eclipse icon; this will provide you with the option to create a new AWS project, as shown in the following screenshot:

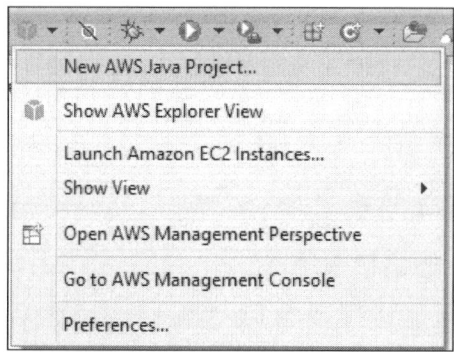

2. Here, you need to select **New AWS Java Project**. Clicking on this option for the first time will give you a few sample codes from AWS and will ask you whether you want these sample codes to be part of the project.

3. Check the **Amazon DynamoDB Sample** checkbox for the first time to understand the syntax of the DynamoDB table operations.

4. Once done, select the AWS account that is already configured or configure a new AWS account.

5. Click on the **Next** button to proceed, as shown here:

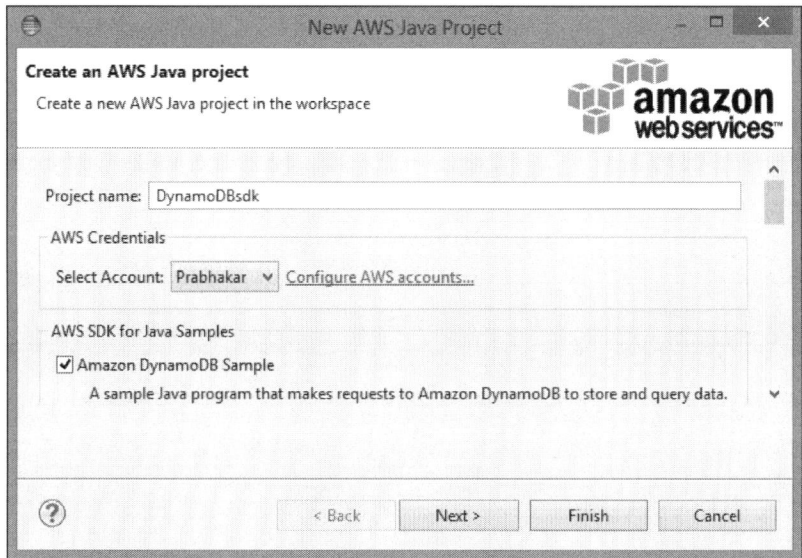

6. Clicking on the **Next** button will create a new project with the name specified in the preceding screenshot. In the `src` folder of the project, the credentials file will be made available by default. The sample DynamoDB code will also be available in the default package of this `src` folder under a file named `AmazonDynamoDBSample.java`, as shown in the following screenshot:

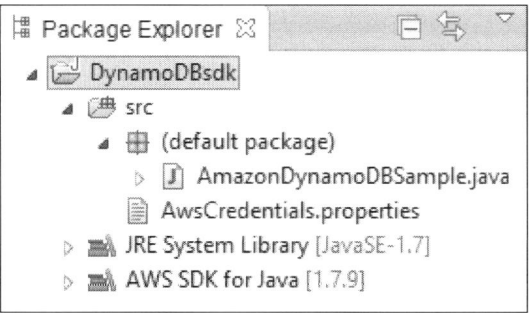

Since the sample code is provided by AWS, I don't want to get into trouble by providing the code here. So we will see what this sample code does. First and foremost, it creates a table named `my-favorite-movies-table` in the **US_WEST_2** region. Once you run this code, you need to open the AWS Explorer and refresh Amazon DynamoDB, as shown in the following screenshot:

Make sure that you're selecting the correct region (**US_WEST_2**) in the AWS Explorer; otherwise, you will not see the table getting created.

Double-clicking on the table name will open the following window, showing the contents of the table:

In this table, **name** is the only key attribute of the `String` type. The **fans** attribute is of the `StringSet` type. The **rating** attribute is of the `String` type, and year is of the `Number` type.

The sample code provided will not have the code to create any indexes. In the following topics of this chapter, we will discuss everything in detail. First, you will create a new class named `AwsSdkDemo` in the same project.

In this DynamoDB class (named `AwsSdkDemo`), you are going to perform the following DynamoDB operations:

- Initialize your AWS credentials
- Define the table attributes
- Define the key schema (of the table and indexes)
- Define the provisioned throughput

- Create the table with the preceding parameters
- Describe the table
- Add (insert) items to the table

Java SDK operations

There are five user-defined private functions that are being invoked in the following code; we will see each and every function in detail:

```
public class AwsSdkDemo {
static AmazonDynamoDBClient client;
initializeCredentials();
String tableName = "dynamodb_table";
if (Tables.doesTableExist(client, tableName)) {
    System.out.println("Table " + tableName + " already EXISTS");
}
else {
    ArrayList<AttributeDefinition> attributeDefinitions =
        getTableAttributes();
    ArrayList<KeySchemaElement> keySchemaElements =
        getTableKeySchema();
    ProvisionedThroughput provisionedThroughput =
        getProvisionedThroughput();

    CreateTableRequest request = new CreateTableRequest()
        .withTableName(tableName)
        .withAttributeDefinitions(attributeDefinitions)
        .withKeySchema(keySchemaElements)
        .withProvisionedThroughput(provisionedThroughput);
    CreateTableResult result = client.createTable(request);

    Tables.waitForTableToBecomeActive(client, tableName);
    TableDescription tableDescription = client.describeTable(
new DescribeTableRequest()
        .withTableName(tableName))
        .getTable();

    System.out.println("Created Table: " + tableDescription);
    putItems(tableName);
}}
```

The first method, `initializeCredentials`, is used to load your AWS credentials and authenticate you to AWS for running the program in order to perform the DynamoDB operation.

For all kinds of DynamoDB operations that you wish to perform, it must be done through the following client:

```
static AmazonDynamoDBClient client;
```

The following block of code will initialize the table name to the local variable. Then, the `if` condition will check whether the table already exists with this name (in the client-configured region) and returns a Boolean value. If the table already exists, then the SYSO message will be printed.

```
String tableName = "Tbl_Book";
if (Tables.doesTableExist(client, tableName)) {
    System.out.println("Table " + tableName + " already EXISTS");
}
```

The following block of code will create a `CreateTableRequest` method with attributes such as `TableName`, `AttributeDefinitions`, `KeySchema`, `provisionedThroughput`, and `indexes`:

```
CreateTableRequest request = new CreateTableRequest()
    .withTableName(tableName)
    .withAttributeDefinitions(attributeDefinitions)
    .withKeySchema(keySchemaElements)
    .withProvisionedThroughput(provisionedThroughput);
```

The following line will submit the table creation request through the DynamoDB client:

```
client.createTable(request);
```

The following line of code will pause the further execution of the code until the table becomes active (it is most probably used before putting items in the table):

```
Tables.waitForTableToBecomeActive(client, tableName);
```

The following code will request to describe the table name passed as a parameter to the client:

```
client.describeTable(new DescribeTableRequest()
    .withTableName(tableName))
    .getTable();
```

The following code will update a table with the passed `UpdateTableRequest` instance:

```
client.updateTable(updateTableRequest);
```

The default location of the credential file is $USER_HOME/.aws/credentials. However, you have to keep your credentials file at $USER_HOME/.aws/config, so that the SDK can easily identify it. The following different operations are performed by the various lines of the code:

- The first line of the `try` block will load the default AWS credentials
- The next line will configure the DynamoDB client with the loaded credential
- The next line will initialize the region to US_WEST_2, which is Oregon
- The last line of the `try` block will set the region for the DynamoDB client to US-WEST-2

In the case of an improper location of the credential file, the following exception will be thrown:

```
private static void initializeCredentials() throws Exception {
AWSCredentials credentials = null;
try {
    credentials = new
          ProfileCredentialsProvider().getCredentials();
    client = new AmazonDynamoDBClient(credentials);
    Region usWest2 = Region.getRegion(Regions.US_WEST_2);
    client.setRegion(usWest2);
} catch (Exception e) {
    throw new AmazonClientException(
          "Invalid location or format of credentials file.",e);
}
}
```

The following function will prepare an `ArrayList` method, which adds all the `AttributeDefinition` methods to it. Each `AttributeDefinition` method will take two parameters: first is the attribute name and the second is the attribute type. In the following code, we are defining the two attributes:

```
private static ArrayList<AttributeDefinition> getTableAttributes() {
    ArrayList<AttributeDefinition> attributeDefinitions = new
          ArrayList<AttributeDefinition>();
    attributeDefinitions.add(new AttributeDefinition()
          .withAttributeName("hashKey")
          .withAttributeType("S"));
    attributeDefinitions.add(new AttributeDefinition()
          .withAttributeName("rangeKey")
          .withAttributeType("N"));
    return attributeDefinitions;
}
```

The following method will return an `ArrayList` of the `KeySchemaElement` type. Inside this function, you are instantiating an `ArrayList` method of the `KeySchemaElement` type. To the `ArrayList` method, you are adding two `KeySchemaElement` elements. The first element is to set the `hashKey` attribute as the `HASH` key type, and the second element is to set the `rangeKey` attribute as the `RANGE` key type. Finally, you are returning the following `ArrayList`:

```
private static ArrayList<KeySchemaElement> getTableKeySchema() {
    ArrayList<KeySchemaElement> ks = new
            ArrayList<KeySchemaElement>();
    ks.add(new KeySchemaElement()
            .withAttributeName("hashKey")
            .withKeyType(KeyType.HASH));
    ks.add(new KeySchemaElement()
            .withAttributeName("rangeKey")
            .withKeyType(KeyType.RANGE));
    return ks;
}
```

In the following function, we will try to put items (`item1` of the type `Map<String, AttributeValue>`) in the table (the table's name is taken as the input parameter). As we have discussed previously (in the `getTableKeySchema` method), every item must have the primary key attributes (`hashKey` and `rangeKey`). Both the items now have these two attributes.

In the first item (`item1`), including the primary key attributes, you will add two more attributes, namely, `numberSet` (the `NumberSet` type) and `stringSet` (the `StringSet` type). In order to add the attributes, you must call the correct method of the `AttributeValue` class depending on the type of attribute, as shown here:

```
private static void putItems(String tableName) {
    Map<String, AttributeValue> item1 = new HashMap<String,
AttributeValue>();
    item1.put("hashKey", new AttributeValue().withS("hash1"));
    item1.put("rangeKey", new AttributeValue().withN("1"));
    item1.put("stringSet", new AttributeValue()
            .withSS(Arrays.asList("string1", "string2")));
    item1.put("numberSet", new AttributeValue()
            .withNS(Arrays.asList("3","2","1")));
    PutItemRequest putItemRequest = new PutItemRequest()
```

```
            .withTableName(tableName)
            .withItem(item1);
    client.putItem(putItemRequest);
}
```

The following method will return a `ProvisionedThroughput` instance with the populated write and read throughput capacities for your table. The long number (2L) here means the maximum read or write data size per second. This is usually measured in KB/s. Here, you are restricting the read/write speed to 2 KB/s:

```
private static ProvisionedThroughput getProvisionedThroughput() {
    ProvisionedThroughput provisionedThroughput = new
    ProvisionedThroughput()
                .withReadCapacityUnits(2L)
                .withWriteCapacityUnits(2L);
    return provisionedThroughput;
}
```

DynamoDB local

DynamoDB local is a local, client-side database, which emulates the DynamoDB database in your local system. This is pretty helpful when developing an application that uses DynamoDB as the backend. Every time after writing a module, in order to test whether the code works fine, you need to connect to Amazon and run it. This will consume a lot of bandwidth and a few dollars. To avoid this, you can make use of DynamoDB local and test the code locally. Once the testing is done, you can make your application use the AWS DynamoDB service. To do this, follow these three steps:

1. Download DynamoDB local from `http://dynamodb-local.s3-website-us-west-2.amazonaws.com/dynamodb_local_latest`.

2. Start the DynamoDB local service (it must be JRE6 or higher).

3. Point the code to use the DynamoDB local port.

 The URL provided in *Step 1* might become obsolete after some point of time. In that case, visit `http://docs.aws.amazon.com/amazondynamodb/latest/developerguide/Tools.html`, where the link for downloading DynamoDB tools will be made available.

The downloaded file might be a zipped file (tar.gz, .zip, or .rar). We need to extract it to a location. I have extracted it to C:\dynamodb, as shown in the following screenshot:

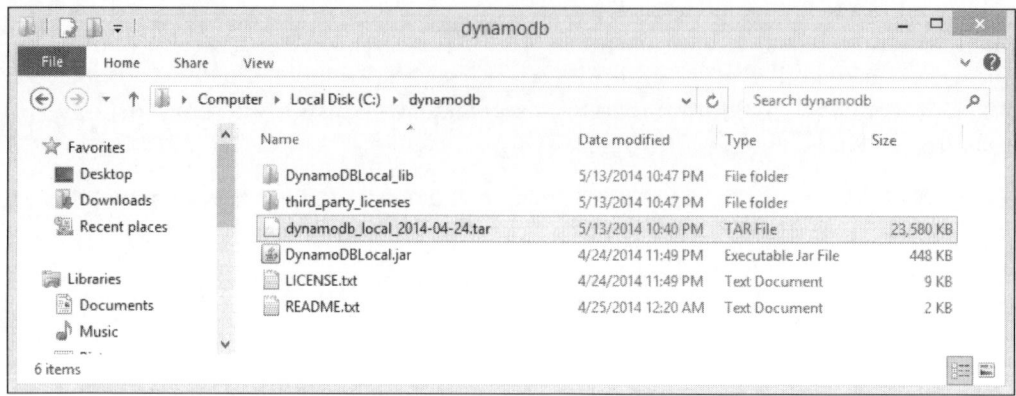

Starting DynamoDB local is very easy. First, you need to change the working directory using the cd command, and then you can start DynamoDB local on port 8888 using the following command:

```
java -D java.library.path=./DynamoDBLocal_lib -jar DynamoDBLocal.jar
-port 8888
```

Even the java -D java.library.path = ./DynamoDBLocal_lib -jar DynamoDBLocal.jar command is enough to start DynamoDB local, but the command starts it on port 8000, which is occupied by my PC. That's why I use port 8888, as shown here:

```
Microsoft Windows [Version 6.2.9200]
(c) 2012 Microsoft Corporation. All rights reserved.

C:\Users\ADMIN>cd C:\dynamodb

C:\dynamodb>java -Djava.library.path=./DynamoDBLocal_lib -jar DynamoDBLocal.jar
-port 8888
2014-05-18 23:21:12.855:INFO:oejs.Server:jetty-8.1.12.v20130726
2014-05-18 23:21:12.945:INFO:oejs.AbstractConnector:Started SelectChannelConnect
or@0.0.0.0:8888
```

Once DynamoDB local is started, it's easier to configure the client. We need to make changes in the three lines of the `initializeCredentials` method (as discussed in the *DynamoDB operations using CLI* section of this chapter). We need to insert a new line pointing to the DynamoDB localhost and port using the `client.setEndpoint()` method, as shown in the following code. Then, you need to remove other client-related setters such as `setRegion`.

```
private static void initializeCredentials() throws Exception {
    AWSCredentials credentials = null;
    try {
            credentials = new   ProfileCredentialsProvider()
                .getCredentials();
    } catch (Exception e) {
            thrownew AmazonClientException(
            "Invalid location or format of credentials file.",e);
    }
    client = new AmazonDynamoDBClient(credentials);
    client.setEndpoint("http://localhost:8888");
    //Region usWest2 = Region.getRegion(Regions.US_WEST_2);
    //client.setRegion(usWest2);
}
```

After this, if you run the `AwsSdkDemo` class, it will give you the following output in the console (where DynamoDB local is started):

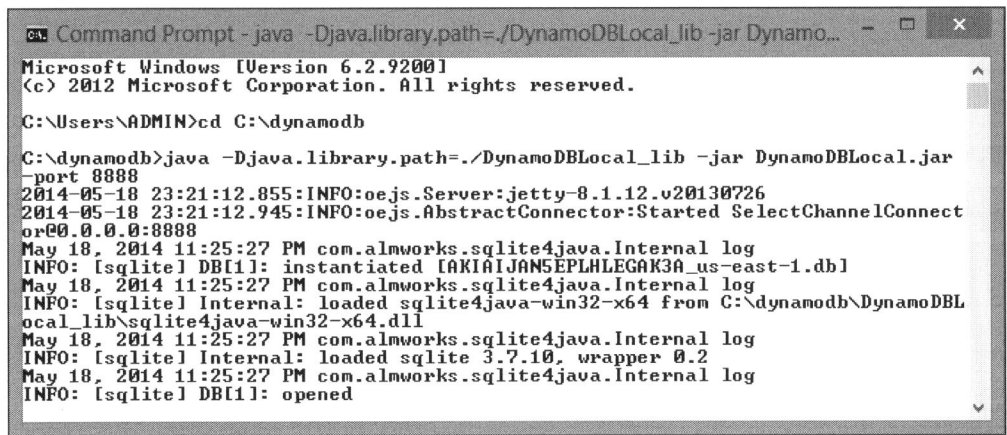

DynamoDB local stores all this data in the local SQLite database.

Performing DynamoDB operations using CLI

Even though the former two interfaces provide an easy usage of DynamoDB, the command-line interface provides good flexibility and, for the advanced programmers, it makes life simple by reducing the number of clicks so you can write commands and program to do certain redundant jobs instead.

To get the AWS CLI, go to the link mentioned in the following screenshot:

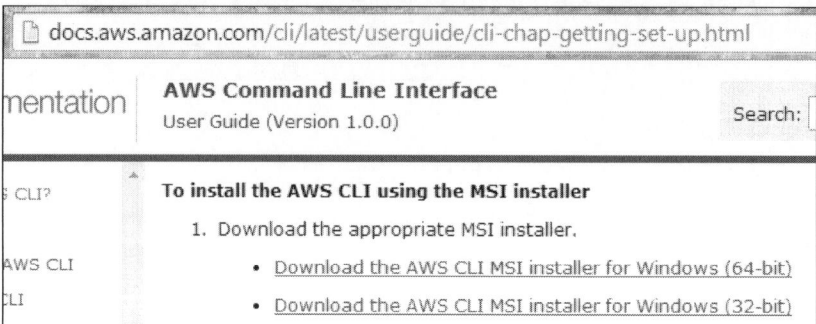

Visit `https://s3.amazonaws.com/aws-cli/AWSCLI64.msi` to download the AWS CLI setup. Once the installation is complete, go to following path in the command prompt (the path might differ based on the platform). Run the `aws configure` command to configure the CLI with your AWS credentials. Pressing the *Enter* key will prompt you to provide four options, as shown in the following screenshot:

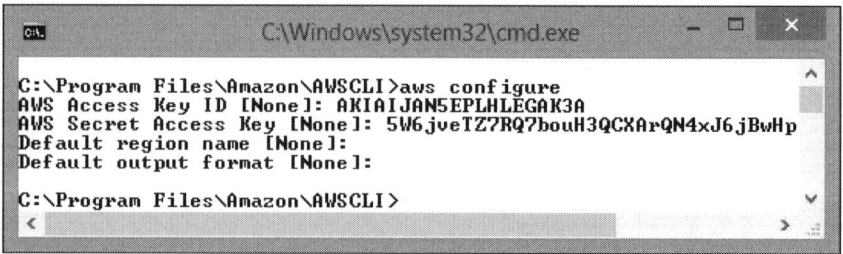

Now you will see one of the simplest DynamoDB commands, which is table creation. We are going to create the same table (but without secondary indexes) that you created using the Management Console with the help of the following command:

```
aws dynamodb create-table --table-name dynamodb_table

--attribute-definitions AttributeName=hashKey, AttributeType=S
AttributeName=rangeKey, AttributeType=N
```

```
--key-schema AttributeName=hashKey, KeyType=HASH AttributeName=rangeKey,
KeyType=RANGE
```

```
--provisioned-throughput ReadCapacityUnits=2,WriteCapacityUnits=2
```

We can retrieve all the table names in the configured region using the `aws dynamodb list-tables` command. To describe a table, use the `aws dynamodb describe-table --table-name dynamodb_table` command.

The following code shows how an item can be inserted in the DynamoDB table. This command purely depends on the OS in which AWS CLI is installed. For Windows 8, the command is as follows:

```
aws dynamodb put-item --table-name dynamodb_table --item {\"hashKe
y\":{\"S\":\"hash1\"},\"rangeKey\":{\"N\":\"1\"}, \"numberSet\":{\"
NS\":[\"1\",\"2\"]}}
```

```
--return-consumed-capacity TOTAL
```

For other platforms, if the command is throwing an error, you just need to replace `\"` with `"`, as shown here:

```
aws dynamodb put-item --table-name dynamodb_table --item {"hashKey":{"S":
"hash1"},"rangeKey":{"N":"1"}, "numberSet":{"NS":["1","2"]}}
```

```
--return-consumed-capacity TOTAL
```

Otherwise, type `aws dynamodb put-item help` to retrieve the format in which the request has to be made. The command used to scan a table with the name is `Tbl_Book` is `aws dynamodb scan --table-name Tbl_Book`. There are several other commands available in the AWS CLI. We can get help from these commands using the `aws dynamodb help` command. This command will list the following options (some options which we have already discussed are not listed here; they are `create-table`, `describe-table`, `list-tables`, `put-item`, and `scan`):

- `batch-get-item`
- `batch-write-item`
- `delete-item`
- `delete-table`
- `describe-table`
- `get-item`
- `help`
- `query`
- `update-item`
- `update-table`

The RDS command-line tool

We don't need to install a separate tool in order to perform the RDS operations. We can use the same tool that you have used in the previous section while discussing the DynamoDB command-line tool. The only thing that changes here is the command. All of your DynamoDB commands began with aws dynamodb, but here they should begin with aws rds, as shown in the following screenshot:

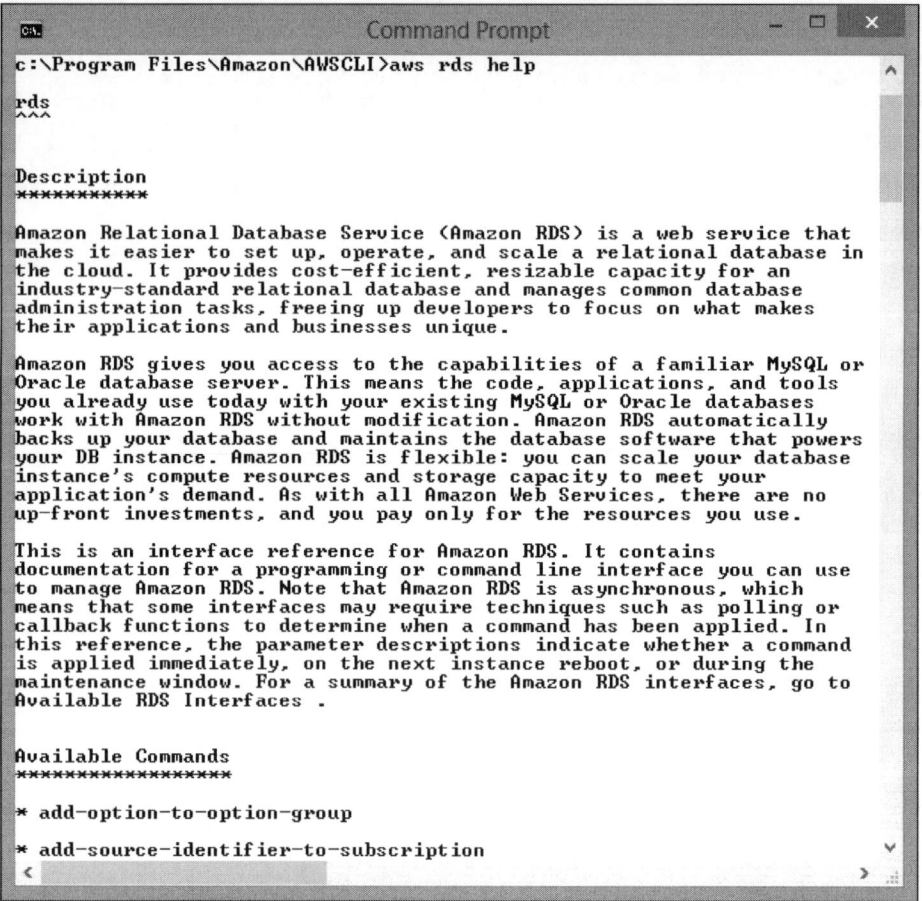

As shown in preceding screenshot, the aws rds help command will display all the possible RDS operations. At present, the SDK's command line supports 54 RDS operations. It won't be possible to list all of them, so let's skip this part. We can get the syntax and more information on each command by typing help along with the command. For example, if you want more details about the list-tags-for-resource command, then you should type aws rds list-tags-for-resource help in the command line.

Summary

In this chapter, you learned the features and uses of managed databases. You started the chapter by discussing the aspects of the NoSQL database DynamoDB. Then you performed table and item operations on DynamoDB. After that, you learned about the best practices and relational database services called Amazon RDS. You also configured and created a MySQL instance, then established a connection to your instance through the MySQL workbench and executed a JDBC code that makes use of this Amazon RDS instance. Finally, you learned about the various tools and libraries for these database services.

In the next chapter, you will learn about Amazon's deployment and management services.

5
Deployment and Management

AWS provides application management and deployment services that help you build, deploy, and scale your web applications instantly. You can use these application management and deployment services to influence other AWS services without having to manage each of them discretely and manually. In this chapter, you will learn about the following topics:

- AWS CloudFormation
- Amazon CloudWatch
- Amazon Identity and Access Management
- Application deployment using AWS Elastic Beanstalk

AWS CloudFormation

Amazon CloudFormation is a method used to initiate environments easily. This means that when you begin a CloudFormation environment, you will be able to launch precise AMIs with meticulous key pairs on predefined instance sizes and behind your AWS load balancers. If any segment of your environment fails to launch, the environment rolls itself in reverse, terminating all the segments along the way. You're going to use a tool that scrutinizes your running environment and creates a CloudFormation template for you.

The tool that you are about to use will give you a template, which will be stored in Amazon S3. Create a bucket to save the template. You have to use CloudFormer, which is a prototype tool that is designed to help you build these templates, and yes, you'll be able to twist the template to eliminate any unrelated instances and you'll also be able to refrain the template as an apposite. The CloudFormer tool is intended to create a starting point for your template. Once created, you can customize it in any manner. CloudFormation and CloudFormer are also accessible via the AWS console. Follow these steps to start with Amazon CloudFormation:

1. Go to the CloudFormation service from the listed AWS services and click on the **Create New Stack** button.

2. Select the CloudFormer sample template from the listed templates and name it `AWSCloudFormer` before clicking on the **Continue** button, as shown here:

3. Accept the terms and continue through the **Review** page.

4. The console will display **CREATE_IN_PROGRESS** for a while. When it's being completed, go to the **Outputs** tab and mark the URL address of the CloudFormer tool, as shown here:

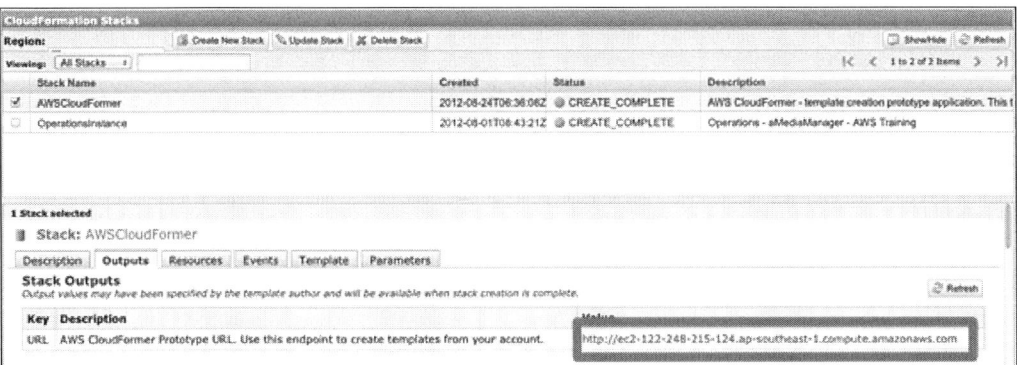

5. Now, try to connect to the tool that is running and start the wizard. Click on **Create Template** and add an explanation that classifies which template this is.

6. You'll be asked to select the resources on a series of screens. Select the load balancer that is associated with your environment, if any, as shown in the following screenshot:

7. Choose your autoscaling group (if any), as shown in the following screenshot:

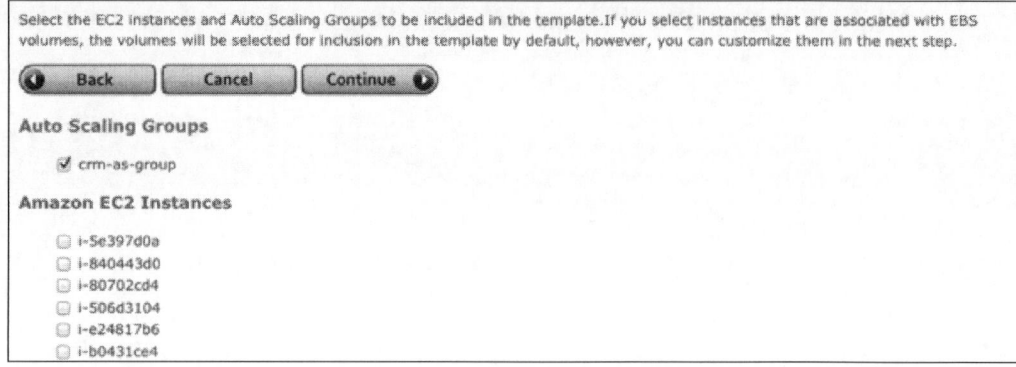

8. Next, select the launch configuration.

9. Select the **Security Group** option that suits you and your environment.

10. Click on **Continue** for the remaining steps. The tool will generate a template and then suggest an S3 bucket in which you can store the template.

11. Use the bucket that you fashioned earlier and click on the **Save Template** button, as shown here:

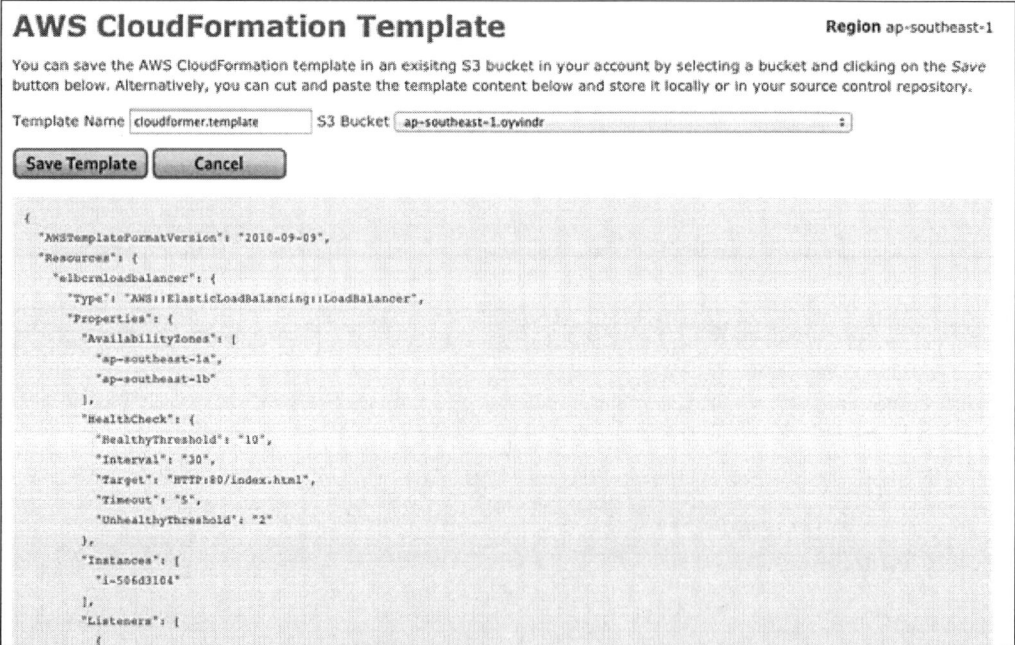

12. Finally, the following page will be displayed and you can launch the stack now by clicking on the **Launch Stack** button, as shown here:

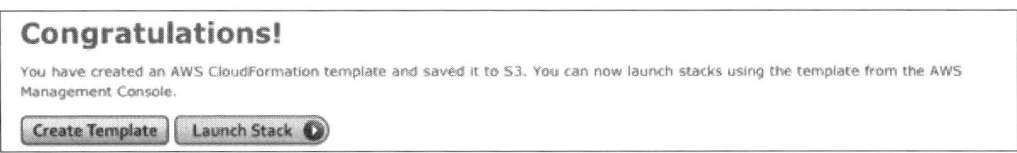

Alarms with Amazon CloudWatch

Amazon CloudWatch is the best monitoring service from Amazon that is used to monitor all of your cloud resources and applications on AWS. Amazon CloudWatch provides metrics to monitor your resources by collecting and tracking data. You can utilize the Amazon CloudWatch metrics to gain insights into resource utilization, application performance, and instance operational health. So, let's go through it with some exercises as practice makes a man perfect!

In this section, you are going to monitor a custom CloudWatch metric. To do this, perform the following summarized steps one by one:

1. Create a custom **Identity and Access Management (IAM)** role for an Amazon **Elastic Compute Cloud (EC2)** instance so that the instance has the permission to write statistics to CloudWatch.

2. Launch the new EC2 server instance.

3. Use **Secure Shell (SSH)** to log in to the server and generate a custom CloudWatch metric.

4. Use CloudWatch to monitor this custom metric.

5. Create a CloudWatch alarm that will be triggered whenever the custom metric, which you have created, drops below the level that you've mentioned.

Now, let's start with the first step, which is creating a custom IAM role for an EC2 instance:

1. On the AWS Management Console, navigate to **Services** | **All services** | **IAM**, as shown here:

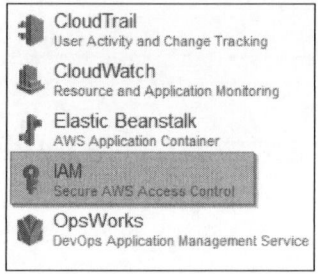

2. In the navigation pane, click on **Roles**, as shown in the following screenshot:

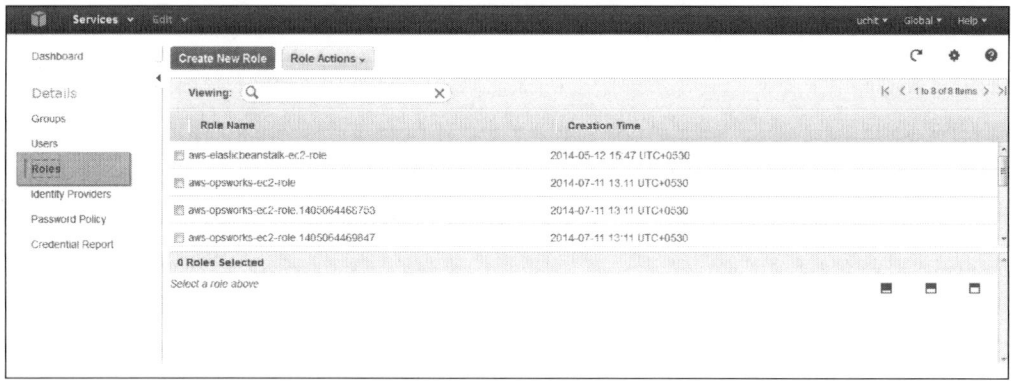

3. Click on **Create New Role** and provide the parameters as needed (in this instance, the role name is uchit, the AWS services role is **Amazon EC2**, and the policy template is **CloudWatch Full Access Template**), as shown in the following screenshot:

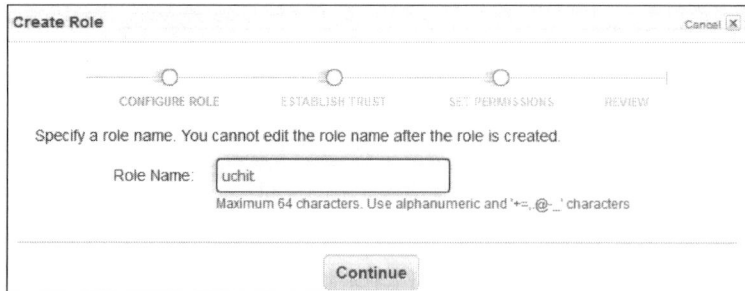

4. Review the policy, click on **Continue**, and then click on **Create Role**.

5. Select the newly created role and on the **Permissions** page, click on **Attach Role Policy**, as shown in the following screenshot:

6. Under the **Select Policy Template** menu, select **Amazon EC2 Read Only Access** and apply it, as shown here:

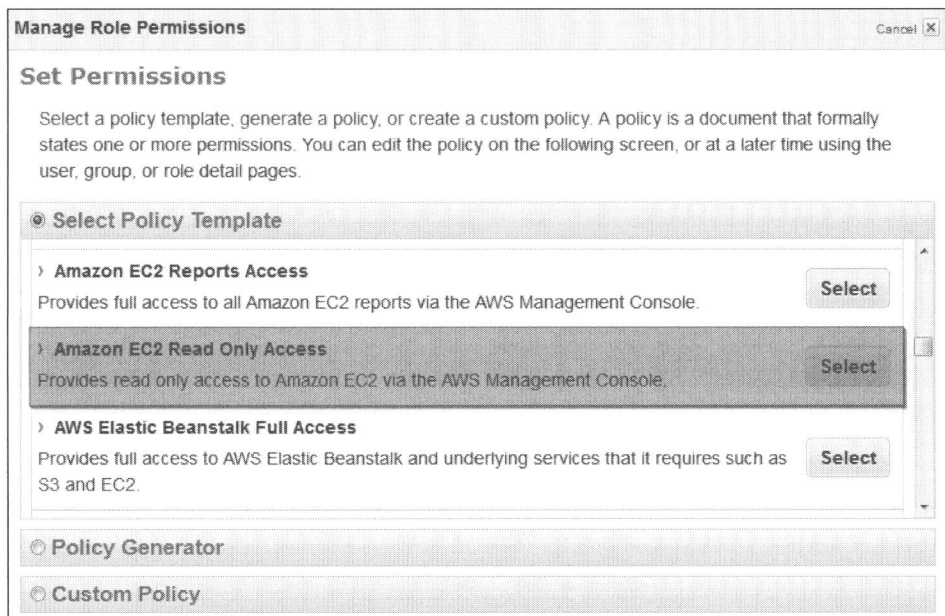

7. Repeat the same procedure from step 5 for the Amazon SQS full access from **Policy Template**.

Until now, you have set up from the IAM side; now, you have to create an EC2 instance with the declared IAM policy. Here, you will monitor the instance's performance in subsequent processes. To create an EC2 instance, follow these steps:

1. Click on **Amazon Management Console** and then click on **EC2**, as shown in the following screenshot:

2. Specify the IAM role and launch the instance, as shown in the following screenshot. Please make sure that you are using the `t1.micro` instance type, which might come with a free tier in your account:

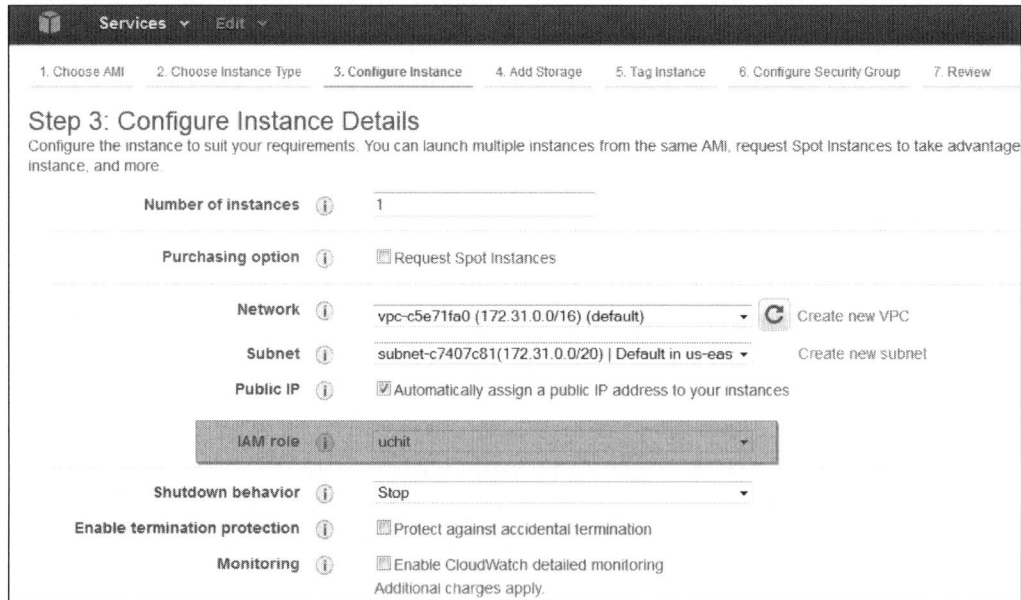

3. Once you are done with launching an instance, log in to the instance using SSH and use AWS CLI to generate a custom metric.

 Make a note of your public IP address in a text file to use it later; it will be called *monitoring-client-ip* in further steps.

4. Copy the AZ value minus the final letter to a text file. This will be your region and will be referred to as `current-aws-region`.

5. Set the environment variable for the region, as follows:

```
export AWS_DEFAULT_REGION=<current-aws-region>
```

6. Use the following command to create the CloudWatch metric:

```
awscloudwatch put-metric-data --namespace  Uchit --metric-name
Test  --value 8 -debug
```

The preceding command will create the sample metric; using this command, you can also create any custom metrics, such as the performance metric or the usage metric. Now, you can see this metric on your CloudWatch dashboard. To monitor the custom metric in CloudWatch, follow these steps:

1. On the AWS CloudWatch Management Console, go to the navigation pane and under the **Metrics** menu, select the **Namespace** option and then click on **Custom Metrics**.

2. After you select **Uchit**, a normal graph will be displayed at the bottom of the page.

3. For the CLI console, use the following command to retrieve the statistics in the CLI console. This command triggers the alarm whenever the metric falls below the designated level:

```
Awscloudwatch get-metric-statistics --metric-name "Uchit"
--namespace="Test" --start-time=$ (date -d yesterday -I) --end-
time=$ (date -d tomorrow -I) --period=400 --statistics="Maximum"
```

To monitor a custom CloudWatch metric, follow these steps:

1. Under the **Alarm Summary** section of the CloudWatch Management Console, click on **Create Alarm**.

2. Select the custom metric and configure **Alarm threshold**; for example, provide the **Name**, **Description**, and **Attention Level** details.

3. Under the **Actions** menu, provide the state of the **Alarm and Notification alerts** settings.

4. Finally, click on **Create Alarm**.

To record a data point with CloudWatch, which can trigger the alarm from the SSH console, use the following command:

```
awscloudwatch put-metric-data --namespace  Uchit --metric-name Test
--value 4 -debug
```

To check the status of the alarm, you can verify it from the AWS CloudWatch Monitoring Console. That's it!

Identity and Access Management

AWS has a shared security section that consists of AWS IAM. AWS IAM permits the formation of distinct users or groups of users with granulated authorizations and even precise services. Authorization levels can be set for any AWS service, including Amazon EC2, letting exclusive security credentials that avert basic users from retrieving statistics that are not related to their job meanings. You can also use IAM to accomplish security credentials such as access keys, passwords, and MFA devices centrally. Active instantaneously, IAM is the **Generally Available (GA)** service among other AWS services now!

IAM includes the following features:

- Complete control over users, groups, and security credentials
- Control over the user's role-based access and security tokens
- Control over the shared AWS resources
- Authorizations based on organizational groups and users
- Centralized networking controls

Accessing IAM

You can work with AWS IAM using the following methods:

- The AWS Management Console
- The AWS **command-line interface (CLI)**

Using any of the preceding access methods, you can accomplish the IAM capitals, for example:

- Create users/groups and assign permissions to them
- Create security credentials (roles and policies) for your users
- Assign passwords to your users and restrict them from particular services

Here, to get familiar with AWS IAM and its usage, we will follow the first method as an overview, and later in this book, we will bring IAM using CLI with other services. Let's check out the first IAM console overview, as shown in the following screenshot:

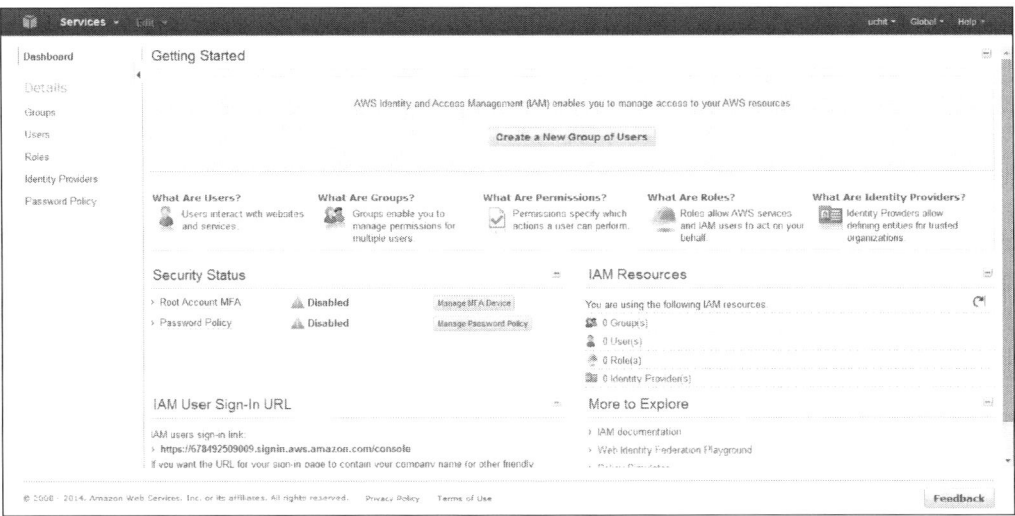

When users sign in to their AWS account, they sign in via an IAM-enabled user sign-in page. For their accessibility, this sign-in page routines a cookie to evoke the user's position so that the subsequent time when a user serves to the AWS Management Console, it automatically calls the IAM-enabled user sign-in page. The navigation tab on the left-hand side (as shown in the following screenshot) allows you to create and manage IAM users, groups of IAM users, their permissions, and their security credentials separately, along with other services:

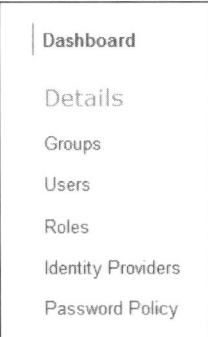

You can select the policy template, which is predefined in the IAM service, or even build your own custom policies using AWS **Policy Generator**, as shown in the following screenshot. The **Permissions** wizard includes a specific template for every service that currently supports IAM, making it easy for you to get started and define policies.

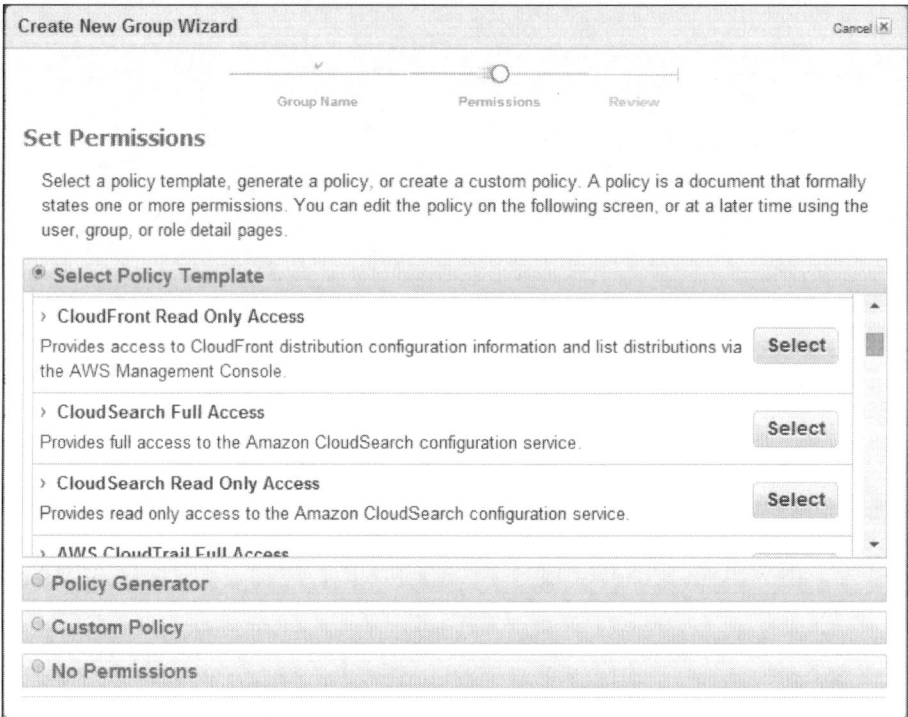

The features that we previously described represent our first overview-based steps toward our long-term goals of learning IAM and its best use cases in the further chapters. However, we have a long journey ahead of us, and we are looking forward to additional integrations, data access methods, and product-based scenarios with AWS IAM.

Authorization and authentication

One of the characteristics that I was concerned about to derive work at AWS was my intellect that the cloud can be a pleasant and logical residence where we can figure out security solutions; now, two of my beloved notions, positioning security in the cloud and quickening the espousal of multifactor authentication.

There are two imperative ideologies that are essential to confirm that precise people are undertaking the right things in the information system. They are as follows:

- **Authentication**: This is how you demonstrate your uniqueness avowal. AWS won't accept you as genuine until you are able to exhibit an acquaintance of a clandestine that AWS can validate. Typically, it's your username and password; it could also be the private key (secret key and access key) associated with a digital certificate (here, we call it X.509 in AWS). Authentication classifications send definite secrets over the wire in no time; in its place, the enigmas are used to compute a difficult-to-reverse message. Since apparently you are the only person who knows your secret, your claim is valid in any system.

- **Authorization**: This is what you're permitted to look at once the cloud grants you access to services. The following screenshot shows the security credentials page:

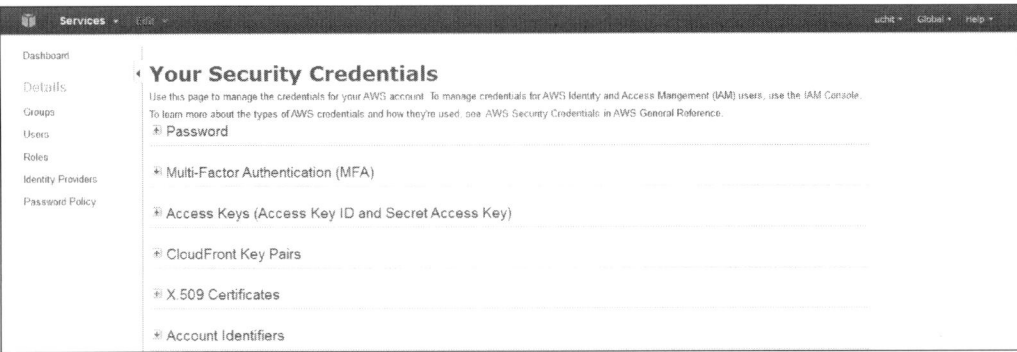

A multifactor authentication device in AWS alleviates this base problem by demanding an additional problem of proof. Authentication factors come in the following varieties:

- **Roughly you know**: This consists of a password, passphrase, key, pin, and response to a challenge

- **Somewhat you have**: This consists of a token, smartcard, mobile phone, passport, and wristband

- **Rather you are or do**: This consists of a middle- and theft-resistant biometric individual

In AWS, for authentication, you can use the two-factor authentication devices, and for the connection and retrieval of data, you can use secret keys, access keys, and the X.509 certificates. These things can be found in the **Security Credentials** menu under the **AWS Management Console** option, as described in the preceding screenshot. They also provide the **Multi-Factor Authentication (MFA)** device, which can be used for two-factor authentication. The following screenshot shows two types of MFA devices, **A virtual MFA device** and **A hardware MFA device**:

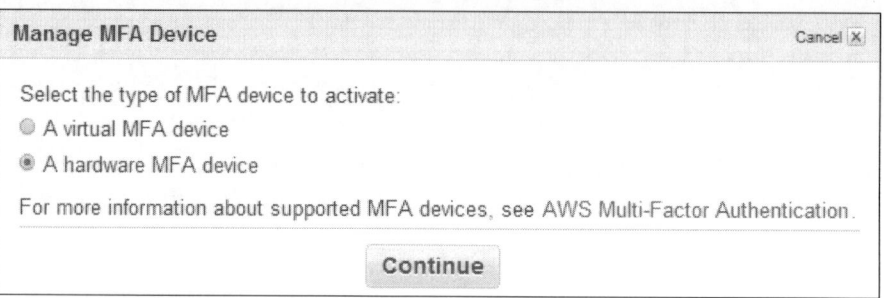

You can purchase your MFA device, if you want, at `http://onlinenoram.gemalto.com/`, as shown here:

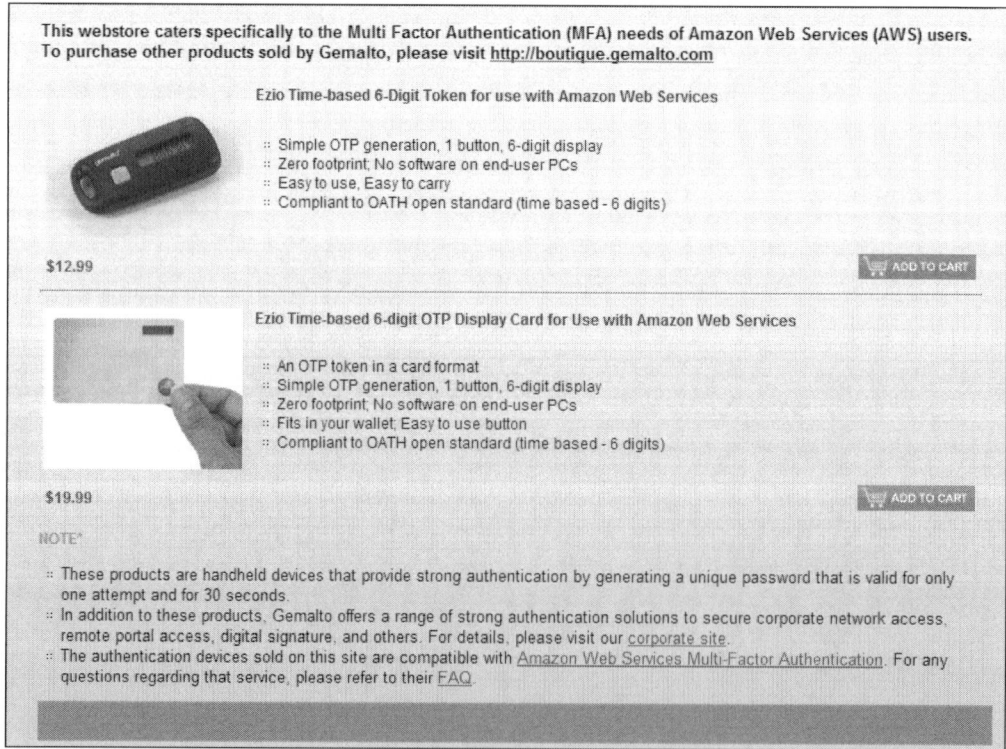

There are two types of MFA devices available on this site that differ in their characteristics and pricing. As per your requirement, you can buy an MFA device and secure your AWS environment using the two-factor authentications.

Application deployment using AWS Elastic Beanstalk

To start with AWS Elastic Beanstalk, you have to first learn some basics of AWS SDK and its toolkit. The AWS toolkit for Eclipse will install and configure the latest version of the AWS SDK for the platform you have selected. Using Eclipse, you can easily manage, customize, build, and deploy any of the samples included in the SDK packages. To install the AWS toolkit, follow these steps:

1. Navigate to the website `aws-amazon.com/sdk-for-java`.

2. Click on **AWS Toolkit for Eclipse**, as shown in the following screenshot:

3. There is an alternative way to configure this. Download Eclipse Juno/Luna from `https://www.eclipse.org/downloads/`.

4. Start Eclipse.

5. Click on **Help** and then click on **Install New Software**.

6. In the **Work with** field, type `http://aws.amazon.com/eclipse` and then press the *Enter* key.

7. In the list that appears, expand **AWS Toolkit for Eclipse**.

8. Add a check mark next to **AWS Toolkit for Eclipse** to download it.

9. Click on **Next** and the Eclipse wizard will, by default, take you through the other installation procedures.

To access AWS through the toolkit for Eclipse, you have to configure the Eclipse toolkit with your access key ID and secret access key, which should be available to you in your AWS account. In addition to allowing the toolkit for Eclipse to create your account, your access keys are also used to sign the requirements that are based on web services to AWS. By allowing the requests to web services, it ensures that only approved programs can make such requests. Moreover, by associating the access keys to every web service request, AWS will be able to track the service usage for billing and monitoring purposes.

The access keys will have a combination of an access key ID and a secret access key, which will be used to sign in the programmatic logical request that you will compose from the application source code to AWS to access different resources. If you don't have access keys, you can create them from the AWS Management Console. For this, go to **Security Credentials** and select **Access Key ID** from the available options, as shown in the following screenshot:

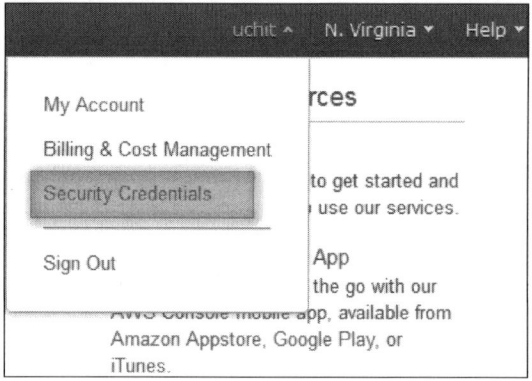

Always keep your security key confidential to guard your account and never e-mail it. Do not share it with a third-person from your organization, even if there is an investigation from AWS or from any other channel.

To add your access keys to the Eclipse toolkit, follow these steps:

1. Open Eclipse's **Preferences** dialog box and click on **AWS Toolkit** located in the sidebar.
2. Type your access key ID in the **Access Key ID** field.
3. Type your secret access key in the **Secret Access Key** field.
4. Click on **Apply** or **OK** to store your access key information.

The following screenshot shows an example of a configured **AWS Toolkit Preferences** screen with a default account:

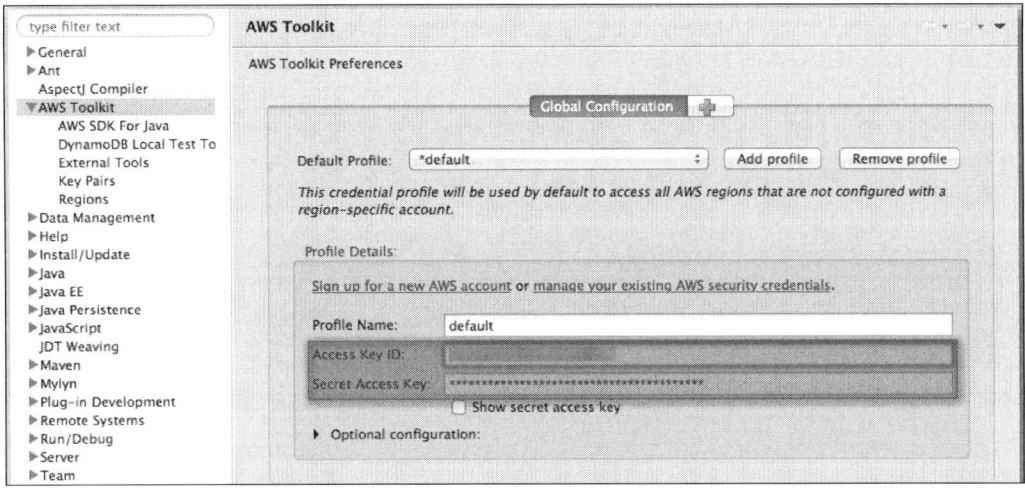

The **Preferences** dialog box enables you to add the access information for more than one AWS account by selecting a profile. Multiple accounts can be functional. In this, they enable the developers and administrators to split resources that will be used for the development stage from resources that will be used in the production stage.

To add another set of access keys, follow these steps:

1. On the **AWS Toolkit Preferences** screen, go to the **Preferences** dialog box and click on the **Add Account** button.
2. Add your new account's details to the **Account Details** segment.
3. Choose an evocative name for the **Account Name** and enter your access key details in the **Access Key ID** and **Secret Access Key** fields.
4. Click on **Apply** or **OK** to save your access key details.
5. You can repeat this procedure for as many sets of AWS account information that you need.

The toolkit for Eclipse can also obtain your Amazon EC2 key pairs from the AWS account. However, you will need to associate your private keys with them to use them in the toolkit for Eclipse manually. To view your Amazon EC2 key pairs in the toolkit for Eclipse, follow these steps:

1. Open Eclipse's **Preferences** dialog box; click on the triangle next to **AWS Toolkit**, given in the sidebar to show the additional categories of the toolkit for Eclipse settings, and configure it, as shown in the following screenshot:

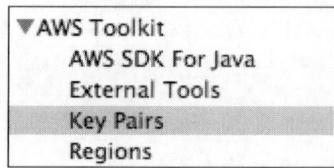

2. Go to **Key Pairs** and Eclipse will show you a list of the available key pairs in this window. If a key pair has a red-colored **X** mark next to it, you will need to link a private key to the key pair to use it with your current use case, as shown here:

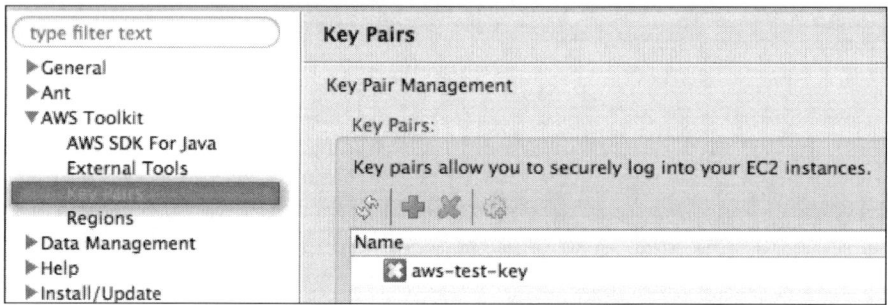

3. Right-click on the key pair and from the context menu, choose the **Select Private Key File** option, shown as follows:

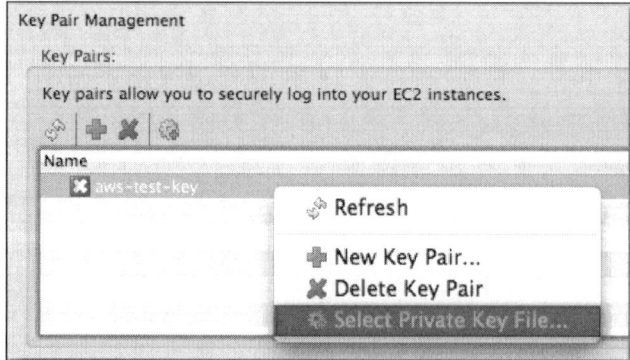

4. Navigate to the private key file and select it to associate it to your key pair.

To deploy the web application, follow these steps:

1. In the Eclipse toolbar, click on the AWS icon and then click on **New AWS Java Web Project**.

2. In the **New AWS Java Web Project** dialog box, select **Travel Log** under the **Start from** area of the dialog, which is a sample Java web application. Enter a name, myTravelLog, in the **Project name** field, as shown in the next screenshot.

3. Click on the **Finish** button. The toolkit will create the project and the project will be shown in **Project Explorer**.

4. If the **Project Explorer** window is not visible in Eclipse, from the **Window** menu, click on **Show View** and select **Project Explorer**.

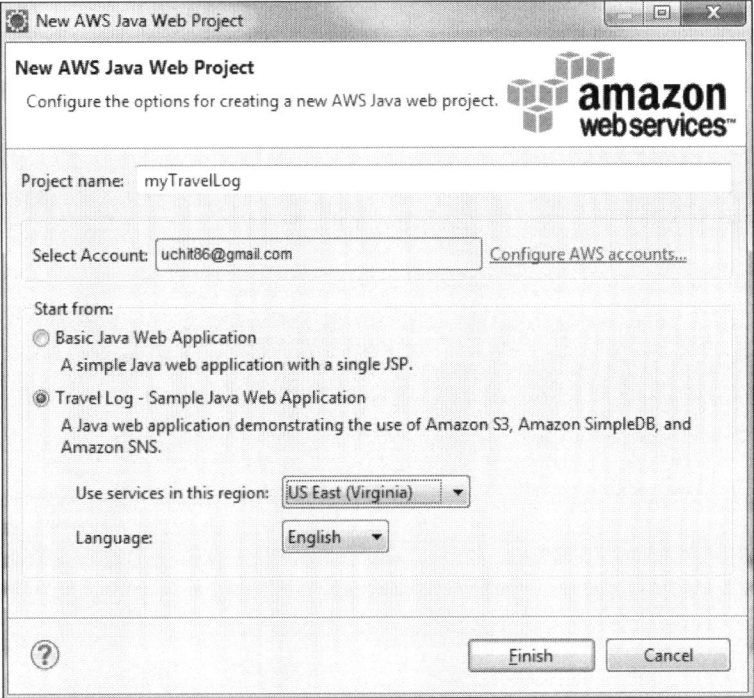

5. The **AWS Java Web Project** dialog box will allow you to choose the region in which your web application will be deployed and run. Here, we will select **US East (Virginia)** as it is the cheapest in our case:

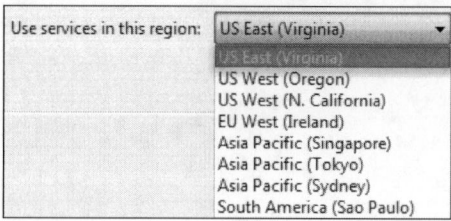

6. In the **Project Explorer** window, right-click on the **myTravelLog** application and select the **Run on Server** option from the **Run As** menu.

7. You can use the sample code, which is provided to run and test your deployment.

8. In the **Run on Server** dialog box, click on **Manually define a new server** and then select **AWS Elastic Beanstalk for Tomcat 7** from the list of the given server options.

9. Enter a name, such as `TravelLogServer`, in the **Server's host name** field or give a suitable name of your choice.

10. Finally, select **Always use this server** when running this project and then click on **Next**, as shown in the following screenshot:

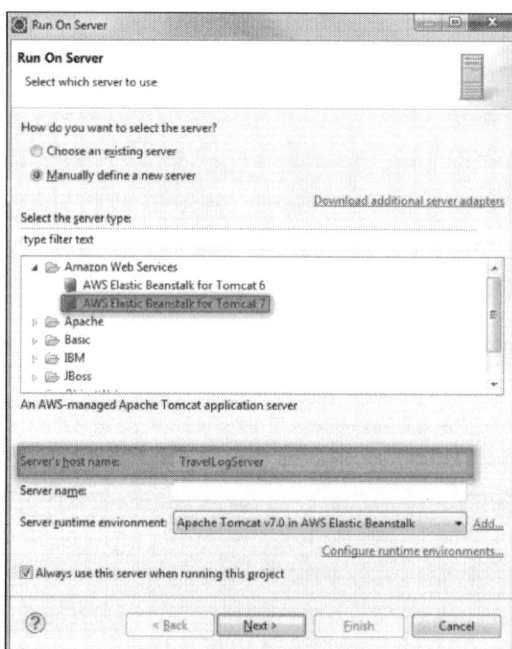

11. In the **Run On Server** box, provide an application name, such as
    `myTravelLogApp`, and an environment name, such as `myTravelLogEnv`, as
    the information for your reference and then click on **Next**, as shown in the
    following screenshot:

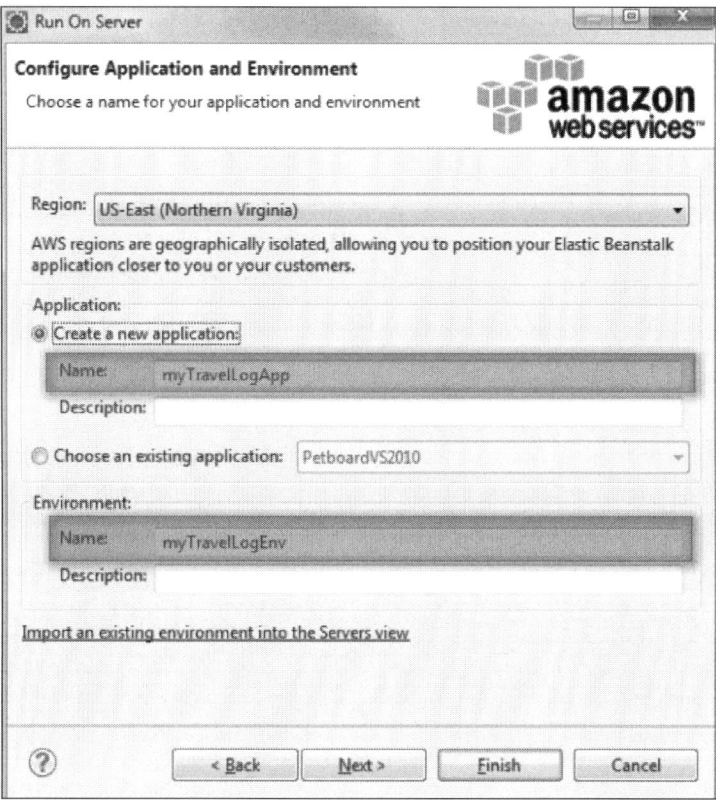

12. The **Advanced configuration** dialog box in the **Run On Server** menu enables
    you to specify additional parameters for your web application deployment
    reference, such as the IAM role, CNAME, notification e-mail address, and
    so on.

13. Before deploying your application to the AWS Beanstalk Container, the
    toolkit will show you a dialog box in which you can set a **Version Label**
    to version your deployment. The AWS toolkit will generate a unique
    version label based on the current time.

14. Click on **OK**, as shown here:

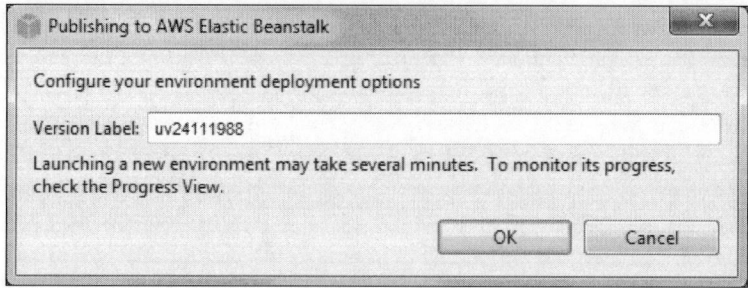

15. While your application is being deployed, the AWS toolkit will display a progress status bar, as shown in the following screenshot:

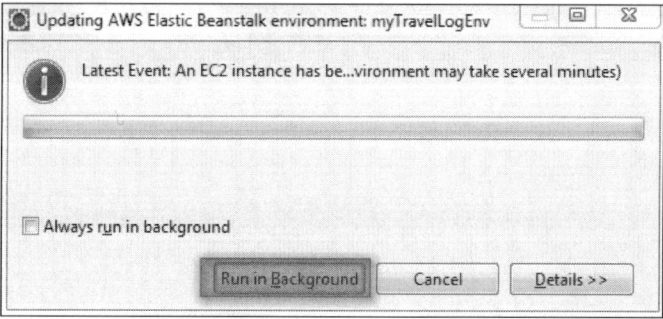

16. When the deployment completes, you will be able to see the following page. This is the user interface for the travel log application, which will be running on your Amazon EC2 instance:

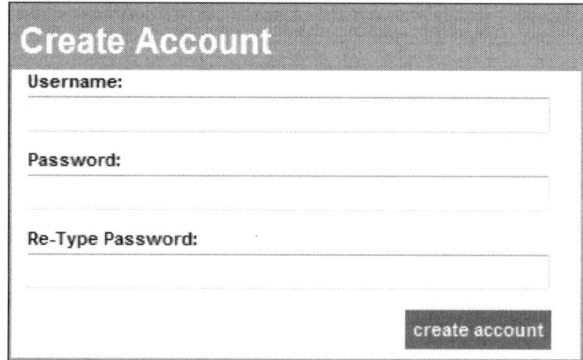

The preceding example shows the deployment of Elastic Beanstalk using the AWS SDK toolkit.

Summary

In this chapter, you learned some of the deployment and monitoring services. In the first section, you learned AWS CloudFormation and its usages with different configurations. Later, you went through the importance of the AWS CloudWatch alarms and learned how you can create your own monitoring mechanisms for your resources using AWS CloudWatch. After this, you explored an important concept of AWS called IAM. You saw the basics of authorization and authentication. Finally, you learned about application deployment using the AWS Elastic Beanstalk service via SDK and code libraries.

In the next chapter, you will learn about the AWS SNS service and will see how this service is important for your web architecture. You will also learn how to leverage the benefits of AWS SNS by configuring it with your application.

Working with the AWS Simple Notification Service – SNS

6

AWS provides mobile services that help you monitor your applications and files in real time. As of now, AWS provides the following three mobile services:

- **Amazon Cognito**: This service is used to manage the AWS user identities (when they access your AWS resources). This service allows you to specify granular access policies to the AWS users accessing your resources.
- **Mobile analytics**: This service is used to monitor the data usage of your applications.
- **SNS**: This service allows you to send push notifications to the mobile (and many more) endpoints.

In this chapter, you will learn about SNS and the following topics will be covered:

- Identifying what AWS SNS is
- Exploring the baseline concept of SNS
- Exploring the SNS service models
- Accessing SNS using the Management Console
- Sample code and libraries of the AWS SNS service

Identifying Amazon SNS

Simple Notification Service (SNS) is a flexible, fast, and fully managed push messaging service for mobile devices. With SNS, you can publish a message once and deliver it one or more times. So you can choose to direct unique messages to individual mobile devices with a single publish request. All the published SNS messages are stored redundantly across multiple availability zones to prevent the messages from being lost.

In the former chapters, you created an alarm that sends an e-mail intimation to kprabha1989@gmail.com if the provisioned throughput exceeds 80 percent; sending e-mail, SMS, or HTTP messages or notifications to the user when a specific condition occurs is the basic use case of SNS.

The baseline concepts of Amazon SNS

Before learning about Amazon SNS, you need to understand a few **Java Message Service (JMS)** terminologies. To understand this better, let's take a look at an illustration where you have registered your mobile number and e-mail ID with your bank. So, whenever you make any card transactions, you will get SMS and e-mail intimations. The JMS terminologies are as follows:

- **Topic**: This is a distribution mechanism (identified by a unique topic name) to publish messages. Let's give the topic a name such as PrabhakarDebit.

- **Endpoint**: This is the receiver (or subscriber) of the topic message. This usually will be a mobile number, e-mail ID, and so on. For example, in this case, the PrabhakarDebit topic will have two endpoints. The first endpoint will be a mobile number and the second endpoint will be an e-mail ID.

> A topic can have any number of endpoints; each endpoint may or may not use the same protocol. For example, more than one mobile number can be an endpoint for the PrabhakarDebit topic.

- **Protocol**: This is the manner in which the topic message is delivered to the subscriber. The possible protocol values are HTTP, HTTPS, e-mail, e-mail-JSON, SMS, Amazon SQS, and an application.

- **Subscription**: This is the process of adding subscribers to the topic. For each and every endpoint, a separate subscription has to be made and the subscription must be confirmed by the endpoint. Only after the confirmation, the topic messages will be delivered to the endpoint.

The following diagram shows you the SNS message delivery for a topic. Whenever a message is published to an SNS topic, the notifications will be sent to all the subscribers, irrespective of the endpoint type. The endpoint type can be SQS, HTTP or HTTPS, SMS, or e-mail.

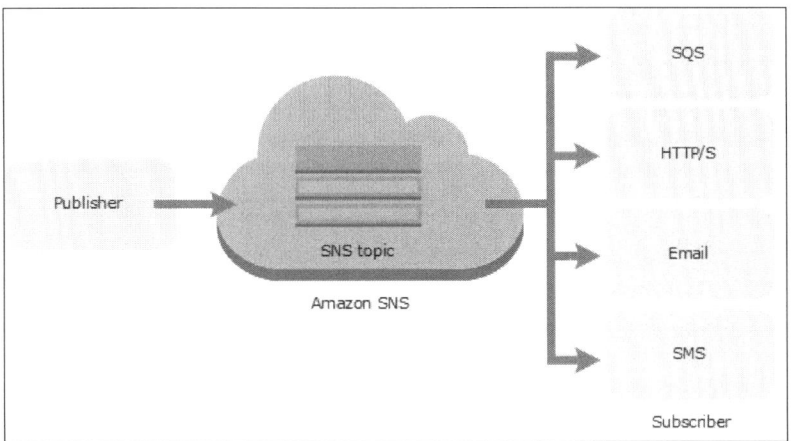

The service models of Amazon SNS

Amazon SNS provides many service models, out of which five of the services are of utmost importance. In some of these offerings, SNS will be aiding them (the example with Amazon CloudWatch, SQS, and so on), and in other cases, you will learn the service varieties provided by SNS. You will see these in a sequence.

Usage in CloudWatch

CloudWatch is one of the services offered by AWS which enables you to monitor your resources in real time. However, everybody has a busy life, and they have better things to do than keeping an eye on CloudWatch's real-time graphs all the time. Amazon SNS and CloudWatch are already integrated by AWS. Instead of sitting in front of the PC all the time to keep an eye on your resources, you can set a condition and whenever a certain condition is set by you in CloudWatch, you can send a notification to any endpoint using SNS. This saves a lot of time.

Mobile push notifications service

Amazon SNS has the ability to push notifications directly to any mobile platform using the device's ID as the endpoint identifier. As of now, SNS supports push notifications to six devices, as shown in the following diagram. So, along with other endpoints, a topic can directly push notifications to the devices simultaneously, as shown in the following diagram:

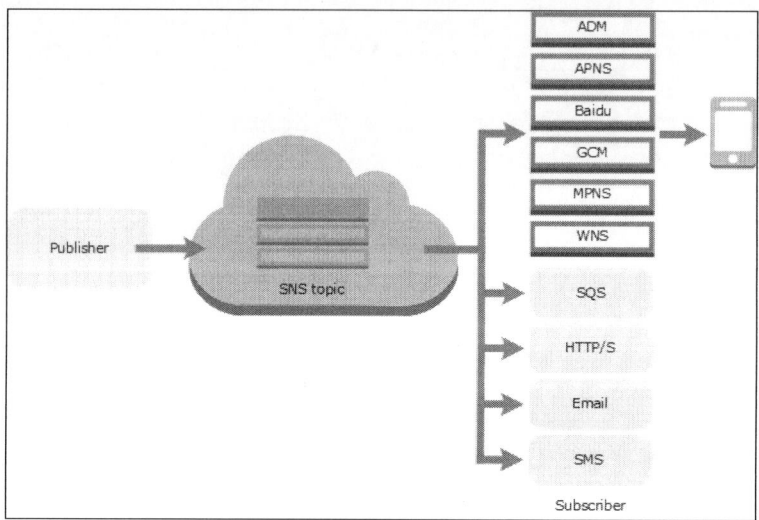

Conjunction with the SQS queues

If a topic publishes millions of messages simultaneously, which are subscribed by millions, then some of the messages might not reach the subscriber. This is because of the absence of a pooling mechanism in SNS. This is where SQS comes into the picture. AWS allows you to divert all your SNS messages to an SQS queue, thereby making the delivery of those messages 100 percent guaranteed.

The SMS notifications service

One of the simplest and reliable notifications is SMS because it consumes nearly zero data charges and the notification is provided for free by almost all the service providers. If you make the SNS endpoint (for the corresponding mobile numbers) for an SMS subscription to an SNS topic, then the message will be delivered as an SMS.

The HTTP/HTTPS messaging service

In the case of push notifications to mobile devices or an SMS notification or e-mail notification, there might be some delay involved for the subscriber to respond to the notification. So, sometimes you need to send these notifications to the REST endpoints, which can automatically take the necessary actions instantaneously (as soon as the message of the topic is received).

Accessing SNS using the Management Console

In the Management Console, SNS will be available in the **Mobile Services** section. To begin with SNS, click on the **SNS** option, as shown in the following screenshot:

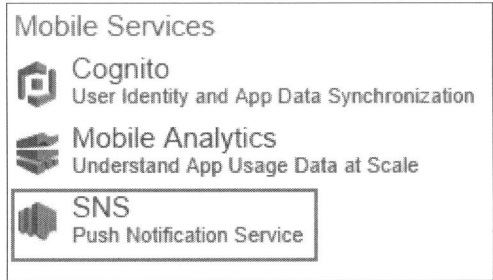

Clicking on this icon will take you to the SNS dashboard. The dashboard consists of the following four sections:

- The **Navigation** section
- The **Getting Started** section
- The **My Resources** section
- The **Additional Actions** section

These sections are shown in the following screenshot:

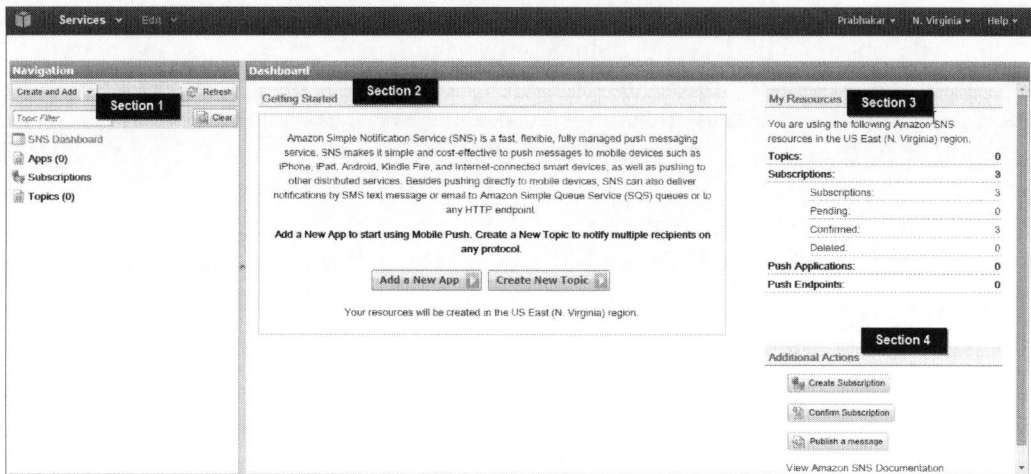

As the name suggests, the **Navigation** section consists of a link to navigate back to the SNS dashboard, manage all the apps used by you, and manage the subscriptions and topics. Accessing this page for the first time will show the **Apps(0)** and **Topics(0)** links, as you haven't created any SNS topic or application yet. This is the most important and frequently-used section. The **Navigation** section will be visible on almost all the pages.

The **Getting Started** section has an overview of SNS and its strengths. This section has two buttons. The **Add a New App** button is used to register an application to send the push notifications to mobile devices. The **Create New Topic** button is used to create a new SNS topic. Creating an SNS topic will be the primary operation.

The **My Resources** section shows you a detailed account of the SNS resources acquired by you. Even though you are accessing SNS for the first time, why is it that it is showing three subscriptions as confirmed? The answer lies in the *AWS Glacier* section of *Chapter 2*, *Working with the AWS Storage Services*. In this section, you created a vault and added three archives to it using the Java SDK. For every archive you created, an SNS (and SQS) client is present to notify the status of the Glacier vault. All these numbers are real-time values accounting to SNS resources in this region only.

The **Additional Actions** section has links for topic-related operations, such as creating and confirming subscriptions to a topic and publishing messages to a topic.

If you want to take a look at all the subscriptions, you can click on the **Subscriptions** link available in the **Navigation** section. One click and it will show the page, as shown in the following screenshot. You can see all the three subscriptions listed, and a checkbox will be available on the left-hand side of the subscription. If you wish to delete any of these subscriptions, you can check the corresponding checkbox and click on the **Delete Subscriptions** button. We will discuss this page in a while, after creating an SNS topic.

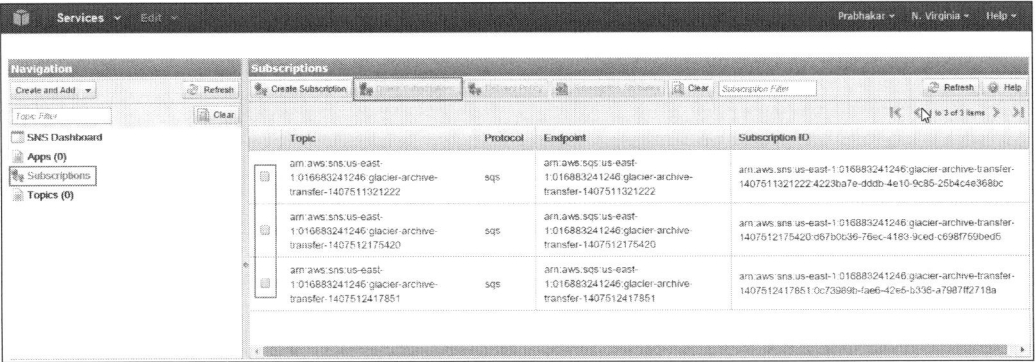

Creating an SNS topic

Clicking on the **Create New Topic** button will result in the following page. It asks for two parameters. The first parameter is **Topic Name**, which is mandatory, and the second parameter is **Display Name**, which is mandatory for the SMS protocol. For all other protocols, the display name is optional. Once you have provided the necessary details, you need to click on the **Create Topic** button, as shown in the following screenshot:

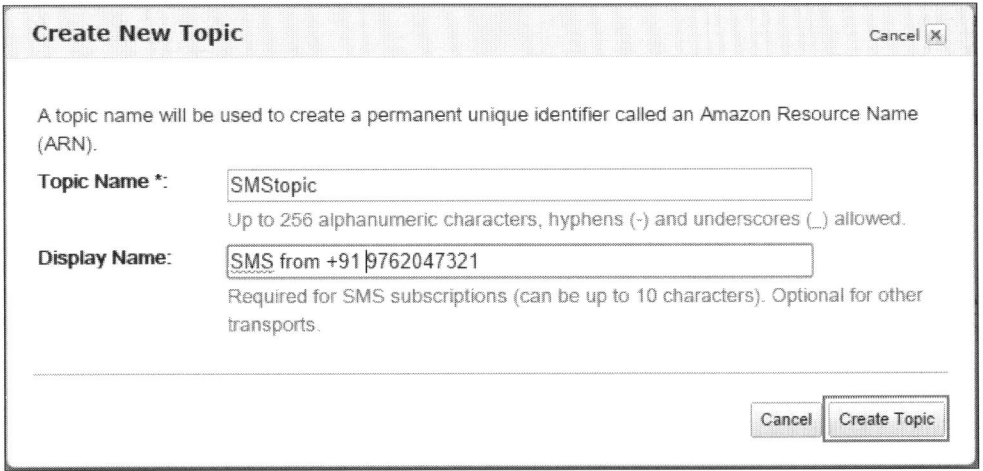

You can see the created **SMStopic** option in the following SNS dashboard when you expand the **Topics (1)** link in the navigation section. Clicking on **SMStopic** will show you the **Topic ARN** and other details. The topic ARN is used to delete, subscribe, unsubscribe, and edit the permission of the topic. So, for all the API or SDK calls, you need to make a note of this ARN.

The topic ARN will usually be in the `arn:aws:sns:<region-name>:<subscriber>:<topic-name>` format. In the preceding screenshot, the **Region** name is **us-east-1**, **Topic Owner** is **016883241246**, and the topic name is **SMStopic**. The subscriber value is unique for every AWS user. So, even if you delete this topic (from **us-east-1**) and create it again with the same topic name, **Topic ARN** will remain the same (or in other words, it will be recreated in the same region).

Adding a subscription to a topic

Even if you have the topic ready, unless someone subscribes to the topic, all the messages published to the topic are a waste of time. It's like you have a key, but you don't know what it unlocks. To add a subscriber to **SMStopic**, you need to click on the **Create Subscription** button. Once you do this, the following page will be shown. The topic will be preloaded as **SMStopic**, and you can choose one of the following protocols. At the endpoint, you need to specify the necessary values. For example, if you need to create an **SMS** (protocol) subscription for this topic, then you need to enter the mobile number in the **Endpoint** textbox, as shown in the following screenshot:

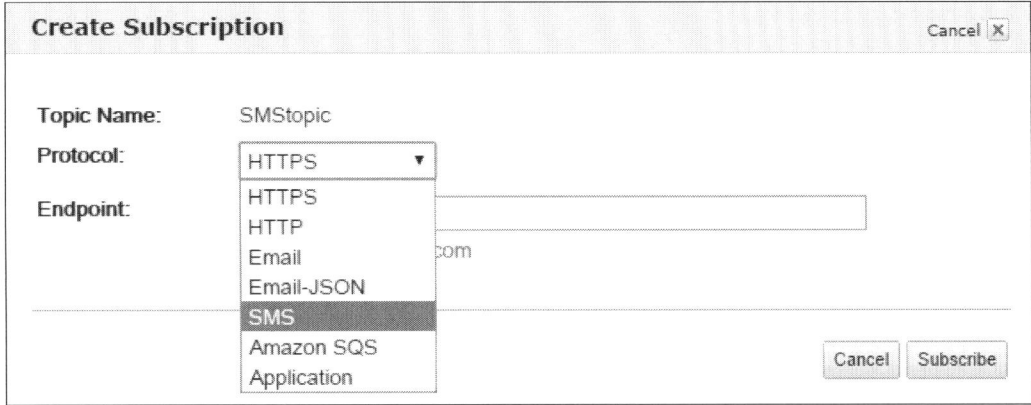

After adding the necessary values, if you click on the **Subscribe** button, you will be taken back to the **Topic Details** page. You will be able to see the SMS subscription (which you have added in the previous step) in the **PendingConfirmation** status. An SMS will be sent to the mobile number, asking for a subscription confirmation. Once it is confirmed, the subscription ID will be updated with a new ARN, as shown in the following screenshot:

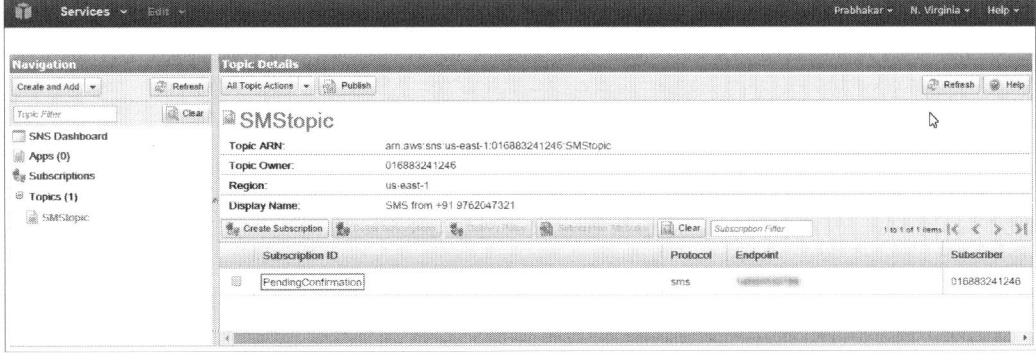

If you need to add an e-mail subscription to **SMStopic**, you can do so by clicking on the **Create Subscription** button and following the same steps that you performed for the SMS subscription, but here you need to select the protocol as e-mail and the endpoint as an e-mail ID. Once you do this, a confirmation e-mail will be sent to the ID entered by you in the endpoint textbox, as shown in the following screenshot:

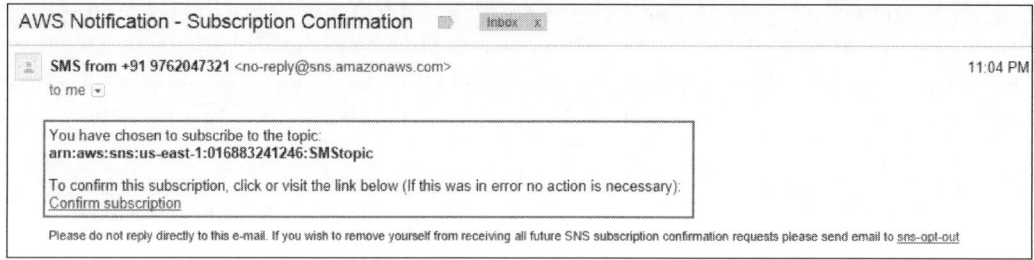

You need to click on the **Confirm subscription** link to confirm the subscription. The confirmation page will show you the subscription ID, as follows:

Once the subscription is confirmed, you can see the subscription ID (which is an ARN and is mandatory to manage the subscription) **arn:aws:sns:us-east-1:016883241246:SMStopic:74f39925-f28c-4f53-827f-0259e6120e9b**. However, the subscription ID of the SMS subscription (until you confirm) will remain as **PendingConfirmation**, as shown in the following screenshot:

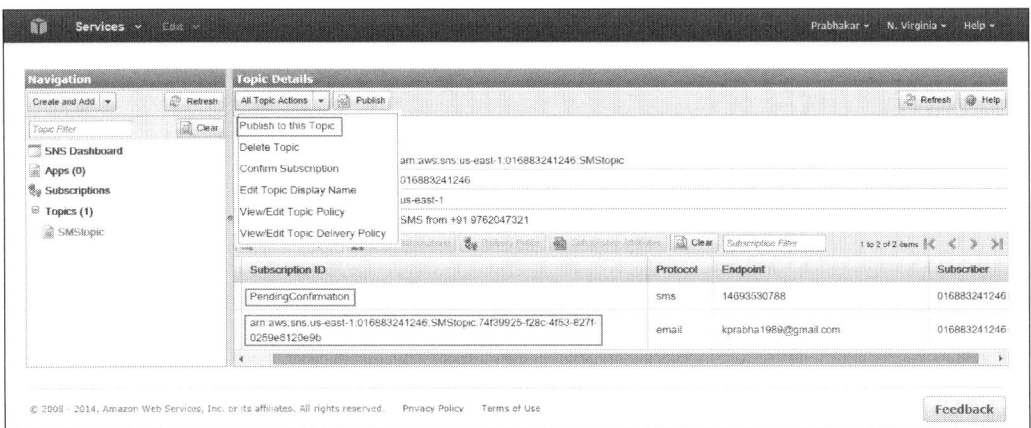

Topic actions

Having created and subscribed to a topic, the next step is to learn about the frequently performed topic actions. In the **Topic Details** section, if you click on the **All Topic Actions** dropdown, it will show those actions. The possible actions are as follows:

- Publish to the topic
- Delete the topic
- Confirm the subscription
- Edit the topic display name
- View/edit the topic policy
- View/edit the topic delivery policy

Publishing to the topic

The next step is to publish a message to **SMStopic**. To do this, you need to select the **Publish to this Topic** option available in the **All Topic Actions** dropdown (as shown in the preceding screenshot). Once you select this option, the **Publish** page will pop up, asking you for the following information. You can specify the **Subject** and **Message** options and then click on the **Publish Message** button. This message will be delivered to all the subscribers of **SMStopic**.

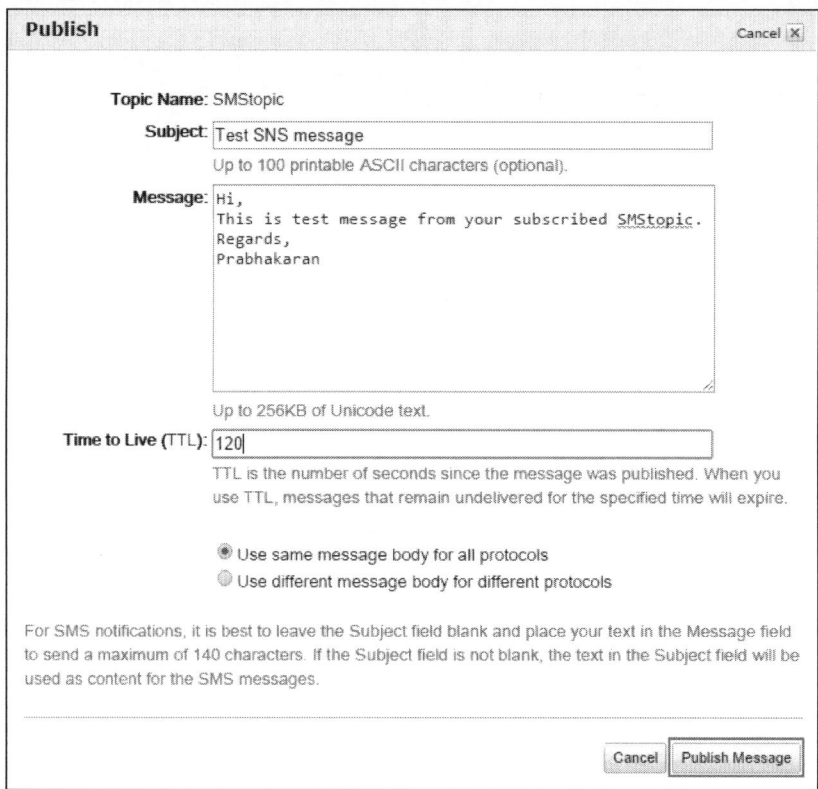

If you check your mail box (which is subscribed to **SMStopic**), you will see the message published by you, as shown in the following screenshot. Even if you look at the mobile subscribed to **SMStopic**, you will see the same message, shown as follows:

Now, it's time to discuss an important feature of SNS, which is used to send different messages to different endpoints (which differ by protocol). For example, for all the mobile numbers, the same SMS message should be sent, whereas for all the e-mail IDs, a different message should be sent. In the **Publish** page, there are two radio buttons, which you will have to take a look at once again, as shown in the following screenshot:

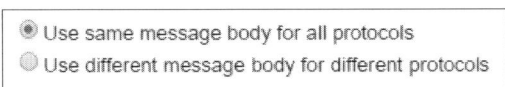

While publishing your first message, you have used the first option. If you want to specify a different message for different protocols, then you should select the second radio button. Selecting the second option will change the page, as shown in the following screenshot. You can specify different messages for different protocols and then click on the **Publish Message** button:

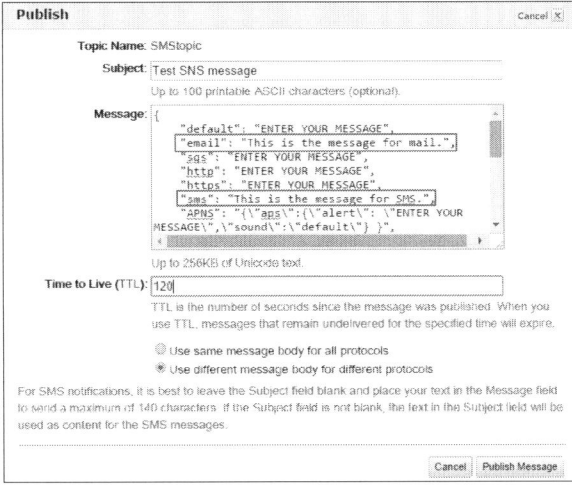

Topic policy actions

When you select an action, the **View/edit topic policy** option will show you the following page. You can set the policy in two ways: first, using the basic view, and the second using the advanced view. You will learn about the basic view now. It has two sections.

The first section, **Publishers**, will help you to specify who can publish the message to the topic. Selecting the **Only me** option will not allow others to publish messages to the topic. Selecting the **Everyone** option will allow anyone and everyone to publish messages, and selecting **Only these AWS users** will allow only specific AWS users (whose account IDs are specified and separated by a comma).

The second section, **Subscribers**, has four options in total. The first three options are the same. So, you will directly go to **Only users with endpoints that match**. If you choose this option, then you can specify the endpoints (which can subscribe to this topic) with wildcard characters. Along with this, you can select the protocols that are allowed for self subscription by the subscribers themselves, as shown in the following screenshot:

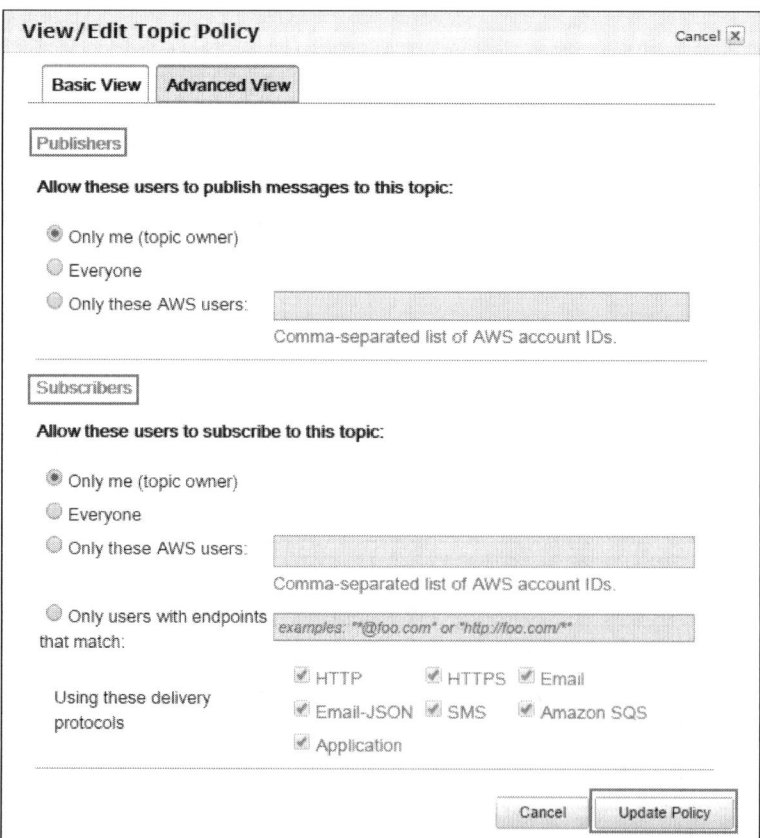

If you select the advanced view, the following page will open, which will ask you to specify the JSON to change the topic policy. If you want to allow a self-subscription for the topic with the policy (allow the endpoints that end with @infosys.com for all the possible protocols), then you need to set JSON.

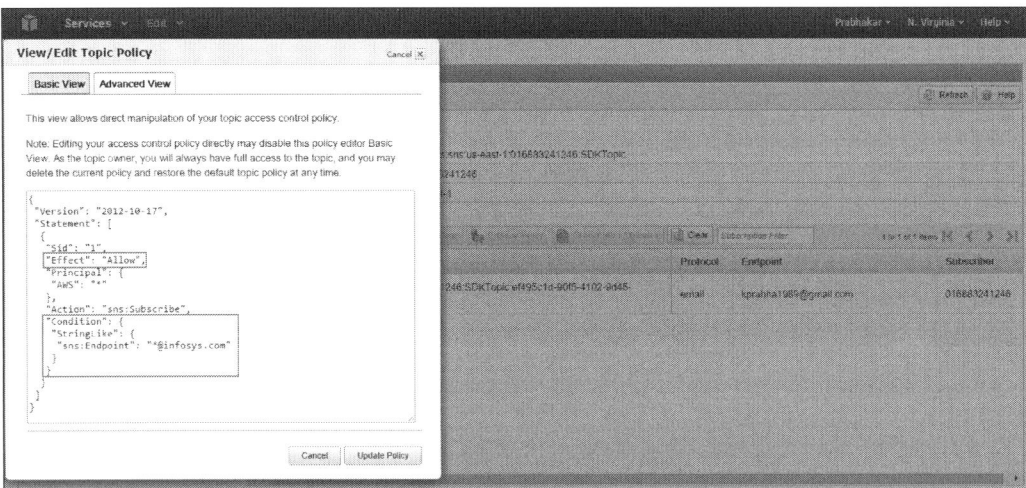

Topic delivery policy actions

Selecting the **View/edit topic delivery policy** option will show you the following page. These policies are used to specify how the topic messages are to be delivered, and in case of any errors, the number of times a retry can be performed, and so on. You can set the policy in two ways. First, we will use the basic view and then use the advanced view. Now you will learn about the basic view. One highlight of this delivery policy is to specify the **Retry backoff function**. This is used to specify the period after which the failed delivery should be resent.

You can choose one of the options (**Linear**, **Arithmetic**, **Geometric**, or **Exponential**). If you choose **Linear**, then for every failed delivery, the delivery will be same after the same period of time. For example, after every 2 seconds, a failed delivery will be retried. If you choose **Exponential**, then a retry will be made for an exponential period of time. For example, the first retry will be made after 2 seconds, the second retry will be made after 4 seconds, then 8 seconds, then 16 seconds, and so on. In addition to this, you can override the subscription-based policy with this one by checking the **Ignore subscription override** checkbox.

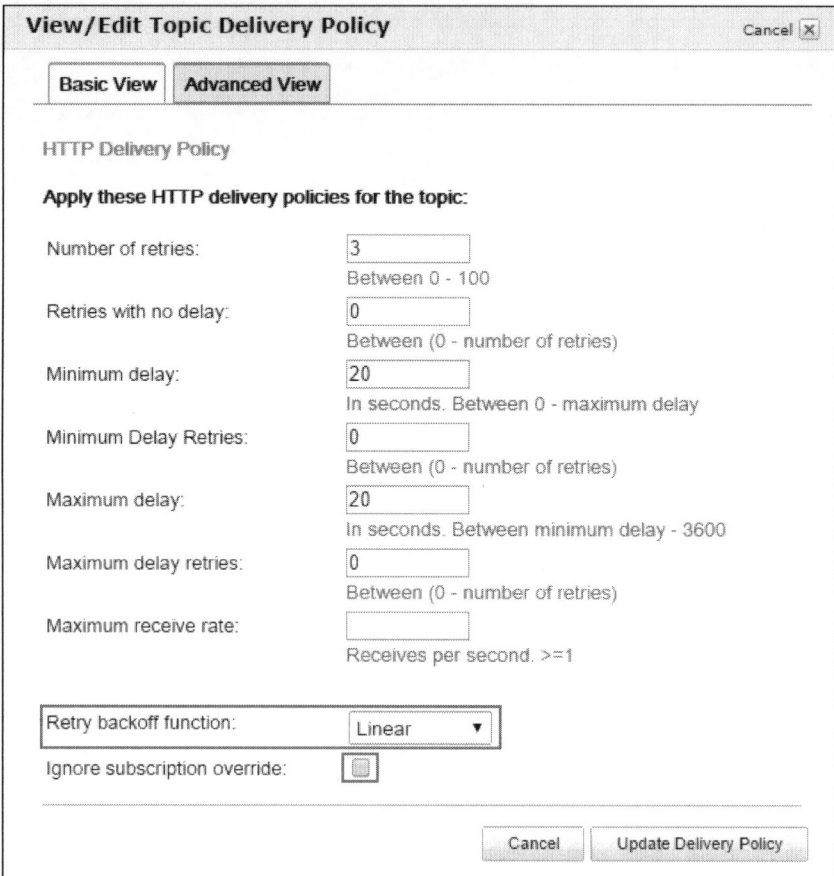

Selecting the **Advanced View** tab will show you JSON, as shown in the following screenshot. All the options are the same; the only difference is that it will be represented in a different way:

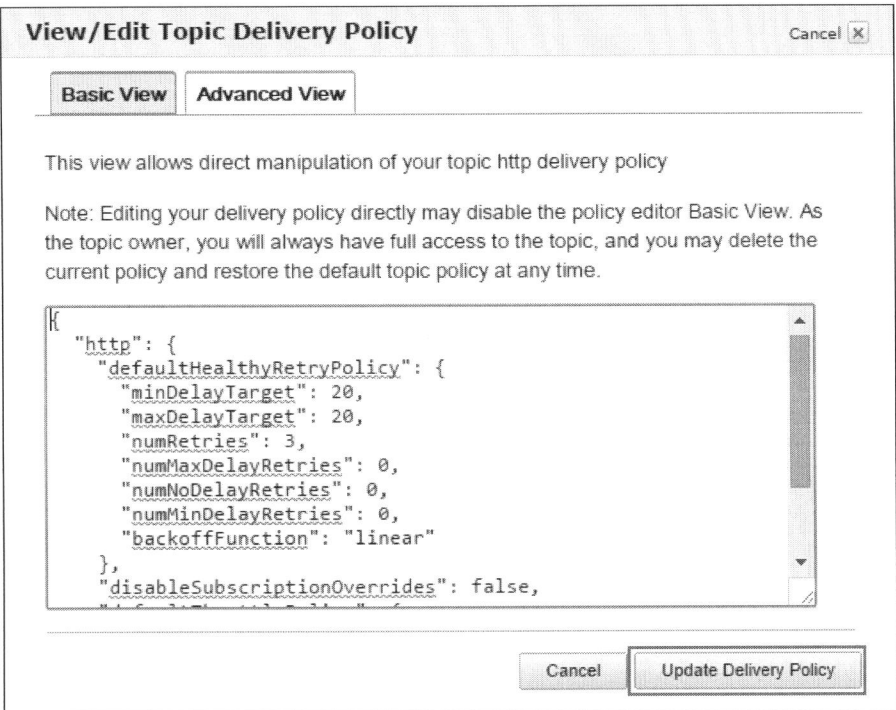

The sample code and libraries of SNS

Amazon SNS doesn't have any specialized tools, so you are going to learn about the Java AWS SDK (using the Eclipse plugin) and the CLI tool configured by you in *Chapter1, An Introduction to AWS*. In this section, you will learn how to perform the operations performed by you in the Management Console using the preceding tools.

Performing SNS operations using the Eclipse AWS SDK

The Eclipse AWS SDK provides libraries to perform SNS operations. Even though you have already created an SNS topic in the *AWS Glacier* section of *Chapter 2, Working with the AWS Storage Services*, you will see it in detail here.

The code used to create an SNS topic using the Java SDK is as follows:

```
ProfileCredentialsProvider credentials = new
ProfileCredentialsProvider();
AWSCredentials credential = credentials.getCredentials();
AmazonSNSClient client = new AmazonSNSClient(credentials);
CreateTopicRequest topic = new CreateTopicRequest();
    topic.setName("SDKTopic");
    topic.setRequestCredentials(credential);
CreateTopicResult topicRequestResult = client.createTopic(topic);
String topicArn = topicRequestResult.getTopicArn();
System.out.println(topicArn);
/* Will print topicArn as "arn:aws:sns:us-east-
1:016883241246:SDKTopic" */
```

If you execute this code (by placing it inside a main method), it will create an SNS topic named SDKtopic in us-east-1, North Virginia region (which is mentioned in your credentials file while configuring the AWS plugin for Eclipse). This code will also return a CreateTopicResult instance that you can use to retrieve the topic ARN. So, topicRequestResult.getTopicArn() will return the topic ARN, which is **arn:aws:sns:us-east-1:016883241246:SDKTopic**, as shown in the following screenshot:

Once you have the topic ARN, you can easily add subscribers to the topic by executing the following code:

```
SubscribeRequest subscribeRequest = new SubscribeRequest();
    subscribeRequest.setTopicArn(topicArn);
    subscribeRequest.setRequestCredentials(credential);
```

```
    subscribeRequest.setEndpoint("kprabha1989@gmail.com");
    subscribeRequest.setProtocol("email");
SubscribeResult subscribeResult =
client.subscribe(subscribeRequest);
```

The preceding code will subscribe an email endpoint to an e-mail ID, kprabha1989@ gmail.com. A confirmation mail will be sent to the e-mail address. After the owner of the endpoint confirms the subscriptions, a subscription ID will be updated in your topic subscription page.

Right now, you have a topic and some subscribers for the topic. So, the next action item to be performed is to publish to the topic. The following code publishes a message to SDKtopic:

```
PublishRequest publishRequest = new PublishRequest();
    publishRequest.setSubject("AWS SNS message through Eclipse
SDK");
    publishRequest.setMessage("This is a sample mail sent through
                Eclipse.\nRegards,\nPrabhakaran K");
    publishRequest.setTopicArn(topicArn);
    publishRequest.setRequestCredentials(credential);
PublishResult publishResult = client.publish(publishRequest);
```

Once you execute the preceding code, the message will be sent to all the confirmed subscribers of SDKtopic. The following screenshot shows the message. At any point of time, a subscriber (by themselves or by the topic owner) can be unsubscribed from the topic using the link, as shown in the following screenshot:

The unsubscribe link will have a lot of information; **arn:aws:sns:us-east-1:016883241246:SDKTopic:ef495c1d-90f5-4102-9d45-e5fca1c8929d** is the subscription ID and the endpoint is kprabha1989@gmail.com.

If you need to unsubscribe from SDKtopic using the Java code, the following code will serve the purpose:

```
UnsubscribeRequest unsubscribeRequest = new UnsubscribeRequest();
    unsubscribeRequest.setRequestCredentials(credential);
    unsubscribeRequest.setSubscriptionArn("arn:aws:sns:us-east-
                    1:016883241246:SDKTopic:ef495c1d-90f5-4102-
9d45-e5fca1c8929d");
    client.unsubscribe(unsubscribeRequest);
```

The following code will provide all the subscription permissions to the endpoints that end with @infosys.com on SDKtopic:

```
Condition endpointCondition = SNSConditionFactory
    .newEndpointCondition("*@infosys.com");
Policy policy = new Policy().withStatements(
    new Statement(Effect.Allow)
            .withPrincipals(Principal.AllUsers)
            .withActions(SNSActions.Subscribe)
            .withConditions(endpointCondition));
client.setTopicAttributes(
    newSetTopicAttributesRequest(topicArn, "Policy",
        policy.toJson()));
```

Last but not least, the following code is used to delete the topic from your account. You can do this by passing the topic ARN and your credentials:

```
DeleteTopicRequestdeleteTopicRequest = new
DeleteTopicRequest(topicArn);
    deleteTopicRequest.setRequestCredentials(credential);
client.deleteTopic(deleteTopicRequest);
```

Performing SNS operation using the CLI tool

As you have already learned, the creation of a topic requires only a topic name as the mandatory parameter. The command that is used to create a topic is shown in the following screenshot along with its response. The command is `aws sns create-topic --name <topic-name>`. This command's response will return the topic ARN, shown as follows:

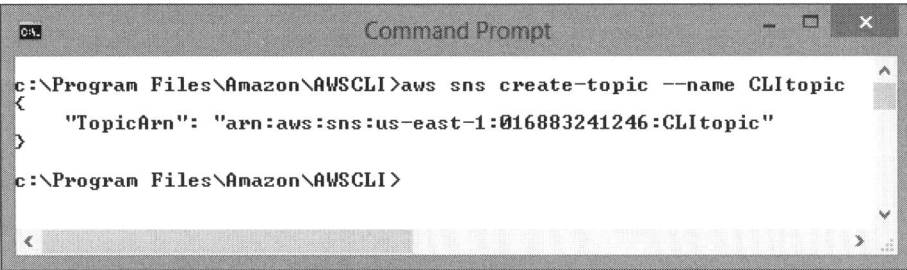

You can subscribe to this topic using the ARN with the following command:

```
aws sns --topic-arn <topic-arn> --protocol <protocol-name> --
notification-endpoint <endpoint>
```

The command shown in the following screenshot adds two e-mail subscribers (kprabha1989@gmal.com and kprabha1989@gmail.com) to CLItopic. Both of these commands will give the response a pending confirmation because these subscriptions need to be confirmed by the endpoint owner:

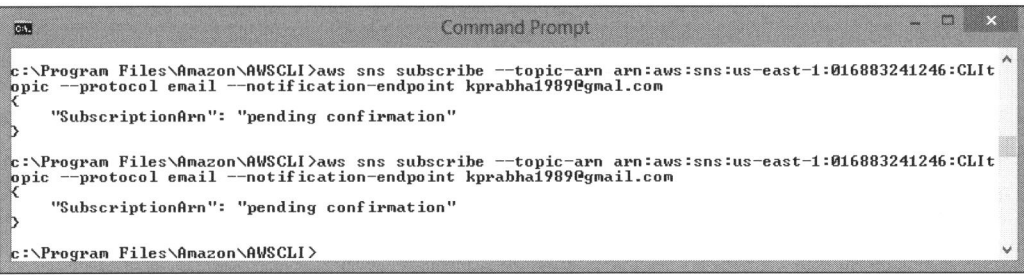

The following screenshot is taken after I have confirmed the subscription to one of the e-mail IDs. You can see this in the following **Subscription ID** status too:

If you want to list all the subscriptions of all the topics created by you, you can use the `aws sns list-subscriptions` command, as follows:

```
c:\Program Files\Amazon\AWSCLI>aws sns list-subscriptions
{
    "Subscriptions": [
        {
            "Owner": "016883241246",
            "Endpoint": "kprabha1989@gmal.com",
            "Protocol": "email",
            "TopicArn": "arn:aws:sns:us-east-1:016883241246:CLItopic",
            "SubscriptionArn": "PendingConfirmation"
        },
        {
            "Owner": "016883241246",
            "Endpoint": "arn:aws:sqs:us-east-1:016883241246:glacier-archive-transfer-1407512417851",
            "Protocol": "sqs",
            "TopicArn": "arn:aws:sns:us-east-1:016883241246:glacier-archive-transfer-1407512417851",
            "SubscriptionArn": "arn:aws:sns:us-east-1:016883241246:glacier-archive-transfer-1407512417851:0c73989b-fae6-42e5-b336-a7987ff2718a"
        },
        {
            "Owner": "016883241246",
            "Endpoint": "arn:aws:sqs:us-east-1:016883241246:glacier-archive-transfer-1407511321222",
            "Protocol": "sqs",
            "TopicArn": "arn:aws:sns:us-east-1:016883241246:glacier-archive-transfer-1407511321222",
            "SubscriptionArn": "arn:aws:sns:us-east-1:016883241246:glacier-archive-transfer-140751131321222:4223ba7e-dddb-4e10-9c85-25b4c4e368bc"
        },
        {
            "Owner": "016883241246",
            "Endpoint": "kprabha1989@gmail.com",
            "Protocol": "email",
            "TopicArn": "arn:aws:sns:us-east-1:016883241246:MailTopic",
            "SubscriptionArn": "arn:aws:sns:us-east-1:016883241246:MailTopic:82ef026c-12d4-49b8-b147-5e9a1a75fdca"
        },
        {
            "Owner": "016883241246",
            "Endpoint": "kprabha1989@gmail.com",
            "Protocol": "email",
            "TopicArn": "arn:aws:sns:us-east-1:016883241246:CLItopic",
            "SubscriptionArn": "arn:aws:sns:us-east-1:016883241246:CLItopic:8cd736bf-1e90-43a4-9505-71fdb91b730b"
        },
        {
            "Owner": "016883241246",
            "Endpoint": "arn:aws:sqs:us-east-1:016883241246:glacier-archive-transfer-1407512175420",
            "Protocol": "sqs",
            "TopicArn": "arn:aws:sns:us-east-1:016883241246:glacier-archive-transfer-1407512175420",
```

If you want to list all the subscriptions for `CLItopic`, you should use the `aws sns list-subscriptions-by-topic --topic-arn arn:aws:sns:us-east-1: 016883241246:CLItopic` command, as shown in the following screenshot:

```
c:\Program Files\Amazon\AWSCLI>aws sns list-subscriptions-by-topic --topic-arn arn:aws:sns:us-east-1
:016883241246:CLItopic
{
    "Subscriptions": [
        {
            "Owner": "016883241246",
            "Endpoint": "kprabha1989@gmail.com",
            "Protocol": "email",
            "TopicArn": "arn:aws:sns:us-east-1:016883241246:CLItopic",
            "SubscriptionArn": "PendingConfirmation"
        },
        {
            "Owner": "016883241246",
            "Endpoint": "kprabha1989@gmail.com",
            "Protocol": "email",
            "TopicArn": "arn:aws:sns:us-east-1:016883241246:CLItopic",
            "SubscriptionArn": "arn:aws:sns:us-east-1:016883241246:CLItopic:8cd736bf-1e90-43a4-9505-
71fdb91b730b"
        }
    ]
}

c:\Program Files\Amazon\AWSCLI>
```

The response to the command will have all the required information (which was available in the Management Console's subscription page) such as owner id, endpoint, protocol, topic-arn, and subscription-arn.

Similarly, you can publish a message to a topic using the `aws sns publish --topic-arn <topic-arn> --subject <message-subject> --message <message-body>` command. This command will send the message ID as the response, as shown here:

```
c:\Program Files\Amazon\AWSCLI>aws sns publish --topic-arn arn:aws:sns:us-east-1:016883241246:CLItop
ic --subject "SNS CLI" --message "Sample SNS message through CLI tool"
{
    "MessageId": "75a6aefc-0617-52b5-b6d1-e27be853f99c"
}

c:\Program Files\Amazon\AWSCLI>
```

You can see the message's subject (**SNS CLI**) at the top of the following screenshot and the message body highlighted beneath it:

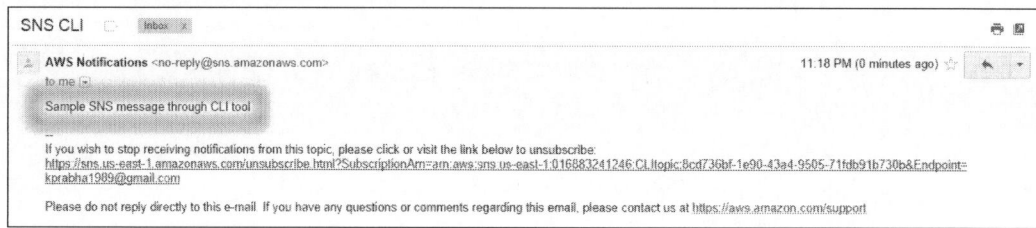

There are numerous ways to unsubscribe to a topic. The simplest way to do this is by clicking on the unsubscribe link in the preceding screenshot (of the e-mail). If you need to unsubscribe using the command prompt, then you need to get the subscription ARN and pass it to the `aws sns unsubscribe --subscription-arn <subscription-arn>` command, as shown in the following screenshot:

To delete a topic from your account, you should have the topic ARN with you. Once you have it, you can execute the `aws sns delete-topic --topic-arn <topic-arn>` command, as shown here:

There are many more SNS operations that are possible with the AWS CLI tool. You can list all the commands using the `aws sns help` command. If you specifically want help or the syntax of one of these commands (for example, the `add-permission` command), you can use the `aws sns add-permission help` command, as shown in the following screenshot:

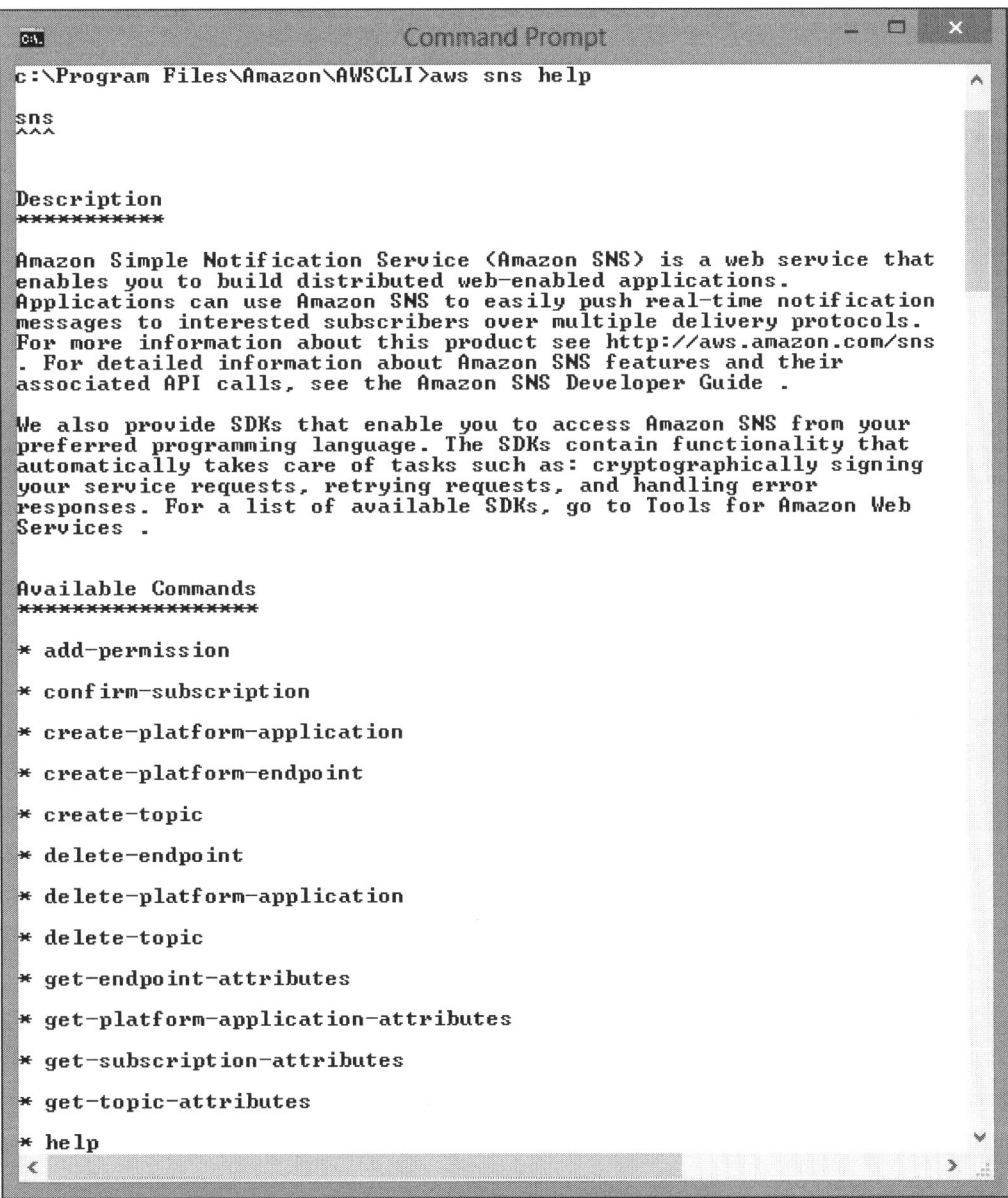

Summary

You started the chapter by learning about the SNS service. You learned the use case, how it is being used by other AWS services, and how you have used SNS in the former chapters. After this, you explored the terminologies and concepts behind SNS. Then, you moved the focus to discuss the service models offered by SNS. Finally, you learned how to perform SNS operations using the Eclipse Java SDK and the CLI tool.

The real advantage of SNS can only be realized if it is queued properly so that none of the subscribers miss any of the topics that the user has subscribed to. Even in the *AWS Glacier* section of *Chapter 2, Working with the AWS Storage Services*, you used SNS in conjunction with SQS—an Amazon queuing service.

In next chapter, you will learn more about SQS and see how it can be integrated with SNS.

7
Working with AWS SQS

Amazon **Simple Queue Service** (**SQS**) is an extremely scalable messaging queue service offered by AWS. Amazon SQS can be used to decouple tasks of different workings within the existing system, which exchange data or a chain of data, to perform sovereign tasks. In this chapter, you will learn the following topics:

- AWS SQS
- SQS's service object models
- The baseline concept of SQS

AWS SQS

Amazon SQS gives you a trouble-free method to set up queues of messages that you can use to supervise workflows or to queue up the work to be performed. This can be an alternating for many other **Message Queuing Services** (**MQS**), such as Microsoft's MSMQ, IBM's MQSeries, and so on. SQS can be used for message-oriented, architecture-based applications. Amazon SQS also allows us to save important data which might be lost in case the entire application goes down or if any component becomes unavailable.

Amazon SNS is a utility service that enables robust messaging for your application as well as adds a flow to it. You can propel a solitary message to manifold subscribers via multiple protocols; for example, you can concurrently post something to a website via HTTP or HTTPS POST and also by sending an e-mail with an equivalent message. Messages can be up to 8 KB long, plus the subject of the message can be up to 100 characters in length.

The baseline concept and object models of SQS

There are multiple things to take into consideration before you start with Amazon SQS. Consider the following points:

- You have to assign a unique name to every queue. The name of the queue or a subset of the queue can have the same initial characters.

- A queue can be empty if you haven't sent any messages to it or deletion happened in the queue from your side. Deletion can be done at any point of time in the queue.

- A queue will retain messages until four days after their creation. Moreover, you can increase this period to 14 days after the message has been sent.

- Amazon SQS can delete your queue without any prior notification if the following actions are not performed on the queue for 30 consecutive days:

  - `SendMessage`
  - `ReceiveMessage`
  - `DeleteMessage`
  - `AddPermission`
  - `RemovePermission`
  - `GetQueueAttributes`
  - `SetQueueAttributes`

Properties of a distributed queue

There are some basic terms and rules—you can call them guidelines—which can help you to design your application and use Amazon SQS effectively.

These properties are described as follows:

- **Message order**: From the point of view of AWS, they will do their best to give you messages in the same order that you sent them but there is no guarantee of this. It's good to send your messages with sequencing information, so that later on you can get your messages in an order from that sequence information if something messed up your sequence at transition.

- **At-least-once-delivery**: From AWS's point of view, your messages will be replicated on multiple servers to give you the advantage of **High Availability (HA)** and redundancy. However, because of this, if something goes wrong, AWS won't delete your message from any server and you will receive that message more than once. So, you should develop your application in such a way that it has some provision if the same message comes more than once.

- **Message sample**: The retrieving behavior will depend on the following polling methods:

   - **Short polling**: While retrieving messages from the queue, Amazon SQS will sample a subset of the servers and give messages only from those servers. This means that your specific raised request might not return all the messages from the queue. So, a best practice might be to continuously retrieve all the messages successfully.
   - **Long polling**: This allows SQS to wait before sending a response until the message is available in the queue.

To enable long polling in AWS SQS from the Management Console, follow these steps:

1. Create a new queue for the AWS SQS console by clicking on **Create New Queue**, as shown in the following screenshot:

2. In the newly opened dialog box, provide an appropriate name for the queue, as shown here:

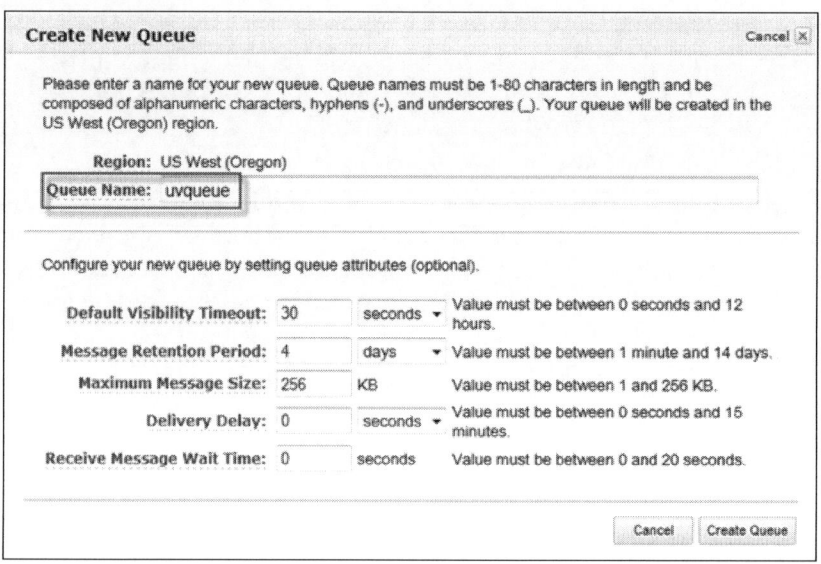

3. Provide any positive value, from 1 second to 20 seconds, in an integer format only in the **Receive Message Wait Time** field, as shown in the following screenshot:

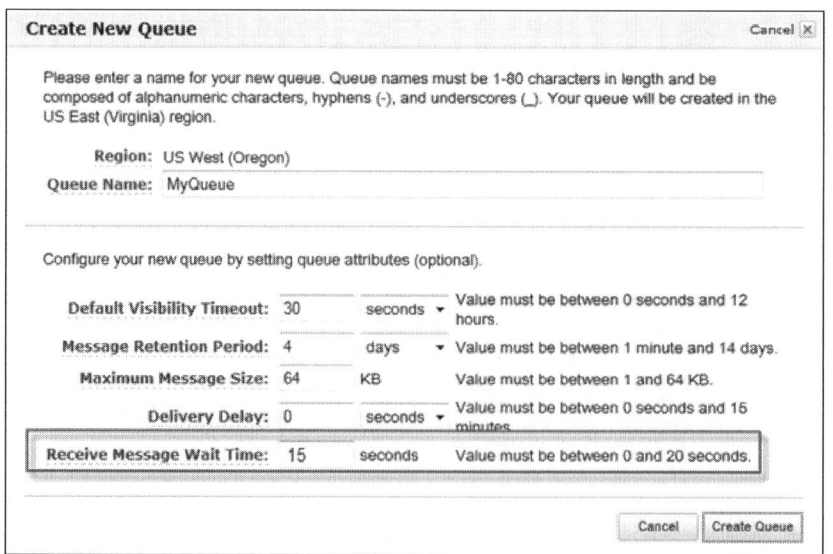

4. As the final step, just click on **Create Queue**.

The life cycle of an Amazon SQS message

To understand Amazon SQS in a very simple manner, you should know the message life cycle of Amazon SQS. So, let's try to understand this using the following steps:

1. As shown in the following diagram, **Component 1** sends a message **X** to a queue, and the message is redundantly distributed across the AWS SQS servers over the AZs:

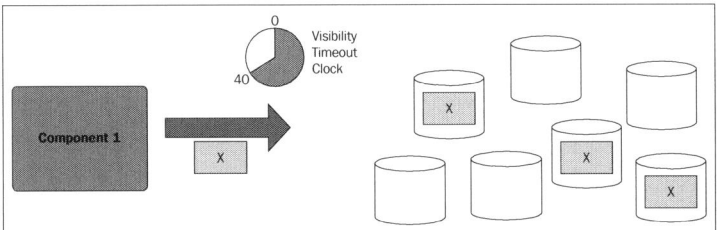

2. When **Component 2** is ready to process the message, it will take the message from the queue and the message **X** will be returned. While **X** is being processed, it will be there in the queue and won't receive a request for the time period of the visibility timeout, as shown here:

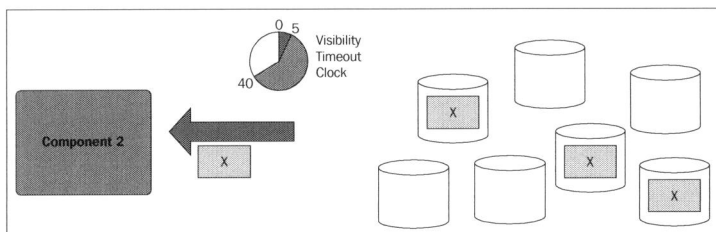

3. **Component 2** will delete the message **X** from the queue to shun the message from being received and processed another time on the occasion the visibility timeout expires, as shown in the following diagram:

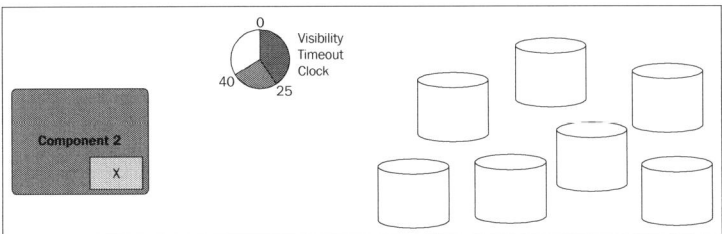

Until now, you learned the basics of AWS SNS and its models/life cycle. Now, you will see how you can use AWS SNS with your application. You can also use the SDK for the following operations.

Code and libraries of the AWS SQS service

You saw how to create the SNS topic in the previous section. Now, you will learn how to publish it and how to start SNS using CLI.

To publish a message, follow these steps:

1. The publisher sends the messages to the topics. So, in the topics list, click on the **Publish to Topic** button to start.

2. You will get a **Message** box, as shown in the following screenshot. Enter your message in it:

You will get a confirmation message stating that it has been done successfully. After this, you can check your mail box.

To start AWS SNS from AWS CLI, you have to install the CLI tools for it on your instance. To do this, follow these steps:

1. Update your existing packages using the following command:

   ```
   sudo apt-get update
   ```

2. After completing the update process, install Java using the following command and verify it:

   ```
   sudo apt-get install openjdk-6-jre-headless
   java –version
   ```

   If you get the following output, it means that Java was installed successfully:

   ```
   java version "1.6.0_24"
   OpenJDK Runtime Environment (IcedTea6 1.11.3) (6b24-1.11.3-
   1ubuntu0.12.04.1)
   OpenJDK Client VM (build 20.0-b12, mixed mode, sharing)
   ```

3. Download the AWS SNS tools using the following command:

   ```
   wget http://sns-public-resources.s3.amazonaws.com/
   SimpleNotificationServiceCli-2010-
   03-31.zip
   ```

4. Unzip the ZIP file using this command:

   ```
   sudo apt-get install unzip
   sudo unzip SimpleNotificationServiceCli-2010-03-31.zip
   ```

5. Create one directory for SNS and copy your unzipped directory here using the following command:

   ```
   sudomkdir /usr/lib/AmazonSNS
   sudo mv SimpleNotificationServiceCli-1.0.3.3/
   /usr/lib/AmazonSNS/
   ```

6. Create a credentials file and provide your access key ID and a secret key in it, as follows:

   ```
   cd /usr/lib/AmazonSNS/SimpleNotificationServiceCli-1.0.3.3/
   sudocp credential-file-path.templatecredentials.cnf
   sudonanocredentials.cnf
   ```

7. Create a shell script and run it to check your SNS tools and configuration as follows:

   ```
   vi sns.sh
   ```

8. Add the following lines to your script file:

```
#!/bin/bash
```

```
export
AWS_SNS_HOME=/usr/lib/AmazonSNS/SimpleNotificationServiceCli-
1.0.3.3
```

```
export AWS_CREDENTIAL_FILE=$AWS_SNS_HOME/credentials.cnf
```

```
export JAVA_HOME=/usr/lib/jvm/java-6-openjdk-i386/
```

```
export
PATH=$PATH:/usr/lib/AmazonSNS/SimpleNotificationServiceCli-
1.0.3.3/bin
```

```
java -version
```

9. To run this file, make it executable with a suitable permission as follows:

```
sudochmod +x ./sns.sh
```

```
sudochmod +x /usr/lib/AmazonSNS/SimpleNotificationServiceCli-
1.0.3.3/bin/*
```

10. To run the file, use the following command:

```
sh sns.sh
```

11. To publish the message, use this:

```
sns-publish arn:aws:sns:ap-southeast-1:777890292532:CRM --
message "Hello from the great Uchit Vyas....LOL" --subject
"I'm UV" --region ap-southeast-1
```

Your message and topic will be created successfully. Now, in order to make the file executable for events, follow these steps:

1. Various Linux distributions run at different run levels on boot time. In my case, Ubuntu AMI is operating at run level 2. You can test yours with the following command:

```
runlevel
```

You will get the following output:

```
ubuntu@ip-172-31-10-128:~$ runlevel
N 2
ubuntu@ip-172-31-10-128:~$
```

2. Create a file named `sns-notify` under the `/etc/init.d/` directory with the following content:

```
#!/bin/bash
export AWS_SNS_HOME=/usr/lib/AmazonSNS/
SimpleNotificationServiceCli-
1.0.3.3
export AWS_CREDENTIAL_FILE=$AWS_SNS_HOME/credentials.cnf
export JAVA_HOME=/usr/lib/jvm/java-6-openjdk-i386/
export PATH=$PATH:/usr/lib/AmazonSNS/SimpleNotificationServiceCli-
1.0.3.3/bin
START=`date`
sns-publish arn:aws:sns:ap-southeast-1:777890292532:CRM --
message "A fresh server just launched on $START " --subject
"AWS Alert!" --region ap-southeast-1
```

3. Create a symbolic link to add the file to the `rc.d` directory in order to run a script on every boot up after making it executable, as follows:

```
Sudo chmod +x sns-notify
```

4. For the symbolic link, use the following command:

```
cd /etc/rc2.d
sudo ln -s ../init.d/sns-notify S99sns-notify
```

5. Date your `rc` scripts with this command:

```
sudo update-rc.dsns-notify enable 2
```

Now, try to stop and start your instance or reboot your system. At the boot time of the instance, you will get an e-mail notification in your mailbox if everything works fine.

For SDK users, follow these syntaxes to start with AWS SNS:

1. After getting the SDK from AWS, add references of the following namespaces to your class:

    ```
    Amazon.SQS;

    Amazon.SQS.Model;
    ```

2. Declare an object to provide your access key ID and secret key as follows:

    ```
    AmazonSQSClientobjClient = new AmazonSQSClient
        ("YourAmazonCloudAwsAccessKeyId", "
    YourAmazonCloudAwsSecretAccessKey");
    ```

3. Create your SQS queue using the following code:

    ```
    CreateQueueResponsequeueResponse = new CreateQueueResponse();

    queueResponse = objClient.CreateQueue(new
    CreateQueueRequest()
            { QueueName = "DemoQueue" });
    ```

4. To get lists of the existing queues, use the following code:

    ```
    ListQueuesResponseobjqueuesResponseList = new
    ListQueuesResponse();
    objqueuesResponseList = objClient.ListQueues(new
    ListQueuesRequest());
    ListQueuesResult Result =
    objqueuesResponseList.ListQueuesResult;
    ```

5. Send a message to the queue with the following code:

    ```
    stringmyQueue =
    uv.QueuesList.SelectedItem.Value.ToString();

    objClient.SendMessage(new SendMessageRequest()
        { MessageBody = uv.txtMessage.Text, QueueUrl = myQueue
    });
    ```

6. To receive a message from the queue, use this:

    ```
    stringmymessage = string.Empty;
    stringmyQueue = uv.QueuesList.SelectedItem.Value.ToString();

    ReceiveMessageResponse queueReceiveMessageResponse = new
    ReceiveMessageResponse();
    ```

```
queueReceiveMessageResponse = objClient.ReceiveMessage(new
ReceiveMessageRequest() {
QueueUrl = myQueue, MaxNumberOfMessages = 10 });

MyReceiveMessageResultobjMyReceiveMessageResult = new
MyReceiveMessageResult();
objMyReceiveMessageResult = queueReceiveMessageResponse.
MyReceiveMessageResult;

List<myMessage> mymessagesList = new List<myMessage>();
mymessagesList = objMyReceiveMessageResult.Message;

foreach (Message objMessage in messagesList)
{
  mymessage += objMessage.Body;
  receiptHandle = objMessage.ReceiptHandle;
}

Session["MessageReceiptHandle"] = receiptHandle;
txtReceivedMessage.Text = mymessage;
```

7. To delete the SQS message, use this:

```
stringmyQueue =
uv.QueuesList.SelectedItem.Value.ToString();

DeleteMessageResponse objDeleteMessageResponse = new
DeleteMessageResponse();
objDeleteMessageResponse = objClient.DeleteMessage(new
DeleteMessageRequest()
{ QueueUrl = myQueue, ReceiptHandle =
Session["MessageReceiptHandle"].ToString() });
```

8. Finally, to delete the SQS queue, use the following code:

```
stringmyQueue =
uv.QueuesList.SelectedItem.Value.ToString();

DeleteQueueResponsemymyqueueDeleteResponse = new
DeleteQueueResponse();
mymyqueueDeleteResponse = objClient.DeleteQueue(new
DeleteQueueRequest()
                { QueueUrl = myQueue });
```

In this way, you can perform various operations on AWS SQS and can integrate SQS into your application. To understand how AWS SQS can be integrated with other applications in real time, we will see batch processing on AWS and learn how AWS SNS is helpful in it. Here, we will go through the basic batch processing steps by horizontally using Amazon EC2 for computing and Amazon SQS for message queuing. To create a batch processing cluster, you will use the AWS Management Console, as follows:

1. Launch and configure the EC2 instance, which will work as a template for the worker node in your cluster.

2. Create an AMI from the instance.

3. Use SQS to task queues for passing messages to your EC2 instances.

4. Launch the Auto Scaling group.

5. Schedule work via a task queue.

6. Observe the output.

In this batch processing cluster, the worker nodes in your cluster will convert a number of different images into a single montage image. A worker node will download the images from the URLs provided by you and will stitch them into a single montage image using the ImageMagick tool. Let's start performing this operation one by one. You have to start by creating an IAM role.

Creating an IAM role

Your batch processing node will communicate with the queuing service SQS to get the processing instructions and will put it into S3. To do this, follow these steps:

1. Go to the AWS IAM console and from the left-hand side pane, select **Roles**. Then, click on **Create New Role**, as shown in the following screenshot:

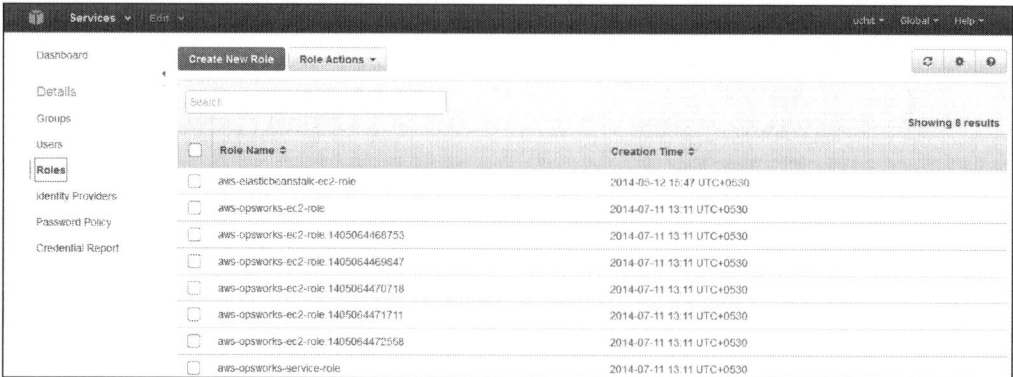

2. Give the role the name `BatchProcessing` and click on **Continue**.

3. In **Select Role Type**, select **Amazon EC2**.

4. Locate the **Amazon SQS Full Access** policy and click on **Select**, as shown here:

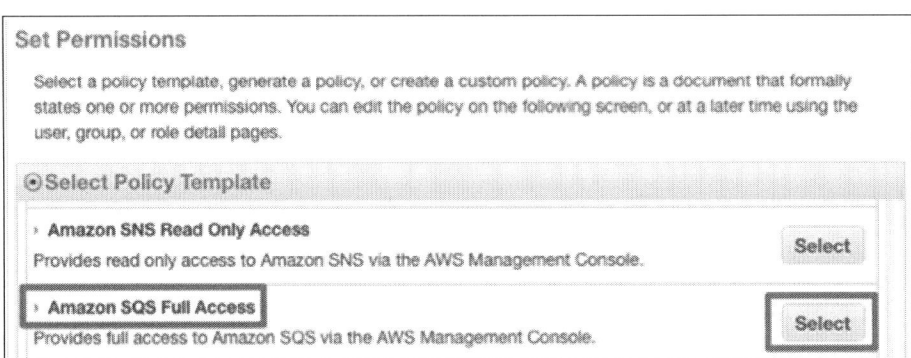

You have to add an additional permission to S3, which you can do using the following steps:

1. Select the newly created role and click on the **Attach Role Policy** button at the bottom of the window to attach another policy.

2. Find Amazon S3 full access and apply it as another policy.

Until now, you are done with the IAM roles and policy creation. Now, it's time to move on toward the EC2 section to launch the master EC2 instance. Launch the EC2 instance having Linux OS with a configuration script for ImageMagick and the batch processing software, as follows:

1. Configure the **Instance Details** panel, as follows:

    1. Provide the `BatchProcessing` role.

    2. Expand the **Advanced Details** section (scroll down to locate it).

    3. Provide the download and configuration script as the user data, as shown in the following screenshot:

```
#!/bin/bash

# Install ImageMagick, a Python library, and create a directory
yum install -y ImageMagick
easy_install argparse
mkdir /home/ec2-user/jobs

# Download and install the batch processing script
# The following command must be on a single line:
wget -O /home/ec2-user/image_processor.py https://us-west-2-aws-training.s3.amazonaws.com
/architecting-lab-3-creating-a-batch-processing-cluster-3.1/static/image_processor.py
```

> To install Image Magik

2. Configure **Security Group** called `BatchProcessing` and make sure that port 22 (SSH) is opened.

3. Review the configuration and launch the instance.

4. Log in to your instance via PuTTY or a similar tool.

After logging in, you will see the `jobs` directory and the `image_processor.py` script.

 For Mac or Linux OS, there is no need to convert the `.pem` file to `.ppk`, but you have to change the permission to `600` using the `.pem` file and then log in.

It's time to create an AMI from the launched instance, so go to the Amazon EC2 Management Console and follow these steps:

1. Select your respective instance and from the **Actions** menu, select the **Create Image** option.

2. Provide the necessary details, such as **Image Name**, **Image Description**, and so on, and then create the AMI.

 Your instance will be rebooted once and then you will lose SSH connectivity at the time of image creation.

Initially, the newly-created instance will be in a pending state, but eventually it will change to the available state.

Creating SQS tasks

To dispatch work from the input queue and to view the results via the output queue, you have to go to the Amazon SQS console and perform the following steps:

1. Click on **Create New Queue** and configure it by providing the following necessary inputs:

    ° **Queue Name**: `input`

    ° **Default Visibility Timeout**: `90 seconds`

2. Create another queue named as the `output` queue.

3. Now, select the `input` queue and from the **Queue Actions** menu, select **Send a Message**.

4. Provide the image URLs that you want to use here. You can even put your images in the S3 bucket and provide the S3 URL.

5. Click on **Send Message** and then click on the **Close** button.

To hold the output of your worker nodes, you need to configure the S3 bucket, as follows:

1. Select **S3** from the **All services** menu.

2. Click on **Create Bucket** and provide the necessary information, as shown in the following screenshot:

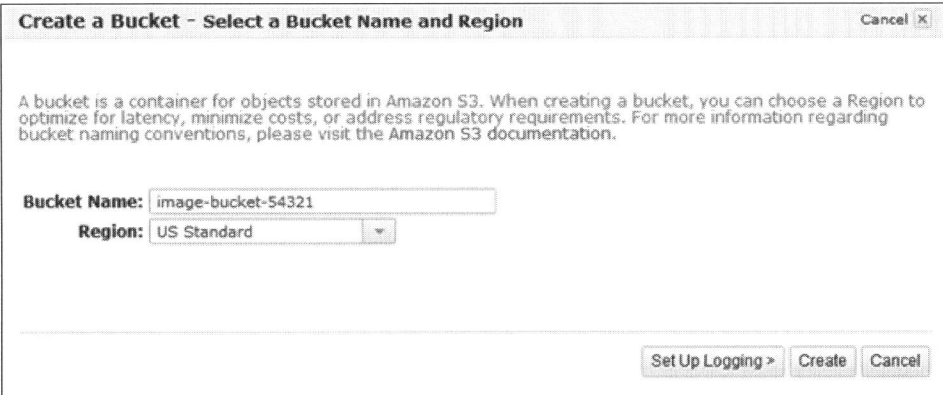

3. Click on **Create** and you are ready to go with S3.

By creating all this, you are ready to launch the worker nodes within the Auto Scaling group. Using the AWS Management Console, you can launch configurations and Auto Scaling using a single mouse-click, and you can even bid for spot instances within these consoles when required.

To start with the configuration, follow these steps carefully:

1. To create the launch configuration, you have to select the AMI and its relevant architecture that suits your application. You have already created the AMI, so select it from the AMI section (from the left-hand side pane) of the EC2 Management Console.

2. To provide the configuration details, you can provide the information in the **Advanced Details** section. Choose the AMI's kernel and RAM disk and optionally fill the details in the user data block, as shown here:

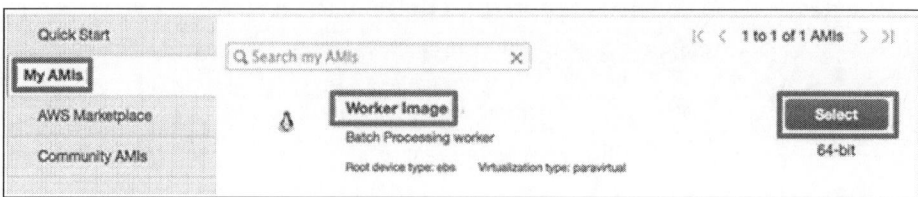

3. You can provide spot instance's bid details if you want. Here, in the **Configure details** panel, you have to provide the **Name** as `Workers` and the **IAM Role** as `BatchProcessing`.

4. In the **Advanced** section, provide your scripts in the **User Data** option, as shown in the following code:

```
#!/bin/bash
/usr/bin/python /home/ec2-user/image_processor.py &
```

5. Provide your necessary storage options in the form of the **Root** device size, EBS volume size, and so on.

6. You can select an appropriate **Security Group** or just add a new customized group named `BatchProcessing`, where you're restricting SSH access to your IP while leaving the HTTP and HTTPS accesses open for the globe.

7. Review the last tab and change the previous choices if required.

8. At last, you've to choose the key pair to access your instances and click on **Create launch configuration**.

Until now, you are done with the launch configuration for the AWS Auto Scaling service, but now you have to configure the Auto Scaling group based on a schedule or policy. So, let's create an Auto Scaling group for your web application, as follows:

1. In the very first tab, you will see a few choices; for example, **Group name**, **Group size**, **Network**, **Subnet**, and so on with the **Advanced Details** option as well. Here, in the **Advanced Details** section, you can call the AWS load balancer, which will route the traffic based on the policies to your scaled instances. Fill the appropriate details and click on **Next: Configure scaling policies**, as shown here:

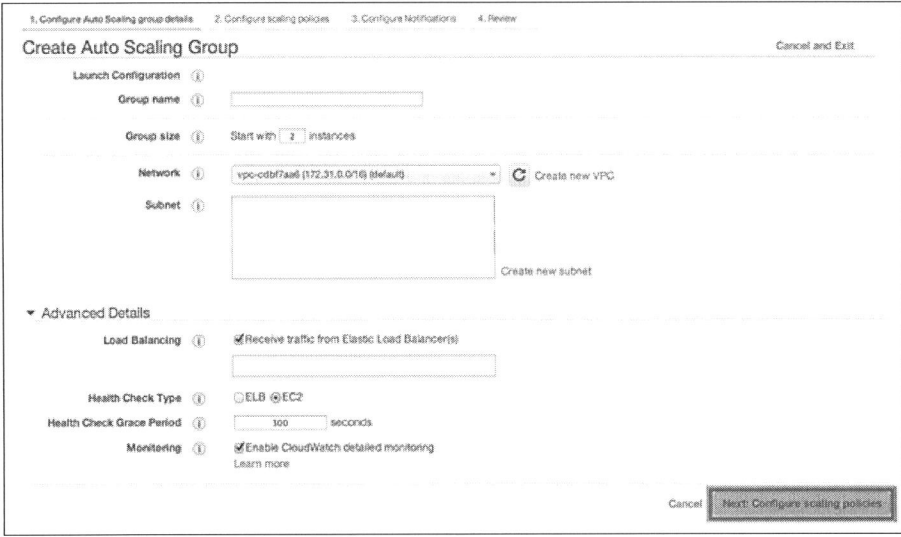

2. The next tab is very important as it allows you to select between the two fundamental scaling plans. Here, there are two options. First is the **Keep this group at its initial size** option which ensures that your group figures out a number of healthy instances equal to the initial size you mentioned. At any point of time, if an instance fails, it will be replaced automatically. The second option is the **Use scaling policies to adjust the capacity of this group** option in which you can select the CloudWatch alarm based on some policies to increase or decrease the number of instance counts.

3. You can set policies for the minimum and the maximum number of instances initiating your Auto Scaling group. You can add CloudWatch alarms easily after some time or in the middle of the deployment, but here, we'll add it now to allow your group to increase its size, as shown in the following screenshot, and vice versa (you can also configure to decrease the group size):

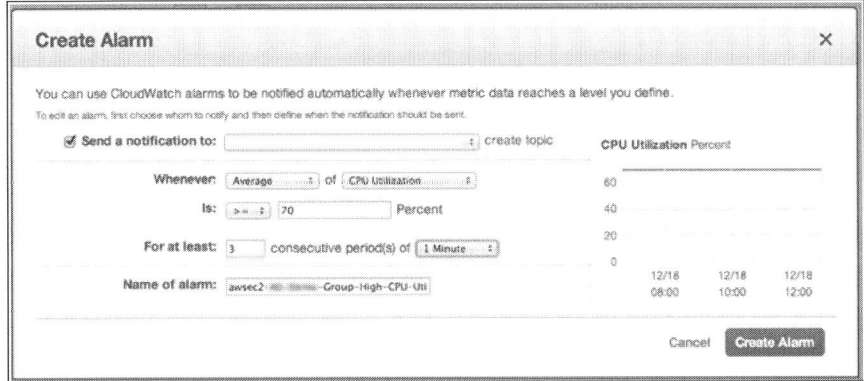

4. You are almost done, so now it's time to configure the notifications relative to your group in order to get updates.

5. The **Review** tab helps you to review the configuration; after clicking on the **Create Auto Scaling Group** button, you will be redirected to a status screen that shows the creation of your resources. If something fails, you're prompted to retry the single resource initiation again with the correction.

So, after initiating, you can see the new scaling activity on your EC2 dashboard, and whenever required, you can make changes to these configurations as per the requirement.

Dispatching work and viewing the results

You have to use the SQS Management Console to put some more messages in your input SQS queue. Your worker node will expect a new-line delimited list of URLs for the images.

Choose your input queue and confirm whether you have a single message in the queue. If a message is not there, check the following:

- The worker node
- The IAM role configuration
- Queue names
- The BatchProcessing role for the instance

The following are the steps to view the output from the output queue:

1. Select the output queue and from the **Queue Actions** menu, select **View/Delete Messages**.

2. Click on **Start Polling for Messages**.

3. Locate your message and click on **More Details** to view the message body.

Monitoring the cluster

You can now go to Amazon CloudWatch to monitor your cluster. As you have already defined the CloudWatch alarm at the time of creating the Auto Scaling policies, you just need to check the metrics from the **Services** menu, as follows:

1. Click on **Browse Metrics**.

2. Click on the **SQS Metrics** header.

3. Choose the line for the following options:

   ○ **QueueName**: `input`

   ○ **MetricName**: `ApproximateNumberOfMessagesVisible`

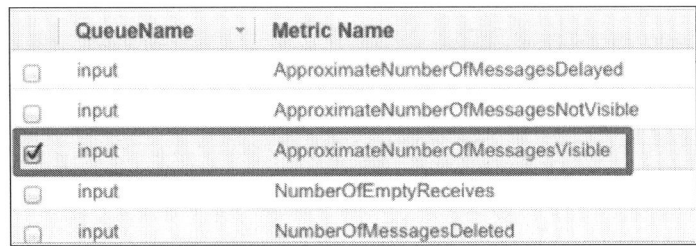

	QueueName	▾	Metric Name
☐	input		ApproximateNumberOfMessagesDelayed
☐	input		ApproximateNumberOfMessagesNotVisible
☑	input		ApproximateNumberOfMessagesVisible
☐	input		NumberOfEmptyReceives
☐	input		NumberOfMessagesDeleted

Check the configuration and you are done here. You can find the usefulness of queues and SQS from the preceding example.

Summary

In this chapter, you saw what AWS SQS is and its basic features. Later on, you went through the life cycle of AWS SQS. Finally, you learned the creation of the SQS topic, its publishing, and AWS SQS using CLI.

In the next chapter, you will get a brief overview of AWS SNS and cover the important operations of AWS SNS with your cloud/in-house applications. Finally, you will learn the basics of AWS SNS with programming.

Building an Application Using AWS

8

We have discussed most of the interesting and useful AWS offerings in the previous chapters. Now, it is time to integrate all those services in an application. Here, we are going to create a web application that is a blend of all the AWS services. In this chapter, we will focus on the following topics:

- An overview of the application
- Tools and software requirement elicitation
- Application implementation and management

An overview of an application

The application that we are going to develop and maintain using AWS is called EducationCloud. This application will provision the EC2 instances to their registered users. We are going to use **Java Server Faces (JSF)** to create the web application; so, the user registration page, login page, dashboard, and every web page will be coded using JSF. In this application, a user will register himself to EducationCloud with his mobile number and e-mail address. During the registration, an SNS topic will be created with his username as the topic name. Both the mobile number and the e-mail address will be subscribed to this topic. The admin will approve the user. Then, the user can request for an EC2 instance (or our custom AMIs). Even if he requests for the instances in VPC, we are going to provision the same. MySQL **Relational Database Service (RDS)** will be used as a database to store this information.

Once the instance request has been approved by the admin, an SMS and an e-mail will be sent to the respective endpoints about the connection details to the instance. As the number of users and instance requests exceed, there is a possibility that some SNS messages might be lost, so we add those to the SQS queues. We are going to store the instance key pairs in S3; once the user downloads it, we will delete them from S3. Finally, we will see how this application can be deployed on Elastic Beanstalk.

Tool selection

We don't need any specific software tools to build our application. We will use the following freeware tools:

- Eclipse IDE (as the development environment) with an AWS plugin setup
- JDK 7 and Tomcat 7.0 (to run our web application locally)
- MySQL connector (to connect to our RDS instance)
- PuTTYgen (to create the `.ppk` file from the `.pem` file)
- PuTTY (to connect to the EC2 instance)

All the preceding software are open source. Since we have already discussed most of these software in the previous chapters, we will move on to the application development.

Creating an application

Now is the time to get our hands dirty by creating our first AWS application (or better known as the application that uses the AWS core services). It is a JSF application, so rather than talking about the decoration of the JSF page and how to make a connection to the MySQL database, we will focus only on the code where we are performing an AWS operation. The application can be downloaded from this book's supporting code files, available on the Packt Publishing website.

Assumptions

For the proper working of the application, the following assumptions must be made. We can even call these points as prerequisites. Even if one of these is missed out, the whole application will fail:

- We should have a bucket with the name `my-keypair` to save the EC2 keys.

- The RDS instance must have an `education_cloud` database with an `admin` account.

- The AWS credentials file must be configured with the admin's AWS account.

- The `publishInstanceCreation` method of the `SNSoperations` class should have the correct subscriber. In the application, it will be hardcoded as `016883241246`. This must be replaced with a proper value.

Users

This application has two kinds of roles for users, namely, admin and non-admin. The admin user can manage instance requests. The following screenshot shows the admin user's dashboard. It consists of two sections. The first section is the **Request section** in which the admin can approve, reject, or waitlist a group of instance requests. This section consists of three links each to navigate to the **Approved requests**, **Pending requests**, and **Rejected requests** pages. The second section is the **Links section**, which has links to add new instances to be made available for the customer or student. The other links are used to test whether the application is running, by requesting and approving the instance and thereby checking the entire workflow.

Our application has another role, which is non-admin (it can be a student or a teacher). We will call this user as the customer. The non-admin user's home page will have links to request for a new instance as well as view and edit the existing requests.

An instance is a collection of the instance type, AMI ID, and kernel ID. These properties are pretty much critical, as choosing an improper combination will result in an exception. In our application, it is the responsibility of the admin to decide on these combinations because it requires expertise. This is the primary operation of our application. Without adding an instance, the customer cannot request any instance. The following screenshot shows the **Add Instance** page. The first parameter is the **Instance Type**, which starts from the low-end (free tier eligible) **T1 Micro** to **i2 8xlarge**. If we want to add information such as the RAM disk size, we can specify it in the description. Then we can click on the **Add Instance** button, which will add this information to the database:

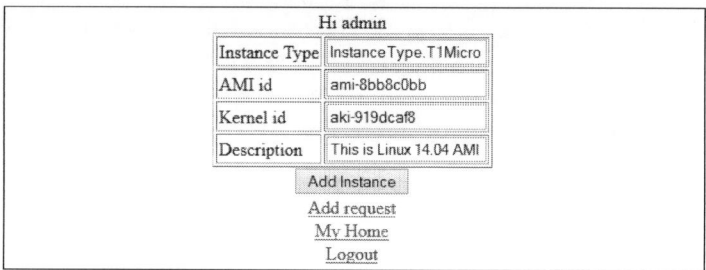

Signing up with EducationCloud

On the login screen, there will be a link to sign up. The signup page will ask for your information, as shown in the following screenshot. Enter your personal information in the first five fields, and the other two fields are used to create your login details.

Once the user clicks on the **Create Account** button, the user's personal details will be added to the Customer table and the login details will be added to the Login table. Simultaneously, an SNS topic will be created by our application with the username as the topic name. In the preceding screenshot, we registered a user with the name kprabha1989. So, an SNS topic will be created with his name as the topic name, and the user will be notified about his request update. The following code is used for topic creation:

```
public void createInstanceTopic(String topicName, String mailId,
        String mobileNumber) {
    CreateTopicRequest topic = new CreateTopicRequest();
        topic.setName(topicName);
        topic.setRequestCredentials(credential);
    String topicArn = client.createTopic(topic).getTopicArn();
    createInstanceSubscription(topicArn, mailId, mobileNumber);
    }
```

In total, EducationCloud uses four tables. The Customer table stores personal information specified during the signup process. The Login table stores the login information for EducationCloud. The Instance table stores information about the instance parameters, such as AMI ID, kernel ID, instance type, and so on (which is the admin module). The fourth table, Request, has information about the instance requested by the user and its status.

The createInstanceTopic function takes three parameters. The first parameter is topicName (which is the same as that of the username), and the next two parameters are mailId and mobileNumber (which are obtained from the personal information entered during signup). The preceding code creates a topic, topicArn (along with mailId and mobileNumber), which is passed to the createInstanceSubscription method. The implementation of this method is shown as follows:

```
private void createInstanceSubscription(String topicArn, String
mailId, String mobileNumber) {
    SubscribeRequest subscribeRequest = new SubscribeRequest();
        subscribeRequest.setTopicArn(topicArn);
        subscribeRequest.setEndpoint(mailId);
        subscribeRequest.setProtocol("email");
    client.subscribe(subscribeRequest);
    if (mobileNumber.contains("+1")) {
        SubscribeRequest request = new SubscribeRequest();
            request.setTopicArn(topicArn);
            request.setEndpoint(mobileNumber);
            request.setProtocol("SMS");
            client.subscribe(request);
    }
}
```

The preceding code subscribes the registered e-mail ID and phone number to the topic. SNS supports all the e-mail IDs, but SMS notification is currently supported only for the US. As soon as we click on the **Create Account** button, the user will get a subscription e-mail for the topic. Once the user clicks on the **Confirm subscription** link, as shown in the following screenshot, the e-mail ID will be subscribed. The same is the case with the mobile number. If the mobile number has +1 (US), then a text message will be sent via an SMS to confirm the subscription.

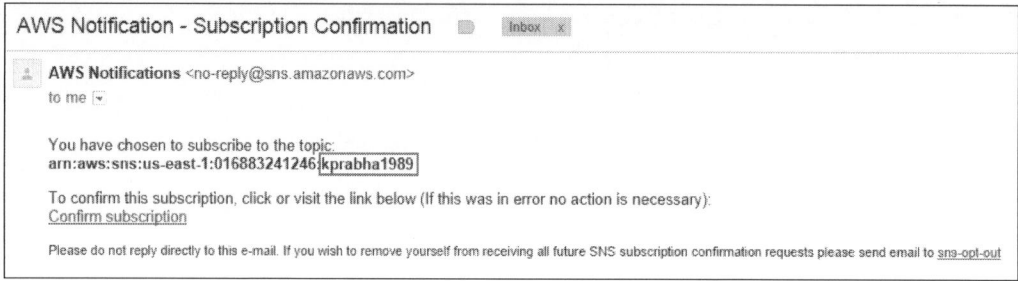

We can verify the subscription by accessing the Management Console, as shown in the following screenshot. Until now, there have been two users in our application (**admin** and **kprabha1989**). The following two topics will serve the purpose for the instance notifications:

Managing an instance request

Until now, we configured the parameters for an instance and registered a customer to our application who subscribed to the notifications. Once the user is done with the subscription, he can request for the available instances. He can choose one of the instances added by the admin using the **Instance Id** drop-down menu. Once he selects the **Instance Id** parameter, the **AMI id**, **Kernel id**, **Instance Type**, and **Description** parameters will be populated automatically.

In addition to this, the user can specify the private key pair, **Key Name**, to be created and the **Duration** for which the instance is needed for practice. Once this is done, he can click on **Send Request**, as shown in the following screenshot. This will not create any EC2 instances. An instance will be created, and the connection details will be mailed (and an SMS will be sent) once the request is approved by the admin.

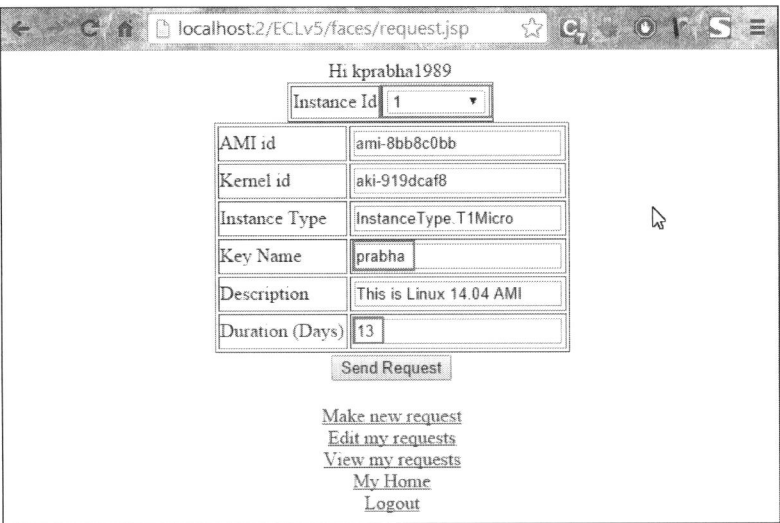

The same information will be available on the **View Request** page, as shown in the following screenshot. Since the request is not yet approved, the **Status** column (of the following table) will show a yellow icon and the checkbox next to this field will be enabled. This will be enabled only if the request is in the pending state. Since the instance is not yet created, the **Instance Id** and **Public DNS** parameters will be empty (as long as they are not approved by the admin):

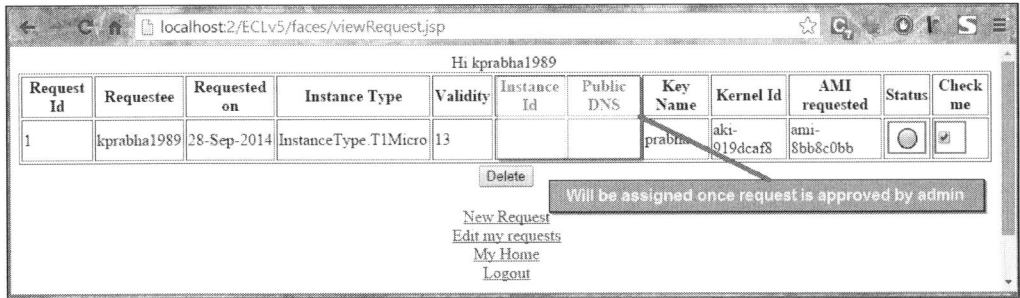

Approving an instance request

The next sequential step shows you how to approve or reject an instance request. The admin home page is the same as the **Pending requests** page. It will show you all the pending instance requests. The last field (column) of the table is a checkbox. The admin can check this button (in the case of multiple requests, the admin can select multiple checkboxes) and then click on the **Approve** button, as shown in the following screenshot:

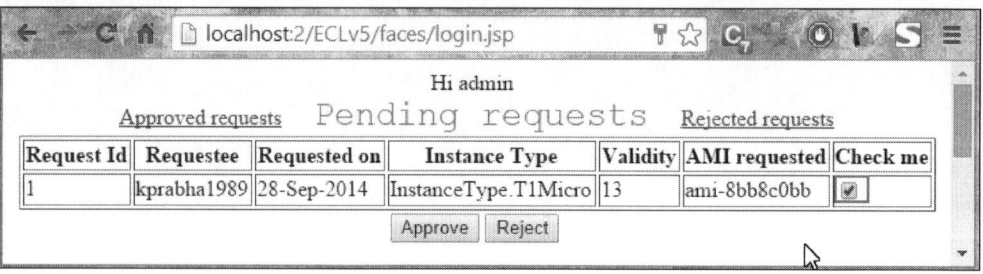

Clicking on the **Approve** button will change the status of the request and will request for the creation of an EC2 instance. The `createInstance` method will be invoked with six parameters, as shown in the following code. This code invokes three local functions, namely, `createKeyPair()`, `getInstancePublicDndName()`, and `getInstanceState()`. Another two functions, `updateRequest()` and `publishInstanceCreation()`, will be invoked to change the status of the request and to send notifications to the registered e-mail and phone.

```
public void createInstance(Integer requestId, String instanceType,
    String imageId, String kernelId, String keyName, String
    topicName) throws Exception {
    String keyPairName = createKeyPair(keyName);
    String keyPairLoc = "https://s3.amazonaws.com/my-keypair/"
        + keyPairName + ".pem";
    RunInstancesRequest request = new RunInstancesRequest();
    request.setInstanceType(InstanceType.T1Micro);
    request.setImageId(imageId);    request.setMinCount(1);
    request.setMaxCount(1);    request.setKernelId(kernelId);
    request.setKeyName(keyPairName);
    RunInstancesResult rs = client.runInstances(request);
    List<Instance> instances = rs.getReservation().getInstances();
    for (Instance instance : instances) {
        String awsInstanceId = instance.getInstanceId();
```

```
String publicDNS = getInstancePublicDnsName(awsInstanceId);
String State = getInstanceState(awsInstanceId);
if (State.equalsIgnoreCase("running")) {
    String emailMsg = "Hi " + topicName
    + ",\nYour instance's public DNS is " + publicDNS
       + ".\nKey pair can be downloaded from " + keyPairLoc;
    RequestEntity e = new RequestEntity();
          e.setRequestId(requestId);
          e.setAwsInstanceId(awsInstanceId);
          e.setKeyName(keyPairName);    e.setDns(publicDNS);
      new RequestService().updateRequest(e);
      new SNSoperations().publishInstanceCreation(
                 topicName, emailMsg);
} } }
```

To put it in a nutshell, the preceding code performs the following functions:

- Creates a key pair and stores it in Amazon S3

- Submits the EC2 instance request

- Tracks whether the instance got created

- Sends the connection details (along with the key pair's location) by an e-mail and a SMS

- Updates the same details in the database (in case the user missed the notification, they can get it from their dashboard)

The following code is used to create a key pair with the name specified by the user (with the millisecond timestamp appended to it). It will add this key pair to the instance request. In order to store this file at an S3 location, the saveKeyPair method of the S3Operations class will be invoked with keyName and the key pair content as a byte array, as shown in the following code:

```
public String createKeyPair(String keyName) {
    keyName += System.currentTimeMillis();
    CreateKeyPairRequest request = new CreateKeyPairRequest();
         request.setKeyName(keyName);
    CreateKeyPairResult keyPair = client.createKeyPair(request);
    String key = keyPair.getKeyPair().getKeyMaterial();
    return new S3Operations().saveKeyPair(keyName,
         new ByteArrayInputStream(key.getBytes()));
}
```

The `saveKeyPair` method of the `S3Operations` class is shown in the following code. In order to make this file available for public download, we set the ACL rule as shown here. It also adds the key pair to the `my-keypair` S3 bucket:

```
public String saveKeyPair(String keyName, InputStream key) {
    AccessControlList acl = new AccessControlList();
    acl.grantPermission(GroupGrantee.AllUsers, Permission.Read);
    PutObjectRequest request = new PutObjectRequest("my-keypair",
            keyName + ".pem", key, null).withAccessControlList(acl);
    client.putObject(request);
    return keyName;
}
```

The following code iterates over all the instances in our account and returns the instance state of the passed `instanceId` parameter. This method will be invoked until the state changes to running, shown as follows:

```
public String getInstanceState(String instanceId) {
    DescribeInstancesResult dir = client.describeInstances();
    List<Reservation> reservations = dir.getReservations();
    for (Reservation reservation : reservations) {
            for (Instance instance : reservation.getInstances()) {
                if (instance.getInstanceId().equals(instanceId)) {
                    InstanceState instanceState = instance.getState();
                    return instanceState.getName();
            } } }
    return null;
    }
```

Once the instance state changes to running, the following method is invoked. The following code is used to get the public DNS of the instance, without which the user cannot connect to the EC2 instance. This code will describe all the EC2 instances for the account. Inside the `for-each` loop, we will check whether the passed `instanceId` parameter is the same as the parameter for the current instance. If this is the case, the public DNS will be returned, as follows:

```
public String getInstancePublicDnsName(String instanceId) {
    DescribeInstancesResult dir = client.describeInstances();
    List<Reservation> reservations = dir.getReservations();
    for (Reservation reservation : reservations) {
            for (Instance instance : reservation.getInstances()) {
            if (instance.getInstanceId().equals(instanceId)) {
                    InstanceState instanceState = instance.getState();
                    return instance.getPublicDnsName();
    } } }
    return null;
    }
```

Once a key pair is created and stored and the instance becomes available, the DNS and the key pair location will be published as an e-mail and an SMS to the registered endpoints of the topic, as shown in the following code:

```
public void publishInstanceCreation(String topicName, String emailMsg)
{
    PublishRequest publishRequest = new PublishRequest();
    publishRequest.setSubject("Education cloud- details");
    publishRequest.setMessage(emailMsg);
    publishRequest.setTopicArn("arn:aws:sns:us-east-
            1:016883241246:"+ topicName);
    publishRequest.setRequestCredentials(credential);
    client.publish(publishRequest);
}
```

The e-mail sent for the user request is shown in the following screenshot. It will have information about the public DNS and S3 location, where the key pair that corresponds to this instance is stored:

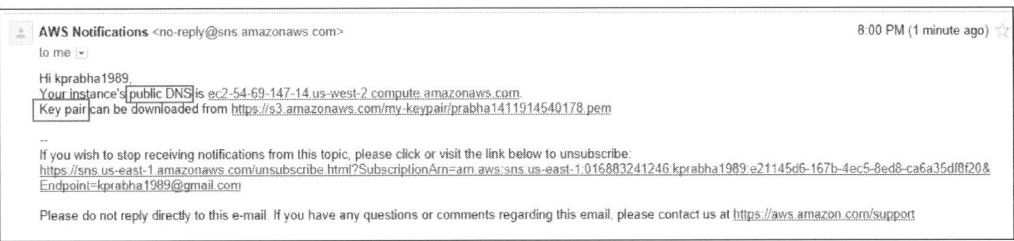

We can verify the same details in the Management Console, as shown in the following screenshot. The three most important parameters (**Instance ID**, **Public DNS**, and **Key pair name**) are highlighted.

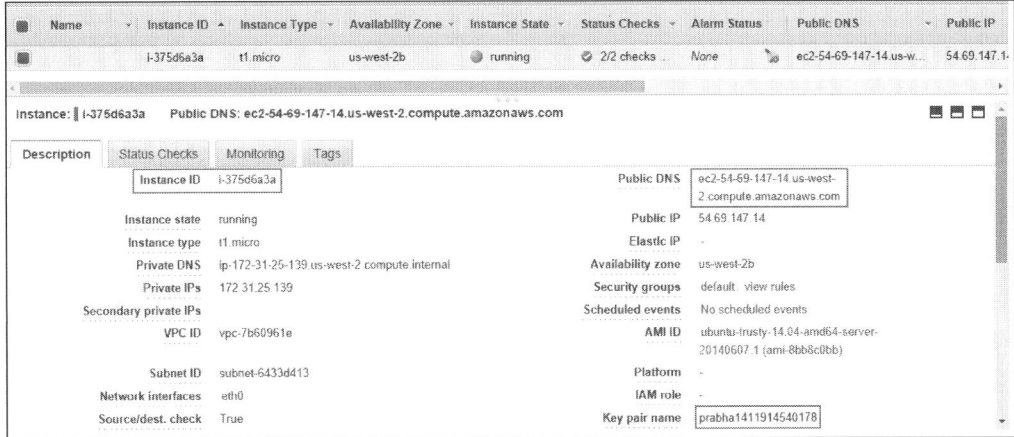

If the user logs in to the application, the same information is shown in the dashboard. Previously, the status icon was yellow; now, it has changed to green (since the request is approved and the instance is provisioned). The checkbox to delete the request is disabled. This will be enabled only if the status is pending, otherwise (approved or rejected) it will be disabled, as shown in the following screenshot:

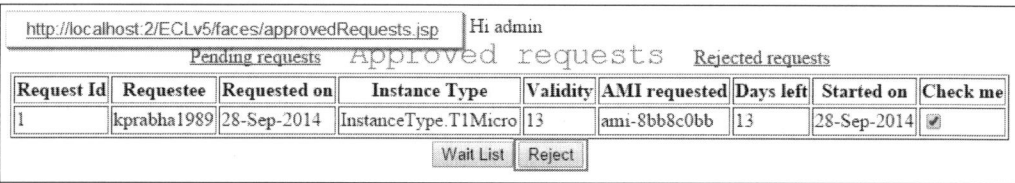

Rejecting an instance request

In the admin dashboard, if the admin has to reject the request and terminate the instance, they can check the corresponding checkbox and click on the **Reject** button. This will terminate the instance, as shown in the following screenshot:

Request Id	Requestee	Requested on	Instance Type	Validity	AMI requested	Days left	Started on	Check me
1	kprabha1989	28-Sep-2014	InstanceType.T1Micro	13	ami-8bb8c0bb	13	28-Sep-2014	☑

The following code terminates the instance request. It can accept a list of `instanceIds`. Each `instanceId` parameter will be iterated, and the instances will be terminated one by one. The execution will stay with the `while` loop until it gets terminated, shown as follows:

```
public void terminateInstance(List<String> instanceIds) {
    TerminateInstancesRequest tir = new
TerminateInstancesRequest();
    tir.setRequestCredentials(credentials);
    tir.setInstanceIds(instanceIds);
    TerminateInstancesResult result =
client.terminateInstances(tir);
```

```
    List<InstanceStateChange> resultList =
result.getTerminatingInstances();
    for (InstanceStateChange instanceStateChange : resultList) {
    while (!getInstanceState(instanceStateChange.getInstanceId())
        .toString().equalsIgnoreCase("terminated"));
    }
}
```

If we access the Management Console, we can infer the same information about the requested instance. We can see the status as **shutting-down**, as shown in the following screenshot:

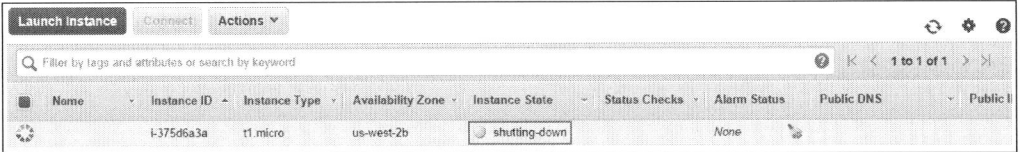

The same information will be made available in the user dashboard. Since the EC2 instance is terminated, the **Instance Id** and **Public DNS** parameters are also cleared, as shown here:

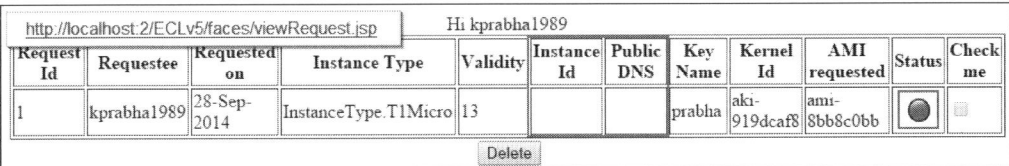

Now, this request will be available in the admin's rejected request page. We can check this request and click on **Approve** to provision the instance again to the user, as shown here:

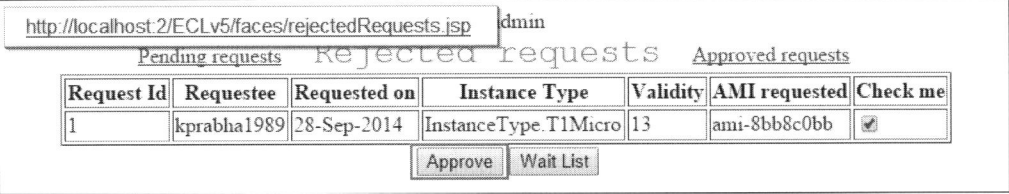

Even though the instance (for the same request) is rejected and approved again, the **Public DNS, keypair,** and **Instance Id** parameters will be different. The following screenshot shows both the e-mails. The first screenshot shows the original e-mail (published when the request is approved for the first time), and the second one shows the latest e-mail received when reapproved:

In the following user dashboard, the **Instance Id**, **Public DNS**, and **Status** parameters will be updated:

Request Id	Requestee	Requested on	Instance Type	Validity	Instance Id	Public DNS	Key Name	Kernel Id	AMI requested	Status	Check me
1	kprabha1989	28-Sep-2014	InstanceType.T1Micro	13	i-8373718e	ec2-54-68-236-76.us-west-2.compute.amazonaws.com	prabha	aki-919dcaf8	ami-8bb8c0bb	○	☐

Delete

Using RDS and Elastic Beanstalk

Since the application that we created is a JSF application, we can see a file named `persistence.xml` in the `src/META-INF` folder. Copy the following content to the `persistence.xml` file and fill up the `RDS-endpoint IP`, `port-number`, `RDS-instance-username`, and `RDS-instance-password` parameters with the RDS instance's details and save the file. Before using the application, make sure that a database with the name `education_cloud` is available in the RDS instance, as shown in the following code:

```
<persistence version="1.0"...>
<persistence-unit name="ECL">
    <class>education.cloud.entity.InstanceEntity</class>
    <class>education.cloud.entity.RequestEntity</class>
```

```
    <class>education.cloud.entity.LoginEntity</class>
    <class>education.cloud.entity.CustomerEntity</class>
    <properties>
     <property name="toplink.jdbc.url" value="jdbc:mysql://<RDS-
    endpoint IP>:<port-number>/education_cloud" />
      <property name="toplink.jdbc.user" value="<RDS-instance-
    username>" />
     <property name="toplink.jdbc.driver" value="com.mysql.jdbc.Driver"/>
     <property name="toplink.jdbc.password" value="<RDS-instance-
    password>" />
    <!-- Some more properties removed -->
    </properties>
    </persistence-unit>
    </persistence>
```

Deploying this application on Elastic Beanstalk will be done in half a dozen clicks if we use the Eclipse IDE. We can right-click on the JSF application and select the **Run on Server** option, which opens a window asking us to choose the proper server. To run it in our local system, we were using Tomcat 7. In order to deploy it in Elastic Beanstalk, we need to select the **AWS Elastic Beanstalk for Tomcat 7** server. A few more windows will pop up, in which we don't do anything, except clicking on the **Next** button. If the AWS plugin is properly configured, then this application will be deployed on AWS Elastic Beanstalk.

Application of the best AWS practices

There are a few security and performance concerns, which we might have come across in the EducationCloud application. Let's summarize those one by one:

- We save the instance key pair in S3 and the file has a read permission for everyone. This should not be the case as it is a major security breach. We must store this somewhere secure, and the read permission should be allowed only to the instance requester.

- Irrespective of whether the instance request is rejected or waitlisted, the EC2 instance will get terminated. So, we can make the application more efficient by stopping the instance (when waitlisting the request) and starting it again (when approving the request).

- There should be a provision for the non-admin user to start and stop an instance, which will reduce the billing amount.

- We cannot sell this application to the third party, as it is against the AWS agreement.

Summary

You started the chapter by discussing the overview of the EducationCloud application. Then we saw the home page and the roles of the admin user and normal user. After this, we logged in as the admin and configured an instance so that it could be requested by the user. Then the user signed up and requested for the instance. We also saw how an e-mail is sent with the connection details and key pair when the request is approved by the admin. Finally, we terminated the instance by rejecting it. The chapter didn't stop there; we also discussed how to integrate RDS and AWS Elastic Beanstalk to this application. At the end, we discussed four points which enhanced the application both performance-wise and business-wise. But the learning doesn't stop here. Since the application is downloadable, we can perform the preceding alterations and call ourselves AWS developers.

Index

D

Dashboard section, RDS 95
database server
  launching, in private subnet 66
distributed queue
  at-least-once-delivery 171
  message order 171
  message sample 171
  properties 170-172
DynamoDB
  about 86
  best practices 94
  item operations 91-93
  libraries 104
  table operations 86-91
DynamoDB local
  about 111-113
  URL, for downloading 111
DynamoDB operations
  performing, CLI used 114, 115
DynamoDB tools
  about 104
  Java SDK operations, performing 107-110
  SDK project, creating 104-106
  URL, for downloading 111

E

EC2
  about 8, 74, 123
  persistent storage, using with 33-35
EC2 instance
  about 50, 51
  creating 126, 127
  custom IAM role, creating for 124, 125
  root device volume, of Amazon EC2 51
Eclipse
  URL 16, 42, 75
Eclipse AWS SDK
  used, for performing SNS
      operations 159-162
Eclipse Juno/Luna
  URL 133

Eclipse plugin
  about 16-22
  using 104
Eclipse toolkit
  access keys, adding to 134, 135
EducationCloud
  signing up with 192-194
Elastic Beanstalk
  using 202, 203
Elastic Block Storage (EBS) 30
Elastic Compute Cloud. *See* EC2
Elastic Load Balancing (ELB) 53
endpoint 144
ephemeral storage 26-29
ephemeral storage size, EC2
  URL 30

F

features, AWS
  AWS Explorer 74
  AWS toolkit 74
FedRAMP Package Request Form
  URL 12
folders, AWS
  Documentation 73
  Lib 73
  Samples 73
  Third-party 74

G

Generally Available (GA) 128
Getting Started section 148
GovCloud 12
Graphics User Interface (GUI) 8

H

handheld devices
  used, for AWS management 8
Hardware/Host 10
High Availability (HA) 171
HTTP/HTTPS messaging service 147
Hypervisor 10

Thank you for buying
AWS Development Essentials

About Packt Publishing

Packt, pronounced 'packed', published its first book "*Mastering phpMyAdmin for Effective MySQL Management*" in April 2004 and subsequently continued to specialize in publishing highly focused books on specific technologies and solutions.

Our books and publications share the experiences of your fellow IT professionals in adapting and customizing today's systems, applications, and frameworks. Our solution based books give you the knowledge and power to customize the software and technologies you're using to get the job done. Packt books are more specific and less general than the IT books you have seen in the past. Our unique business model allows us to bring you more focused information, giving you more of what you need to know, and less of what you don't.

Packt is a modern, yet unique publishing company, which focuses on producing quality, cutting-edge books for communities of developers, administrators, and newbies alike. For more information, please visit our website: www.packtpub.com.

About Packt Enterprise

In 2010, Packt launched two new brands, Packt Enterprise and Packt Open Source, in order to continue its focus on specialization. This book is part of the Packt Enterprise brand, home to books published on enterprise software – software created by major vendors, including (but not limited to) IBM, Microsoft and Oracle, often for use in other corporations. Its titles will offer information relevant to a range of users of this software, including administrators, developers, architects, and end users.

Writing for Packt

We welcome all inquiries from people who are interested in authoring. Book proposals should be sent to author@packtpub.com. If your book idea is still at an early stage and you would like to discuss it first before writing a formal book proposal, contact us; one of our commissioning editors will get in touch with you.

We're not just looking for published authors; if you have strong technical skills but no writing experience, our experienced editors can help you develop a writing career, or simply get some additional reward for your expertise.

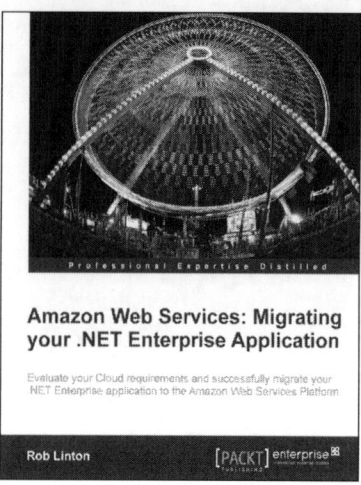

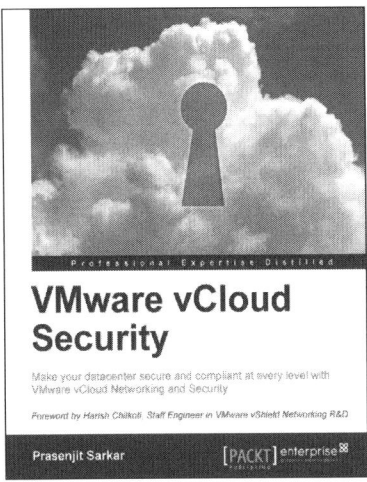

VMware vCloud Security

ISBN: 978-1-78217-096-9   Paperback: 106 pages

Make your datacenter secure and compliant at every level with VMware vCloud Networking and Security

1. Take away an in-depth knowledge of how to secure a private cloud running on vCloud Director.

2. Enable the reader with the knowledge, skills, and abilities to achieve competence at building and running a secured private cloud.

3. Focuses on giving you a broader view of the security and compliance while still being manageable and flexible to scale.

VMware vCloud Director Essentials

ISBN: 978-1-78398-652-1   Paperback: 198 pages

Build VMware vCloud-based cloud datacenters from scratch

1. Learn about DHCP, NAT, and VPN services to successfully implement a private cloud.

2. Configure different networks such as Direct connect, Routed, or Isolated.

3. Configure and manage vCloud Director's access control.

Please check **www.PacktPub.com** for information on our titles

Printed in Great Britain
by Amazon.co.uk, Ltd.,
Marston Gate.